DISCARD

P9-CDW-980

LC
191.4
.S73
1990

Staton, Ann Q.

Communication and
student
socialization

$39.50

DATE			
		OCT 1 8 1990	

SOCIAL SCIENCES AND HISTORY DIVISION

THE CHICAGO PUBLIC LIBRARY
SOCIAL SCIENCES AND HISTORY DIVISION
400 NORTH FRANKLIN STREET
CHICAGO, ILLINOIS 60610

© THE BAKER & TAYLOR CO.

Communication and Student Socialization

Communication and Student Socialization

Ann Q. Staton

Department of Speech Communication
University of Washington

ABLEX PUBLISHING CORPORATION
NORWOOD, NEW JERSEY

SOCIAL SCIENCE & HISTORY DIVISION
EDUCATION & PHILOSOPHY SECTION

Copyright © 1990 by Ablex Publishing Corporation.

All rights reserved. No part of this publication may be reproduced in any form, by photostat microfilm, retrieval system, or any other means, without the prior permission of the publisher.

Printed in the United States of America.

The following publishers have generously given permission to use quotations from copyrighted works:

From *Then Again, Maybe I Won't*, by Judy Blume. Copyright © 1971 by Judy Blume. Reprinted by permission of Bradbury Press, an affiliate of Macmillan, Inc.

From *How Do You Lose Those Ninth Grade Blues*, by Barthe DeClements. Copyright © 1983 by Barthe DeClements. All rights reserved. Reprinted by permission of Viking Penguin, Inc.

From *Ramona Quimby, Age 8*, by Beverly Cleary. Copright © 1981 by Beverly Cleary. Reprinted by permission of Morrow Junior Books (a division of William Morrow and Company, Inc.).

From *Middle School Blues*, by Lou Kassem. Copyright © 1986 by Lou Kassem. Reprinted by permission of Houghton Mifflin Company.

From *The House at Pooh Corner*, by A. A. Milne. Copyright © 1928 by E. P. Dutton, renewed 1956 by A. A. Milne. Reprinted by permission of E. P. Dutton, a division of NAL Penguin, Inc.

From *A Long Way From Home*, by Maureen Crane Wartski. Copyright © 1980 by Maureen Crane Wartski. Adapted and used by permission of Westminster/John Knox Press.

From *Madame Bovary*, by Gustave Flaubert. Translated by Eleanor Marx-Aveling. First printing 1943 of Washington Square Press. Reprinted by permission of Simon & Schuster.

Library of Congress Cataloging-in-Publication Data

Staton, Ann Q.
    Communication and student socialization / Ann Q. Staton.
        p.   cm.
    Includes bibliographical references.
    ISBN 0-89391-551-3; 0-89391-674-9 (ppk)
    1. Education—Social aspects—United States.   2. Students—United
States—Case studies.   3. Communication in education—United States.
4. Socialization.   I. Title.
LC191.4.S73   1990
371.8—dc20   89-78253
                                                                              CIP

746 59279

Ablex Publishing Corporation
355 Chestnut Street
Norwood, New Jersey 07648

SSH
ED

TO MY MOTHER

Table of Contents

Preface

The flurry of back-to-school excitement each year is the high point of autumn in America. Newspapers are filled with advertisements for school clothes and shoes. Local stores send out coupon booklets replete with bargains on notebook paper, backpacks, and pencil boxes. The evening news includes reports of high school football events. Stickers appear on the bumpers of automobiles telling us to drive carefully as "school is open." The milk cartons we purchase in grocery stores and the paper bags we use to carry our groceries are printed with reminders of the opening of school. The pace of life picks up for small towns and cities that host a college or university. Local merchants rejoice that the students are returning. Indeed, the back-to-school phenomenon is a ritual of autumn.

As with most rituals, the back-to-school experience is a regular occurrence. Despite its regularity, however, starting back to school is viewed as a milestone. For young children, entering kindergarten or first grade is a major event in their lives. The children's section of any library or bookstore has a variety of books on starting school (e.g., *The Berenstain Bears Go to School, My First Day at School, The New Girl at School, The O'Hare Family in First Day at School, Shawn Goes to School, Timothy's First Day, When You Go to School*). Magazines abound with articles offering advice to parents on how to make the first school experience a positive one (e.g., "Tips to Help You and Your Child Through the First Days of School"). Parents everywhere try to make the first day of school a special one, whether it be through the purchase of new clothes, a lunchbox, a haircut, or simply a favorite dinner and dessert the night before. And it is rare that a child's scrapbook does not include pictures of the youngster going off to school on the first day.

The significance of starting school does not end after that very first entry at age five or six. Indeed, the beginning of each new school year is considered a passage and is accompanied by various markers. Some years students enter a new grade level, but remain in the same school. With movement into other grade levels, students automatically move into a different school building (e.g., elementary to middle school, middle to high school). These moves are often considered more significant than those which occur from one grade to another within the same school building.

Even for students who are considered to be adults, the passages are still notable. Freshman entry into a college or university is an event often heralded by the whole family accompanying the student to the new school and staying over to help with settling in and unpacking. And for adults over 25 enrolling for the first time (or returning) in a community college, four-year college, or university, the step is a major one. Starting school is an important occasion, regardless of when it occurs during the life cycle.

NEED FOR THE BOOK

Since most state laws in this country require young people to attend school from the ages of seven to 16, it is reasonable to characterize the occupation or career of young people as that of student (Calvert, 1975). Because most American youngsters spend at least 11 years of their lives as students, it is imperative that the student role be understood. It is the student career, specifically *socialization* into the student role and school environment, that is the focus of this book. The book examines how young people learn the role of student and adapt to changes as they progress from one grade level to another and often, from one school to another. This phenomenon of student socialization into school, critical as it is, has been largely unstudied. As Lubeck (1985) observed, "We tend to take it as unproblematic that children are pupils, but we ignore the process by which children become pupils" (p. 111).

ORGANIZATION OF THE BOOK

The book is organized into eight chapters: an introduction, six empirically based chapters of the socialization experiences of students at various age and grade levels, and a conclusion. The grade levels were selected because they are points at which important status passages occur for most students in American society. Each of the empirically based chapters is a report of a qualitative study of young people who experience socialization into a new student role and school situation. As the process is examined across students of various grade levels and situations, differences as well as commonalities emerge which serve to facilitate a more complete understanding of student socialization.

Chapter One, the introduction, sets out the conceptual underpinnings for the subsequent empirical studies of student socialization. Grounded in symbolic interactionism and a dialectical model of socialization, the chapter explicates the examination of socialization from a communication perspective. Three conceptual frameworks are presented that guide the description and analysis of socialization across the grade levels: uncertainty reduction, concern, and status passage.

Chapters Two, Three, and Four present descriptions of elementary and middle school students. Chapter Two is a case study of an all-day kindergarten class where children learn what it means to be students as they experience their first formal schooling. Chapter Three is a case study of a group of third graders as they experience entry into a new school as well as a new grade level. Chapter Four is an examination of sixth graders in two schools as they begin the middle school years and experience the status passage from elementary to middle school.

Chapters Five, Six, and Seven describe the socialization experiences of high school students. Chapter Five examines the perspectives of freshmen during their first semester in high school. Chapter Six describes and analyzes the socialization experiences of a group of tenth, eleventh, and twelfth grade transfer students during the first school term. Chapter Seven reports a study of a group of high school students who are recent immigrants to the United States, including their early experiences in a bilingual orientation program and their subsequent entry into a regular high school program.

Chapter Eight, the conclusion, compares the socialization experience across the span of the student career. Differences and similarities in the socialization of children and adolescents are highlighted. Thus, this book provides readers with an understanding of the process by which young people socialize into new student roles and school environments.

Data for the six empirical studies presented in Chapters Two through Seven were collected over a period encompassing three academic years, from September 1985 to December 1987. The volume presents results of data gathered in 10 different schools (two elementary schools, two middle schools, six high schools), including public and private (two private schools, eight public schools), in a large metropolitan area in the Pacific Northwest region of the United States. Throughout the book, all the names used (of children, of teachers, of schools) are fictitious.

Acknowledgments

I am grateful to a number of people for their assistance with this book. To the co-authors of the several chapters I extend thanks for their fine research work: Dan Cavanaugh of the University of Texas, Kristine Fitch of the University of Colorado, and Dee Oseroff-Varnell of the University of Washington. All were graduate students at Washington during the time the studies reported in Chapters Three, Four, Six, and Seven were conducted. A very special acknowledgment goes to Dee Oseroff-Varnell, now a doctoral candidate at Washington, who worked closely with me and provided invaluable assistance. I also acknowledge the helpful suggestions and criticism of the outside reviewers. To several colleagues I extend thanks for reading various chapters and offering valuable comments: Ann Darling of the University of Illinois, Gustav Friedrich of the University of Oklahoma, and Thomas Scheidel and Donald Wulff of the University of Washington. To other colleagues I express thanks for the encouragement they provided: Randy Hirokawa of the University of Iowa, Martin Todaro of the University of Texas, and Haig Bosmajian and Jody Nyquist of the University of Washington. To the capable staff at Ablex, especially Barbara Bernstein and Carol Davidson, I owe thanks. I also acknowledge the gracious cooperation of the many elementary and secondary school students and teachers who participated in the studies or facilitated data collection.

Finally, to my family, I express heartfelt gratitude. I thank my husband and colleague, Kit Spicer of Pacific Lutheran University, for his insightful criticism of the book and constant encouragement. I thank my sons, Christopher and Nicholas Staton Spicer, for offering their first-hand views and experiences about elementary school, for counting questionnaires, for asking continually how the project was going, and for their understanding on those occasions when I stayed home to write and missed a soccer game, a basketball game, or a Saturday excursion. I thank my father, E. H. Staton, for all the trips he made to Seattle to take care of the boys so that I could work on the book. I thank my mother, Norma Staton (formerly Assistant Superintendent of Elementary Education for the Waco Independent School District), for her enthusiasm about the research, her expert editing, and the public school educator's perspective she provided.

chapter 1
Introduction: Conceptual Overview

Socialization is defined as "the comprehensive and consistent induction of an individual into the objective world of a society or a sector of it" (Berger & Luckmann, 1966, p. 130). As such, there are two major types of socialization: primary, which begins at birth, and secondary, which occurs after primary socialization and continues to recur throughout a person's life. Berger and Luckmann characterize primary socialization as "the first socialization an individual undergoes in childhood, through which he becomes a member of society" (p. 130). Primary socialization is a process that occurs over time and is not a single event; it is a process that is accomplished when an individual becomes a functioning member of society. Although it is impossible to pinpoint an age at which children are considered socialized members of society, it is apparent that young infants are not yet socialized while most five-year olds entering kindergarten are. By the time a child starts kindergarten, she or he is treated as a socialized member of our society.

Secondary socialization, in contrast, is "any subsequent process that inducts an already socialized individual into new sectors of the objective world of his society" (Berger & Luckmann, 1966, p. 130). More specifically, secondary socialization involves learning knowledge relevant to a particular role, internalizing the "subworld" or culture of a role, group, or institution. Thus, it is a process involving cognitive, affective, and normative components (Berger & Luckmann, p. 138). Unlike primary socialization, individuals undergo secondary socialization repeatedly throughout life and often experience such socialization into more than one sector of society simultaneously. A newly married individual, for example, moves to a new city, takes a new job, and joins a new church. This person is learning the role of spouse, becoming a part of a new neighborhood, learning the culture of the new company, and becoming a member of the church community. Secondary socialization occurs in each of these instances.

SCHOOLS AS AGENTS OF SECONDARY SOCIALIZATION

Traditionally, schools in American society have been viewed as important secondary socialization agents for young people. They are characterized as socializing institutions which prepare students for life outside of school as productive adults (Durkheim, 1956; Egan, 1983; Feinberg & Soltis, 1985). Schools are considered people-processing organizations that function to make "long-range, systematic changes in the knowledge, beliefs, attitudes, or skills" of their clients (Wheeler, 1966, p. 57). They seek to accomplish their goals primarily in two ways: (a) by teaching academic content, and (b) by transmitting the values of society.

According to Shulman (1986), students must negotiate two types of curriculum within schools: (a) the manifest curriculum, consisting of classroom content and academic tasks, and (b) the hidden curriculum, comprised of interactional, social, and management dimensions. Overtly, schools teach a variety of cognitive skills and knowledge, such as reading, writing, arithmetic, history, science, and so on. The transmission of such academic content is viewed as important in ensuring an educated citizenry. Less overtly, schools teach a variety of societal norms and values which constitute the hidden curriculum that prepares students for the world of work.

The Hidden Curriculum

The scope of the research on schools as socializing institutions is extremely broad, yet has focused more on the hidden than on the manifest curriculum. Many theorists have advocated that the hidden curriculum serves a sorting function which maintains the unequal social order that exists in American society. As Erickson (1984) comments, "The various activities of schools are organized so that class position is in most instances maintained from one generation to the next" (p. 527).

Influence of classroom social structure on socialization to societal work values. A variety of research has analyzed the way classroom social structure socializes children for the world of work. LeCompte (1978) examined four elementary classrooms (two comprised of low-income, predominantly Mexican-American children and two comprised of middle-class, largely Anglo children) for the type of work behavior enforced in the hidden curriculum. She found that each of the classrooms focused on the transmission of a standard "work norm" through the teachers' verbal and nonverbal behavior. The norms included: (a) conform to authority, (b) conform to a schedule and avoid wasting time, (c) keep busy, (d) maintain order, and (e) equate achievement with personal worth. The results revealed that despite individual teacher differences, the "work norm" dominated in the hidden agenda of all four of the classrooms. She concluded that the socialization function of schooling was to prepare all youngsters for the work-oriented roles and expectations of the larger society.

Anyon (1980) observed five fifth-grade classrooms representing a variety of socioeconomic levels: two working-class schools, one middle-class school, one affluent professional school, and one executive elite school. Her findings revealed that the type of work-related activities encouraged in each of the schools corresponded to the type of occupations engaged in by the students' parents. For example, the working-class schools stressed rote behavior in students with little freedom of choice; the middle-class school emphasized the importance of following directions yet permitted some student decision making; and the affluent professional and executive elite schools encouraged divergent thinking and independence. Language arts was primarily technical in the lower socioeconomic schools, with the emphasis on correct punctuation and grammatical rules; the higher socioeconomic schools emphasized individual creativity and self-expression. Anyon concluded that the experiences in the various schools "differed qualitatively by social class" (p. 90).

Carroll (1981) examined children ages five to 12 in a suburban elementary school and found that the structure of the classroom work guided them toward the principles generally valued in the professional and managerial positions held by their parents. School personnel encouraged the development of "know-how" and motivation in children by introducing them to a "sense of order, regulation, and autonomous action" (p. 52). The classroom social structure that fostered these values included a daily routine of activities, teacher-led projects, and a policy of independent work.

Wilcox (1982) compared children in two elementary schools (one was multicultural, lower-middle class, and the other was all-white, upper-middle class) and found that self-fulfilling prophecies served to socialize youngsters for the hierarchy of work experienced by their parents. She made extensive observations of children that focused on three categories: (a) the values emphasized by the teacher, (b) the student role in the classroom, and (c) the way academic content was presented. She found differences in such aspects as the degree of internal and external control in the classroom, the importance placed on skills of self-presentation, and the degree of orientation to the present and the future. Wilcox concluded that differential patterns of teacher socializing behavior did not reflect the goals of equal educational opportunity.

Socialization function of classroom discipline. Several studies have focused specifically on the socialization function inherent in elementary school discipline practices. Sieber (1978), for example, compared the discipline experiences of children in three elementary schools and discovered that the experiences were preparing children for adult roles similiar to those of their parents. There were variations among schools in such aspects as pupil autonomy in initiating activities, degree of cooperation among students, frequency of behavioral sanctions, and types of rewards and punishments used (e.g., verbal reprimands versus forced repetition of tedious routines).

In a subsequent study drawing from the same data base, Sieber (1979) discussed how the informality of classroom social organization and inexplicitness of rules socialized students for the "often unspoken understandings that later come to inform the child's role behavior in the public sphere, as employee, as client . . . " (p. 281). In a study of teacher–student interaction in two first-grade classrooms during the first two months of the school year, Sieber (1981) explored how teacher reprimands, verbal appeals, rewards, and punishments served a similar socialization function.

School influence on socialization to sex roles. Another line of research has focused on the role of schools in socializing young people to sex roles. A variety of research during the 1970s analyzed school textbooks for their portrayal of sex roles (Federbush, 1974; MacLeod & Silverman, 1973; Trecker, 1974; Women on Words and Images, 1972). Additional studies examined sex-role stereotyping in schools (Lee & Gropper, 1974; National Education Association, 1977; Saario, Jacklin, & Tittle, 1973). Results indicated that women were presented as less informed and less serious than men, and were not given appropriate recognition for their contributions in history and politics.

In a discussion of these same issues, Bates (1988) has described a "gender curriculum" that takes different forms, yet serves a socialization function throughout elementary, junior high, and high school. She highlighted several examples: the segregation of the sexes beginning in kindergarten, the unspoken assumption that girls should like school more than boys, the expectation that girls will be more compliant than boys, the belief that girls are more interested in music, reading, and art than boys, and so on.

Still other research has examined sex-role socialization that is manifested in classroom communication. Brophy and Good (1974), although interested in interaction patterns and not school socialization per se, conducted and reviewed research indicating that teachers interact differently with girls and boys. The implications of such results are that female and male students may receive different messages from teachers about what is appropriate behavior. In an update of this review, Brophy (1985) found that although female and male students still have "somewhat different experiences in most classrooms," teachers do not cause these differences but reinforce existing societal differences (p. 137). Research reviewed by Eccles and Blumenfeld (1985) supported this conclusion: "Nonetheless, when differences occur, they appear to be reinforcing sex-stereotyped expectations and behaviors" (p. 112). In a meta-analysis of research on gender differences in teacher-pupil interactions, Kelly (1988) found that teachers interacted less with girls than with boys, spending an average of

44% of their time with girls and 56% with boys. This male domination in classrooms may socialize students to stereotypical sex roles.

Finally, some research has indicated the opposite, that schools actually function to dispel sex-role stereotypes. Goetz (1981), for example, observed a group of first graders in a rural public school and examined the sex-role socialization messages and expectations they received. She found that teachers introduced students to egalitarian sex roles and broadened their awareness beyond that of the traditional sex roles learned in their homes.

Summary. Thus, a variety of research has examined schools as socialization agents of youngsters to larger society. Although some researchers have found that the hidden curriculum may liberate students from traditional, narrow values of home, others are firm in arguing that "only in a minority of cases does the modern public school function for individuals or for society as Horace Mann envisioned that it would, as the 'balance wheel of democracy' " (Erickson, 1984, p. 527). It may be that classroom life is simultaneously a shadow of the larger society yet constitutive of its own unique context and form.[1]

Socialization into the student role: A needed focus. Compared to the research on schools as socializing institutions, only limited attention has been paid to the ways in which students take on, or socialize into, *their student role in schools.* If being a student is viewed as the "occupation" of young people for a minimum of 11 years for some and more than 20 years for others (Calvert, 1975; Schwartz, 1975), then it becomes important to examine how young people learn the student role initially and adjust as the role and setting change over the duration of the career. In his discussion of classrooms as collectives, Bloome (1985) argues the need to examine the ways students learn the role:

> Students must also learn how to go to school. Children must be socialized into being students . . . . consequently, researchers' questions should address . . . the means by which children become members of the classroom collective. (p. 125)

Thus, socialization into the student role and school environment is a critical and neglected aspect of research regarding the hidden curriculum.

---

[1] Another body of research related to the hidden curriculum is that of the sociolinguistic analysis of classroom discourse. Such research examines actual classroom talk. This research is not reviewed systematically in this chapter because its major emphasis is not on socialization. Interested readers are referred to original research conducted by Cazden (1988) and reported by Wilkinson (1982), and excellent reviews of research by Cazden (1986) and Green (1983).

The nature of the role students take and the sense they make of the new school environment are integral to their success with the manifest curriculum.

Types of Secondary Socialization

As youngsters begin and continue throughout their student career, they experience a process of secondary socialization which takes two forms: (a) occupational or role socialization, and (b) organizational or school socialization.

Occupational or role socialization for the young person in a school setting is a process of learning what it means to be a student. This involves acquiring an understanding of "the values and attitudes, the interests, skills and knowledge" (Merton, Reader, & Kendall, 1957, p. 287) of the student role. Because the role itself is not static, but ever-changing, this process of learning is continuous throughout the student career. Fenstermacher (1986) coins the terms "studenting" and "pupiling" in reference to the student role. "Studenting" incorporates learning but is much broader:

> In the context of modern schooling, however, there is much more to studenting than learning how to learn. In the school setting, studenting includes getting along with one's teachers, coping with one's peers, dealing with one's parents about being a student, and handling the nonacademic aspects of school life. (p. 39)

What it means to be an elementary school student, for example, is quite different from what it means to be a high school student or a graduate student. Early in the school year many kindergarteners are taught the importance of sitting still, listening to the teacher, and raising their hands before speaking out in class. For high school freshmen a new school experience is that of having free time for the first time in nine years of schooling. High school teachers and counselors try to teach ways of managing and using such unstructured time (e.g., a full hour of study hall) productively. The role of graduate student—advanced learner, one who conducts research, one who serves as a teaching assistant—is a distant one from the previous student roles (Darling & Staton, in press; Staton & Darling, 1989). Thus, the student role across the career is constantly changing as students continually face new expectations, demands, requirements, choices, and constraints. Occupational or role socialization, then, is an ongoing process.

The organizational or school socialization that students experience is defined as "the process by which a person learns the values, norms and required behaviors which permit him to participate as a member of the organization" (Van Maanen, 1976, p. 67). Schools are social institutions with organizational structures, each with its own particular culture. In her study of "the sandbox society," Lubeck (1985), for example, discovered two preschool settings within the same city that had discernibly different cultures, each with a distinct set of values and accompanying curricular agendas. What it meant to be a successful student in one environment was not the same as what it meant to be successful in the other. She found that the classroom of low-income black children was one in which youngsters were socialized to the importance of group needs over individual needs, with an emphasis on convergent thinking and group responses to adult directives. For the middle-income white children, the focus was on the individual. Teachers urged children to work alone, offered them choices, and encouraged them to give divergent responses.

Although role socialization and school socialization are distinct entities, they are reciprocal processes that mutually influence one another. As Fernie (1988) explicates in his description of a preschool boy and a kindergarten girl as they enter their first school settings, each school environment defines and encourages a particular student role. Socialization into the student role and into the school environment are interwoven.

Young people experience role and school socialization repeatedly throughout the student career, as they make numerous moves from grade to grade and from school to school. With entry into each new grade level or school, students undergo socialization. Thus, not only must young people learn what it means to be a student, they must also continually learn what it means to be a student in a new school setting.

Phases of Socialization

With respect to role and school socialization, the concept of phases is important. In his study of organizational socialization, Van Maanen (1976) described three phases through which individuals progress: (a) anticipatory socialization, (b) entry or encounter, and (c) continuance or adaptation.

Anticipatory socialization involves the choice phase during which an individual decides to join an organization and begins preparing for the workplace. Students experience this phase as they contemplate starting school for the first time, anticipate the transfer to a different school, or think about what it will be like to advance from middle school to high school.

The second phase is that of *entry* or *encounter* during which a newcomer may experience reality shock as she or he confronts the job situation, both the occupation and the particular organization, for the first time. For students, this phase occurs during the first days and weeks when they begin school as kindergarteners, enter as high school freshmen, or walk into a new school as transfer students. James Dean, in *Rebel Without a Cause*, began the entry phase of socialization when he first stepped onto the campus of the new school, observed and interacted with other students, and felt a sense of alienation.

Continuance or *adaptation* is the third phase during which a newcomer is an accepted member of the organization and makes changes and adaptations as needed to remain in the occupation or the organization. After the initial entry has faded and students begin to "settle" into their roles and into the school, they continue to make their own way and negotiate a student role that is ever changing. Many new students, for example, begin the school year as compliant youngsters who adhere to rules. As these students become comfortable in the school setting, however, some begin to challenge the rules and redefine their student role. A new student in school may start out being very studious, only to become more of a "party-goer" as she or he makes friends and actively participates in the social life of peers.

MODELS OF SOCIALIZATION

It is evident, then, that student socialization is complex and continuous. In order to examine the socialization process, it is necessary to articulate the view of socialization which underlies the book. For many years, socialization has been viewed from a functionalist perspective, a model advocating a deterministic view of the individual in which socialization served to mold people to fit into society (see discussions in Feinberg & Soltis, 1985; Lacey, 1977; Parsons, 1951). Within this perspective, people are considered as passive recipients of a variety of external socializing forces. As applied to student socialization, this view considers the student role a largely static one in which outside agents such as teachers, administrators, and school structure shape students according to an ideal image. The study of student socialization from this perspective, then, involves an examination of the goals and messages of the socializing agents and the ways in which the messages are transmitted to students. For those who take a view of humans as knowing beings, that is, active agents who act in purposive ways (Magoon, 1977), this functionalist model is limited. Although the model has served to generate much research and has identified contextual constraints on socialization, it has not illuminated an understanding of the *process* of socialization.

An alternative perspective to functionalism is what Zeichner (1980) has termed a dialectical model, one in which the emphasis is "on the constant interplay between individuals and the institutions into which they are socialized" (p. 2). This view is of socialization as a "complex, interactive, negotiated, provisional process. The model ... also stresses the importance of man as a creative force, as a searcher for solutions and as possessing a considerable potential to shape the society in which he lives" (Lacey, 1977, p. 22). The implication of this model for the study of student socialization is that students are involved actively in the process. They are not considered mere recipients of socializing messages provided by school authorities, but are dynamic individuals engaged in the formation of their own roles as students. As Erickson, Boersema, Pelissier, and Lazarus (1985) assert, "student status is socially constructed in everyday life in classrooms" (p. 2). Thus, in order to understand the process of student socialization it is necessary to focus on students themselves, their perspectives, and their interactions with others. The assumptions of this book are grounded firmly in the model of socialization as a dialectal process.

SYMBOLIC INTERACTIONISM

Underlying the dialectical model of socialization is the view of human society as symbolic interaction. Although the philosophical conceptualization can be found in various works by Mead (1934, 1938), the perspective has been set forth most explicitly by Blumer (1969):

> The term "symbolic interaction" refers, of course, to the peculiar and distinctive character of interaction as it takes place between human beings. The peculiarity consists in the fact that human beings interpret or "define" each other's actions instead of merely reacting to each other's actions. Their "response" is not made directly to the actions of one another but instead is based on the meaning which they attach to such actions. (pp. 78–79)

Blumer (1969) identifies six "root images" basic to understanding the perspective of symbolic interactionism. Each is important to an analysis of student socialization. First, human groups consist of individuals engaged in action and involved in fitting together various lines of action. Second, society is comprised of individuals who interact with one another. Such social interaction is a process of mutual role taking that constitutes or forms human action. Classrooms and schools are societies composed of students and teachers who interact with one another to fit together their respective lines of action. As a group of kindergarteners fit together their lines of action, for example, they are constructing a society and defining their roles as students within the society. Individual five-year olds come together in a single classroom and negotiate with each other and the teacher to accomodate their diverse lines of action.

A third dimension of symbolic interactionism is that the "world" of each individual consists of objects that derive meaning through interaction with others. With respect to socialization into schools, students derive meaning for the school "objects" salient to them through a process of interacting with others. They bring expectations with them about the new school/student experience, but it is through interaction with others during the entry phase that they derive meaning and make sense of the experience.

A fourth root image is that humans are acting organisms, not merely responding organisms, who engage in self-interaction. Fifth, humans make indications to themselves and actively construct their own action based on their interpretations. Consistent with these perspectives, students are necessarily viewed as active agents who formulate their own interpretations of the school environment and of the student role. This is as true for kindergarteners as it is for high school students, although there may be fewer explicit, external attempts by others to define the role for older students.

Finally, Blumer (1969) states that it is the interlinkage of diverse lines of action which forms joint action and constitutes organizations and institutions. Even for instances of joint action that are repetitive, such as moving to a new grade level or a new school, there is still an interpretive process of formation that occurs. As Blumer indicates:

> The participants still have to build up their lines of action and fit them to one another through the dual process of designation and interpretation. . . . Repetitive and stable joint action is just as much a result of an interpretative process as is a new form of joint action that is being developed for the first time. (p. 18)

Thus, students can be viewed legitimately as newcomers who must fit together joint lines of action each time they enter a different school situation or take on an even slightly different student role. Socialization into schools, then, clearly is not a phenomenon that occurs only with initial entry into formal schooling.

In a conceptual elaboration of the interactionist framework applied to sociology and education, Woods (1983) discusses the viewpoint as concentrating "on the small-scale detail of interpersonal relationships, what people do, and how they react to each other, the patterning of behaviours, the ebb and flow of everyday life" (p. xi). He sets forth several core concepts—contexts (situations that are constructed and interpreted by actors), perspectives (frameworks by which people construct their realities and make sense of the world), cultures (shared rules and codes for speaking and acting), strategies (methods of achieving goals), negotiation (interplay and interaction between people), and careers (stages and transitions in a person's activities)—which encompass interactionism in schools. These concepts are considered throughout the various empirical studies of student socialization described in this book.

COMMUNICATION

When socialization is viewed from a dialectical perspective and human society is seen as symbolic interaction, the function of communication in the socialization process takes on added importance. Human communication is the process by which people attempt to negotiate shared meanings, thereby validating their perceptions. It is a process of interpretation which begins when people assign meaning to the behavior of others and seek to make sense of their environments. At a fundamental level, communication is the process by which people create shared understandings with others in society through symbolic activity (Cronkhite, 1986). Interactants attempt to discover the expectations of others, as well as let their own expectations be known, for appropriate roles and behaviors. They construct roles and achieve understanding through the communicative interplay of negotiation. Thus, as Bernstein (1972) noted, "Individuals come to learn their social roles through the process of communication" (p. 474).

As Stewart (1978) describes a dialogic perspective of communication, the focus is on "the dynamic, complex, context-dependent communicative 'transaction,' 'reciprocal bond,' 'between,' or 'relationship' " (p. 184). This conceptualization of communication is grounded in Buber's (1965) view that a person can be understood only as a person-in-relation. Stewart points out that the concept of "student" is meaningful only "in relation" (e.g., student-to-teacher or student-to-student). This view of communication is consistent with a dialectical model of socialization.

As a way of examining student socialization from a communication perspective, three frameworks are used to guide the description and analysis in subsequent chapters. These include: uncertainty reduction, concern, and status passage.

Gaining Information to Reduce Uncertainty

To understand how communication functions during the socialization process, the book draws upon some of the concepts of uncertainty reduction set forth by Berger and Calabrese (1975) and Berger (1979). They constructed a framework to explain what occurs during the initial stages of interaction between strangers. Their framework rests on the assumption that when people first meet, their primary motivation is to reduce uncertainty about the other and increase predictability. They assert that it is through communication that such explanations and predictions are constructed.

In an expansion and reconceptualization of uncertainty reduction, Berger (1986) notes the importance of person, role, and procedural knowledge if relationships are to progress beyond mere initial interactions and if individuals are to coordinate lines of action. Although Berger does not refer to socialization as such, it is reasonable to view the anticipatory and entry phases of socialization as times of uncertainty that include both initial interactions as well as continued ones. Socialization is a process during which individuals confront new people, circumstances, environments, and expectations. There is generally an urgent need to obtain information about the role and the institution (Louis, 1980).

Research on organizational socialization and the socialization of newcomers to groups suggests that the uncertainty reduction framework may be a productive one. Spicer and Staton-Spicer (1983) identified communication strategies newcomers use to gain information and reduce their uncertainty in group situations. Wilson (1986) applied uncertainty reduction concepts to the study of communication networks during socialization into an organization. In a study of the socialization of academic department chairpersons, Staton-Spicer and Spicer (1987) discussed how uncertainty about a new role is reduced through interaction.

Because socialization into new school situations is a process of entering a new environment and taking on a new student role, it is likely that it is a period accompanied by uncertainty. Thus, it may be fruitful to examine the ways in which students seek information to reduce uncertainty.

Gaining Information and Reassurance to Resolve Concern

A second framework guiding the study of socialization is that of communication concern. A variety of research related to teachers has drawn upon the developmental model of teacher concern (Fuller, 1969). Adapted from this general model, but more specifically focused, communication concern is defined as a constructive frustration or anticipation of a problem situation that involves participation in face-to-face interaction with others (Staton-Spicer, 1983). Staton-Spicer and Bassett (1979) found that concerns could be categorized according to the *self* as a communicator, the *task* of communicating, and the *impact* of one's communication on others. Consistent with previous research on general teacher concerns (Fuller & Bown, 1975; Fuller, Watkins, & Parsons, 1973), they also discovered a developmental sequence. The communication concerns of preservice teachers differed from those of inservice teachers (that is, preservice teachers expressed primarily self and task concerns, and inservice teachers expressed concerns primarily about impact).

In a study of communication concern of student interns during socialization into teaching, Staton-Spicer and Darling (1986) reported that students talked most frequently about the self, then about the task of teaching, and only very little about impact. The communication interactions of the interns were important during their socialization: "It is through talk with others that interns learn about their new role, begin to feel a part of the culture of teachers and of the school community, and relieve some of their own frustrations and uncertainties in order to survive" (p. 228). In a recent essay, Staton-Spicer and Darling (1987) detailed a communication concern framework as a productive way of examining socialization.

Just as the anticipatory and entry phases of teacher socialization can be characterized as times of high levels of concern about self and task, it is also reasonable to expect that students learning new roles or entering new school environments will have concern about self and task dimensions. As suggested by Staton-Spicer and Darling (1987), newcomers are likely to have *self* concerns about their performance in the new role and also about themselves as members of the new school setting. They may well have *task* concerns about what it is they are to do in the new student role, as well as how they are to function in the new school environment. Thus, the framework of communication concern is used to guide the examination of student socialization.

Status Passage

The concept of status passage is used throughout the book as a third framework to guide the understanding of socialization. In his classic *Rites of Passage*, van Gennep (1960) sets forth an analysis of life crises, or status passages, through which individuals progress:

> The life of an individual in any society is a series of passages from one age to another and from one occupation to another.... Transitions from group to group and from one social situation to the next are looked on as implicit in the very fact of existence. (p. 3)

Chapple and Coon (1942) elaborate on the concept of passages: "Each individual undergoes changes in his relations to others, and these changes will upset his own equilibrium and that of others in the system in which he interacts" (p. 506). Socialization itself can be conceived of as a passage through which young people progress in the student career. As students take on different roles and move into new settings, some of the interaction patterns and regularities of their lives are disrupted. Routines must be reestablished. Leemon (1972) argues that such changes are stressful for those who are seeking incorporation into a new group in that new situations are uncertain and accompanied by a risk of failure.

Glaser and Strauss (1971) discuss passages which occur between age-linked statuses as well as those which occur within occupations or organizations. Formally, a change of status occurs every year when students are promoted to the next grade level. Although students take on a new status every year, each passage is not necessarily equal in importance. In the American school system, for example, major status changes occur at the following times: (a) upon first entry into school at kindergarten or first grade, (b) upon entry into middle school at sixth or seventh grade, and (c) upon entry into high school at ninth grade. Additional important status changes may occur at any time that students enter new schools, whether as a collective in the regular process of grade advancement, or as individuals who may transfer into new schools for personal reasons.

In their seminal study of status passages, Glaser and Strauss (1971) identify 17 properties of status passage which can serve as a focus for systematic analysis. An additional important property is drawn from the work of Van Maanen and Schein (1979) who propose tactical dimensions by which organizational newcomers are socialized. Thus, the 18 properties which guide the analysis of socialization in subsequent chapters include:

1. Whether the passage is scheduled or unscheduled—that is, whether the passage is governed by rules about when the change of status should occur and by whom,
2. Whether the passage is regular—that is, whether the passage occurs routinely,
3. Whether the passage is prescribed—that is, whether the passage has a dictated sequence of steps a person must go through in order to accomplish the passage,
4. Whether the passage is desired—that is, whether the person wants to make the passage,
5. Whether the passage is inevitable—that is, whether the passage occurs regardless of other factors,
6. Whether the passage is reversible—that is, whether the passage can be changed,
7. Whether the passage is repeatable—that is, whether the passage can occur more than once,
8. Whether the person in the passage goes through alone, collectively, or in aggregate with others—that is, whether the person experiences the passage in isolation, as a collective/group, or as an aggregate of distinct individuals without a group bond,

9. Whether the person in the passage is aware of the collective or the aggregate—that is, whether those experiencing the passage are cognizant that they are going through the passage together,

10. Whether the persons in the passage may communicate with one another—that is, whether talk and interaction occur among those experiencing the passage,

11. Whether the person has a choice about the passage—that is, whether the person makes the passage voluntarily,

12. Whether the person and other agents have control over the passage—that is, the degree of influence which the passagee and others have over various aspects of the passage,

13. Whether the passage requires special legitimation—that is, whether the passage must have official sanction by an authorized agent,

14. Whether the signs of the passage are clear—that is, the degree to which there are explicit, external indicators that the passage is occurring,

15. Whether the signs of the passage are disguised—that is, the degree to which external indicators of the passage actually may be disguised in an attempt to hide them,

16. Whether the passage is central to the person—that is, how important it is to the person,

17. Whether the duration in passage is important—that is, the importance of the length of time in passage (Glaser & Strauss, 1971), and

18. Whether the passage is formal—that is, the degree to which the passage has defined, structural properties (Van Maanen & Schein, 1979).

These properties serve as focusing points in describing the socialization process across grade levels and school situations.

Summary of the Descriptive Frameworks

The three conceptual frameworks that guide the examination of student socialization from a communication perspective include: uncertainty reduction, concern, and status passage. The frameworks of uncertainty reduction and concern facilitate the understanding of student perceptions and feelings about their socialization experiences (that is, the types of uncertainty they have, the information they need, and the concerns they express). In contrast, the status passage framework is utilized, not to illuminate student perceptions, but to describe the actual process of socialization that students undergo (that is, the characteristics and dimensions of the socialization experiences). These three frameworks provide the conceptual basis from which the research questions in each chapter are derived. Taken in conjunction, they foster an understanding of how communication functions in the student socialization process. (See Figure 1.1 for a display of the conceptual frameworks underlying the book.)

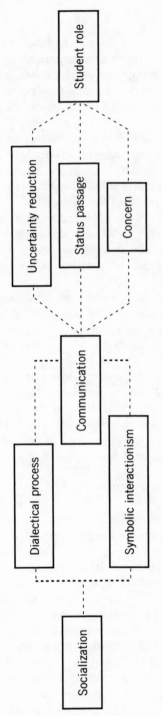

Figure 1.1. Conceptual Frameworks.

16

FOCUS OF THE BOOK

Grounded in symbolic interactionism and a dialectical model of socialization, this book examines socialization into the student role and school environment across the span of the child and adolescent student career. The emphasis is on communication. The central questions addressed across grade levels and new school situations include:

1. What does it mean to be a new student?
2. What is the nature of the communication process by which youngsters take on new student roles in new school environments?
3. What are the critical dimensions of the particular status passage?

Each of the empirical studies reported in Chapters Two through Seven addresses four research questions: Question 1 focuses on the meaning of the new student role; Questions 2 and 3 explore concerns of students, the information they need, and the way communication functions; and Question 4 identifies the salient status passage dimensions. Each chapter addresses parallel research questions in order to allow for a comparison of the socialization process for children and adolescents across grade levels. Literature relevant to the particular grade level or student situation is reviewed at the beginning of each chapter.

A METHODOLOGICAL NOTE

Consistent with a symbolic interactionist perspective for the study of student socialization, the general methodology employed throughout the six empirical studies in the book is interpretive or qualitative (Staton-Spicer, 1982). This approach focuses on "human meaning in social life and its elucidation and exposition by the researcher" (Erickson, 1986, p. 119). The aim is to provide description and analysis of the socialization experience. Across all of the chapters, student perspectives are presented from data derived from interviews, and, for some of the youngsters, written responses to open-ended questions (middle schoolers, freshmen, transfers). In addition, participant observations provided descriptive data about the socialization experiences of all students except for the high school freshmen.

The number of students who participated in the studies varied across grade levels and school situations. At the elementary school level, results were derived from case studies of a single kindergarten class and a single third grade class. At the middle-school level, interviews were conducted with some 100 sixth graders in two different schools. At the high school level, over 750 freshmen from four different schools responded to open-ended questionnaires. Participants in the study of transfer students were 15 youngsters who transferred into a single school. In the immigrant student chapter, nine students were observed at the bilingual center, and two of these were interviewed. Four of the nine were observed and interviewed during the second semester when they transferred to a regular high school. It is important that readers keep in mind these disparities in the number of participants.

There were similarites across the studies in the methods of data collection and analysis. To be certain that readers have a clear understanding, however, each chapter includes a brief description of the particular procedures employed.

chapter 2
Learning to be a Student: Kindergarteners' First School Experiences

This chapter presents a case study of a kindergarten class in a parochial school. It provides a glimpse inside the classroom where a group of five-year olds are making the first passage to the status of "student." The children begin the school year with their own expectations about the role of kindergartener. They engage in social interaction with their teachers and one another to make sense of the first formal school experience and to negotiate a role that is functional within the classroom context. As they make the transition from the private world of home to the public world of school they launch their career as students. Although novices to the career, they are active in defining and shaping the role.

Christopher Robin was going away. Nobody knew why he was going; nobody knew where he was going; indeed, nobody even knew why he knew that Christopher Robin was going away. But somehow or other everybody in the Forest felt that it was happening at last....

After they had walked a little way Christopher Robin said: "What do you like doing best in the world, Pooh?" ... "I like that too," said Christopher Robin, "but what I like doing best is Nothing."

"How do you do Nothing?" asked Pooh, after he had wondered for a long time.

"Well, it's when people call out at you just as you're going off to do it, 'What are you going to do, Christopher Robin?' and you say 'Oh, nothing,' and then you go and do it." "Oh, I see," said Pooh.

"This is a nothing sort of thing that we're doing now." "Oh, I see," said Pooh again.

"It means just going along, listening to all the things you can't hear, and not bothering."

"Oh!" said Pooh....

Then, suddenly again, Christopher Robin, who was still looking at the world with his chin in his hands, called out "Pooh!" "Yes?" said Pooh.

"When I'm–when–Pooh!"

"Yes, Christopher Robin?"

"I'm not going to do Nothing any more."

"Never again?"
"Well, not so much. They don't let you."
(Milne, 1928, p. 159, 168, 169, 175)

Christopher Robin is preparing to embark upon his first formal schooling experience. He has spent his early years enjoying life in The Hundred Acre Wood, passing away many pleasurable hours each day doing "Nothing." Although neither he nor any of his friends utters the word "school," it is undoubtedly that which will soon prevent him from doing "Nothing" any more.

Entry into kindergarten frequently signals the ending of a life filled with relatively free time. No longer are children able to select their own activities, go to the kitchen for a snack whenever they feel hungry, use the bathroom without seeking permission from an adult, or do "Nothing" just because they do not feel like doing anything else. Entry into kindergarten marks the passage from a world of play to a world of work, from moderately structured days to days that are usually highly structured and routinized, from a familiar home environment to an unfamiliar public facility, from interaction with a few significant others to contact with a relatively large number of strangers. These are but a few of the changes that children face as they begin their first school experience. As Moore (1986) observes, entrance into elementary school is:

> a turning point in the child's social and intellectual life. At that point the child enters a cohesive social system to which he or she will belong for many years to come. The school is the major social unit outside of the home where the child must adapt to be considered "competent" and "adjusted." (p. 110)[1]

In today's American society, entry into kindergarten is a reality for most five-year olds. In 1986, 90 percent of all five-year olds were enrolled in a kindergarten program (Spodek, 1986). Although most states do not mandate kindergarten attendance, all support kindergarten as an integral component of the public school system. Kindergarten is generally viewed as the first formal schooling experience (Borman, 1978; Fromberg, 1989; Martin, 1985). In a report on elementary education in America, then Secretary of Education William J. Bennett (1986) quoted one expert as saying: "I don't think kindergarten is an ambiguous issue anymore. It's school and it's here to stay" (p. 59).

This chapter deals with the first formal school experience for a group of five-year olds. The focus is on the challenges they face as they enter

---

[1] For those children who attend preschool, a somewhat similar passage may occur as they leave home and enter a "school" environment.

school for the first time and the ways they socialize into the classroom and school environment.

Learning to be a Student

As Balaban (1985) so aptly states, "Beginning school is an important event" (p. ix). Even for young children with prior experience in daycare or preschool situations, the first encounter with elementary school is "a milestone in their lives and the beginning of the 'big stuff'—the time when one begins to read books and get homework" (Moore, 1986, p. 128). The child must learn what it means to be a student, in contrast to what it means to be "Daddy or Mama's daughter or son," and must establish herself or himself in a student role that is comfortable (Woods, 1980). Although the formal student career is relatively long in duration, usually about 12 or 13 years, it is a transitional career and not a permanent one. As such, it takes on special dimensions.

As discussed in Chapter One, most research on school socialization has examined how schools function as agencies which socialize youngsters for adulthood. Much less attention has been directed to the question of how children learn to be students. With the shift in perspective from a functionalist model of socialization to a dialectical one, however, there has been an increasing call for the examination of how children become students. No longer are students viewed as interchangeable units acted upon by teachers. Indeed, student status is constructed through classroom interaction.

The view of student status, or role, as socially constructed relies upon several critical assumptions. First, students are active agents in the process of forming and developing the role. They are not simply recipients who conform to the expectations of others. This is clearly evidenced as one observes in classrooms and sees students engaging in a wide variety of student roles, for example, class clown or teacher's helper. Second, teachers and students are involved in a reciprocal relationship in which they socialize each other (Grant, 1979). Socialization is a process of mutual influence in which the teacher impacts students, students influence the teacher, and students affect one another. Third, the role of student is developed through interaction with others. Implicit in the view that a role is a *social* construction is the notion that it occurs as students interact and communicate with teachers, staff, other students, parents, and so on. The student role is not built by an individual in isolation, but by persons engaged in social interaction.

Thus, it is important to examine how children construct their first student roles as kindergarteners. Since kindergarten is the first "real" student role for most American children, the role learning that occurs is essential and may well set the tone for the entire student career. The critical question here is not "How does the school socialize kindergarteners for adulthood?," but rather, "What do students need to know in order to function effectively in the classroom?" (Mehan, 1980). Mehan acknowledges the need for students to accumulate a body of academic content, but stresses that such knowledge is not sufficient for competence in the classroom. Students must also demonstrate their competence in the appropriate use of their knowledge:

> The necessity for the integration of interactional form and academic content is readily apparent in elementary school classroom lessons. Although it is incumbent upon students to display what they know during lessons, they must also know how to display what they know. While students are expected to provide substantively correct academic content during lessons, they must be able to provide this information in the appropriate form. (p. 137)

Almost everyone is familiar with the case of an academically gifted child who does not "succeed" in the classroom because of an inability or unwillingness to conform even minimally to a teacher's requirements for appropriate behavior. A bright child who continually flaunts her or his knowledge, ridicules the responses of classmates, or challenges the teacher in an offensive manner is not likely to be viewed as competent in the student role. Thus, socialization into the student role involves a link between academic learning and social learning or interaction (Erickson, 1982; Hamilton, 1983). In the following sections, studies of student socialization into school are reviewed.

Teacher Influence on Student Socialization

Several recent studies have examined the process of student socialization into school with an emphasis on the influence of the teacher. In a study of six first-grade teachers, Blumenfeld, Hamilton, Wessels and Falkner (1979) asserted that successful socialization to the student role is the process by which schools accomplish their dual educational mission of imparting knowledge and developing citizens. They focused on teachers' statements about responsibility in order to understand how children socialize into the student role. From 10 hours of talk in the classroom of each teacher, statements were classified into categories of academic matters, procedural norms, and social/moral norms. Results indicated that open and traditional classrooms differed with respect to academic task structure, but that in general, teachers talked most about procedural matters, somewhat less about academic topics, and still less about social/moral issues. One interpretation they suggest is that "learning the student role initially may be a matter of learning the conventions of carrying out that role. Once the child has learned to sit still, follow instructions and adhere to general procedure, then the work of creating the scholar and citizen can begin" (p. 179).

In an extension of their earlier study, Blumenfeld, Hamilton, Bossert, Wessels, and Meece (1983) and Blumenfeld and Meece (1985) examined 18 classrooms, nine at the first-grade level and nine at fifth grade. Their research goal was to construct a map of socialization into the student role, focusing on teacher talk and its effect on student perception of the role. They found that teachers seem to take on a managerial role filled primarily with reactions to negative events such as disruptions or instances of rule breaking. Thus, "the student is essentially a socializee who absorbs on-the-job experience geared to passive citizenship in an ongoing institution" (Blumenfeld et al., 1983, p. 186).

Rohrkemper (1984) examined the role of the classroom teacher as a socializing agent, exploring the relationship of teacher socialization style to student perceptions and behaviors. Drawing on data from eight elementary school teachers and their students, ranging from first to fifth grade, she concluded that teacher socialization style (inductive or deductive) can be a strong influence on the social cognition and interpersonal behavior of students.

Teacher–Student Interaction in Student Socialization

Finally, there are three reports about the kindergarten year, consistent with the symbolic interactionist perspective of this book, which provide data about how teachers and students interact to construct social norms and rules. Drawing from observations of classroom interaction of two kindergarten classes over a two-year period, the research is based on the premise that "the study of socialization in educational settings is the study of how children and teachers arrive at an interpretation of the instructional content of a message that matches the social or ecological situation at that moment" (Wallat & Green, 1982, p. 102). Through analysis of teacher and student verbal and nonverbal behavior, Wallat and Green (1979) found that children as well as teachers use communication strategies such as clarifying, confirming, focusing, and restating in order to "make social events." They concluded that social rules emerge throughout the course of classroom conversation and are adapted to the flow of interaction.

Drawing on interaction data in a single kindergarten class, Wallat and Green (1982) examined the construction of social norms utilizing a three-step procedure, including: mapping conversation through analysis of verbal and nonverbal cues, identifying social norms through analysis of interaction patterns, and validating results with participants. They concluded that the construction of social norms is an issue of coordination between teachers and students and that "an adequate account of socialization processes must include the meaning of both verbal and nonverbal symbols to this coordination process" (p. 118).

In a third report based on data gathered in two kindergartens over a three-year period, Green and Harker (1982) explored the conversational, social, and cognitive demands for group participation and learning. Their work is based on an underlying assumption that an integral component of what children must learn in schools is how to participate in classroom conversation. Through comparisons of different classrooms, they found that the demands for participation and learning vary with teachers and schools.

Summary

Thus, some research has examined the influence of teacher talk and behavior on student socialization, and teacher–student interaction in the construction of classroom norms. This chapter builds upon and enhances previous research by presenting in-depth description and analysis of the way children take on their first formal roles as students in the first formal school environment.

PURPOSE OF THE CHAPTER

The purpose of this chapter is to provide an understanding of the communication process by which children learn to be pupils. The chapter addresses four research questions:

1. What does it mean to be a kindergartener?
2. What are the key challenges children face in becoming pupils?
3. How do children learn the role of kindergartener?
4. What are the critical dimensions in the passage to the status of kindergartener?

METHOD

Research Setting

The participants of the case study in this chapter were 20 kindergarteners and their teacher in a parochial (Catholic) school during the autumn semester of 1986. Comprising the group of 12 girls and eight boys, were 16 white students, three Hispanic, and one Asian. The teacher, Ms. Lane, was a white female in her ninth year of teaching kindergarten, six of those years in the present school. The school was located in a middle-class neighborhood in a large, West coast city. Tuition was charged but was relatively low. Most of the children were from lower- to middle-income families who made financial sacrifices to place their children in a religious school environment.

One of the requirements for admission was that each family pledge 50 hours of volunteer time annually to the school, either in fund raising activities or in assisting with school functions. The result was an unusually active parent community. Parents, especially mothers, were a common presence in the school—serving as teachers' aides, lunchroom monitors, and playground supervisors.

The school enrolled pupils in kindergarten through eighth grade, with one class at each grade level. There was a stable enrollment of approximately 200 students. Although a parochial school, the only staff person who was a member of the religious community was the librarian. The principal, teachers, and other staff were lay persons. The kindergarten class was a full-day program with an academic orientation.[2] Based on conversations with school staff and parents, it seemed evident that both viewed entry into kindergarten as the first formal schooling experience for the youngsters.

Procedures for Data Collection

There were four data bases for the chapter. First, to determine how children learn the role of kindergartener and to identify the key challenges and critical dimensions they face, observations were made in the school setting. For the first two weeks of school, the researcher was a daily observer. During the remainder of the autumn term, observations were made at least twice weekly. Since the researcher was present from the moment children entered the classroom, her presence seemed to be an immediate "taken-for-granted" by the students. Observations occurred in the regular classroom, in the art class, in the music class, in the math class, on the playground, in the lunchroom, at the Halloween carnival, and at the Christmas program. Of 76 instructional days, the researcher observed on 41 of them for a total of 70 hours. For the most part, the researcher's role was that of an unobtrusive, participant observer. As the

---

[2] There has been a resurgence of full-day kindergarten programs in recent years (Puleo, 1988; Robinson, 1987).

school term progressed the teacher occasionally called on the researcher to provide assistance, ranging from tying shoes to correcting work and answering student questions. The researcher tried to establish a friendly, yet neutral relationship with the children. When the researcher was left alone with the class on several occasions, she maintained the rules established by the teacher. At no time, however, did she report to the teacher about infractions of the rules, thus preserving a relationship of trust with the students. By the end of the observation period, most of the children were comfortable with the researcher, proferring hugs at every visit.

The second data base was a series of four interviews with the students designed to discover their perspectives and meanings about the first school experience. During early June of the previous academic year, the kindergarten teacher administered a readiness test as a prerequisite to entry into the class. After each child's testing was completed, the researcher conducted a 10-minute interview with her or him.[3] The questions focused primarily on the children's expectations about the kindergarten experience. The subsequent three interviews were conducted at the end of the first week of school in September, at the middle of the term, and during the last week of class prior to Christmas vacation.

The third data base was a series of four, scheduled 30-minute interviews with the classroom teacher. The interviews were conducted prior to the beginning of the school year and at monthly intervals throughout the term. Questions were designed to determine the teacher's goals for the class and her perceptions of how the class as a group and students as individuals were socializing into school. In addition, informal conversations with the teacher occurred on an ongoing basis.

A final source of data was that of assorted written documents. Included were notices the teacher sent home to parents, the principal's weekly school bulletin, various class handouts and student work sheets, pupil scores on the Iowa Basic Skills test, and reading readiness test scores.

Procedures for Data Analysis

Data analysis occurred in several stages. During the four months of data collection, the researcher recorded field notes during each daily observation. As suggested by Lofland and Lofland (1984), preliminary analysis began at the outset and occurred throughout, as well as after, the data collection period. Consistent with Smith and Geoffrey (1968), immedi-

---

[3] Ten minutes was a sufficient time period in which to gather needed responses, and seemed to stretch the limits of a kindergartener's attention span for answering direct question.

ately upon leaving the field each day, the handwritten notes were typed and reflections were recorded. The typed notes were scanned with each event or interaction categorized in a preliminary way using analytic induction (Goetz & LeCompte, 1981). At the end of each week the researcher reexamined the notes, reflections, and categories, and typed a summary sheet. At the end of each four-week period, this same sequence of analysis occurred with systematic checking of instances of emergent categories. Finally, after the data collection period ended, subsequent analysis enabled the researcher to refine and condense the categories.

Data collected through interviews with students were analyzed using similar inductive methods. Prior to each autumn interview, the researcher reread the field notes, reflections, categories, and summary sheets from the previous weeks' observations. Students were asked to respond to particular events that had been observed as well as to give their perspectives about kindergarten in general. These data were analyzed by coding openly the children's responses to specific incidents and to what it means to be a kindergartener (Spradley, 1979). The third data set, interviews with the teacher, was analyzed in a similar manner.

Finally, the assorted written documents were examined. These served to expand and supplement the analysis drawn from the interview and observation data (LeCompte & Goetz, 1982).

RESULTS

Question One: What Does it Mean to Be a Kindergartener?

Data to determine the meaning of kindergartener were drawn from interviews with the children. During the first, second, and fourth interviews, children were asked, "What do kindergarteners do?" During the second and fourth interviews, they were also asked, "What does it mean to be a kindergartener?" Responses to the questions were first analyzed separately, but then collapsed because of similarity and overlap. Results are described according to the phases of socialization discussed in Chapter One.

Anticipatory. Three months prior to the beginning of school, children articulated a variety of expectations for what kindergarteners do and for what they would do when they started kindergarten. The responses could be classified into three categories: academic (75%), social (20%), and procedural (5%). Included in the academic category were responses such as: do arithmetic, do "abc's," learn how to read and write, and do homework. The social category was comprised primarily of two activities: playing with kids, and having recess. The procedural category included comments about taking naps and having lunch.

When asked what would be the hardest part of kindergarten, responses included: spelling numbers and letters, doing too much work, learning what's 5 + 5, reading, math, and making things. Katie, a girl who cried every morning of the first week of school, responded that the hardest part would be "when I'm just coming here." When asked why, she replied, "Cause I don't know anybody."

Entry. Three months later, by the end of the first five or six days of class, when asked what kindergarteners do, the children offered a greater number of responses and more specific responses than they had in the spring. The same three categories emerged along with an additional one labeled "development." Consistent with the spring responses, children in September believed that kindergarteners engaged primarily in academic tasks (57%) (e.g., learning, studying, working, doing homework, writing numbers and counting, writing in workbooks), then social activities (30%) (e.g., playing, having friends, having fun), followed by prodedural (8%) (e.g., eating lunch, taking naps), and finally, development (5%) (e.g., being little and getting bigger, getting into bigger schools, having to go to school).

By the end of the first semester, another three-month interval, the youngsters were asked again about the meaning of being a kindergartener. Although children were at the end of their fourth month of school, their articulated definitions of kindergartener were strikingly similar to those given at the beginning of school: kindergarten as academic (59%) (e.g., working on math papers, doing projects, working in workbooks, learning sounds), kindergarten as social (36%) (e.g., going out to recess, having lots of friends, watching movies, having short people, big people and medium-sized people all together), and kindergarten as procedural (5%) (e.g., don't get in trouble, don't break the rules).

Changes in meaning over time. The expectations of this particular group of children about what it means to be a kindergartener and about what kindergarteners do matched very closely the realities they articulated once school was underway. They perceived of kindergarten as primarily an academic experience, but with "fun" activities as well. This perception was consistent with the view expressed by the classroom teacher about her philosophy of kindergarten and her goals for the class. Perhaps because the school was one in which parents were heavily involved, this group of children may have been well-prepared by their parents for the kindergarten experience. The category of "development" was present only during the entry phase, after the first week of class. It may have been that the very first days of school attendance highlighted for children that they were "bigger."

Question Two: What Are the Key Challenges Children Face in Becoming Pupils?

As children become pupils they must make a transition from the usually safe, familiar environment of home to the unfamiliar, less secure, less predictable world of school. As Lightfoot (1978) comments:

> The child takes the precarious journey from home to school, experiences the contradictions between the two settings, and must incorporate the myriad and often dissonant norms and expectations, while the adults seek to shape the environments and define the path in an attempt to assure the child's educational success. (p. 21)

Analysis of the classroom observation data indicates that there are two major challenges that children face as they journey from home to school: (a) making sense of inconsistency, misunderstanding, contradiction, and (b) dealing publicly with private trauma.

Making sense of inconsistency, misunderstanding, contradiction. This category includes instances in which children's intent is misunderstood; teacher talk or behavior is inconsistent; talk or behavior of one teacher contradicts that of another; and teacher talk or behavior is discrepant with what a child believes to have occurred.

Children's intent is misunderstood. There were times when it was apparent to the researcher that a child was not understood by the teacher. Sometimes Ms. Lane was unaware of any problem; at other times she probed for the child's intent, but stopped short of getting it. During a lesson on shapes, she asked individuals to find squares in the room. She called on Jake who pointed to the cover of the record player. Ms. Lane responded as if he had pointed to the record cart. Jake seemed frustrated and shook his head, but did not pursue the error.

During flash card drill one morning, Ms. Lane showed the class a card with a picture of a xylophone. Ned answered that it was "a mob." She was puzzled by his response and quizzed him further, even allowing him to come to the front of the room to look at the card. She finally said, "Oh, a mob of keys," to which he gave a weak nod. He returned to his seat, but it appeared to the researcher that his meaning had not been understood.

Another day, the teacher prepared to read a story to the class, explained that it had no pictures, and said: "Make them in your head." Ellen promptly closed her eyes as the teacher began reading and made hand movements as if she was making pictures of the story. Ms. Lane called to her: "Are you listening? Turn around and look at me." Ellen complied with the request, but looked confused, as if to say she had only been doing as the teacher had directed.

Teacher talk or behavior is inconsistent. Included in this category were instances in which there were discrepancies in something the teacher said or did.[4] As a way of reinforcing the concepts of left and right, Ms. Lane taught the class to play "Simon Says." Although she told the children to raise their hands only when she said "Simon Says," she raised her hands every time to model left and right. Since the children acted in accordance with the behavior she was modeling, not with what she was saying, they ended up confused and could not play the game "correctly." During a lesson on how to say something nice about somebody, David commented that Jake's sweater was nice, a reply that was accepted by the teacher. Jill then said that Jim's pants were nice. Ms. Lane did not accept this comment, however, saying that the remark was about his clothes and not about him. Jill looked puzzled. In a similar vein, during art class, the teacher asked children to draw and color a rainbow. She instructed them carefully about what particular colors to use and in what order, numbering each color. Walt then asked the teacher, "What blue do you think I should use?" The art teacher responded: "I never tell you what colors to use. I let you use your imagination." Walt understandably looked confused.

Other examples of inconsistency children faced had to do with the teacher violating rules. In one instance, the class was taking a standardized achievement test. Because most of the kindergarteners could not read, the teacher read every question aloud. Ms. Lane separated the children, put barriers between them, and instructed them to do their own work. There was one particular question that she found exceedingly difficult. She read the question aloud, but instead of giving the children time to figure out the answer for themselves, told them which response was correct. Several children looked very puzzled. Another instance of the teacher allowing children to break a rule occurred during an in-class birthday party. The birthday child distributed chewing gum as a party favor. Ms. Lane told the class they could chew the gum but must throw it away before they left, since "it's against school rules and you must not walk out of the school chewing gum."

One teacher contradicts another. Included in this category were instances in which the talk or behavior of one teacher contradicted that of another. As previously stated, the children also had music, art, and math teachers as well as the regular classroom teacher. Periodically there were incidents in which what one teacher said or did contradicted that of another. On the first day of art class, the teacher showed the children how

---

[4] Certainly all people, not just teachers, are inconsistent at times in their talk and behavior. In the classroom, however, dealing with instances of inconsistency seemed to be an important aspect of the sense-making process in socialization.

to draw themselves, using basic shapes (e.g., circles, squares) for various body parts and articles of clothing. Some days later the regular teacher was having a lesson on shapes and pointed to objects asking if they could be rectangles. When one child responded yes, an answer that was consistent with the lesson learned in art class, Ms. Lane said no. Another incident occurred when the regular teacher told the children not to put markers in their mouths, that if they returned from art class with marker on their faces she would have to scrub it off with cleanser. In the art class, Edward thought he had marker on his nose and went to the art teacher and asked. Her response was: "Some, but no big deal." Later, when back in the regular classroom, Ms. Lane asked if anybody broke the rule. Edward glanced at the researcher, but remained silent.

Teacher action is discrepant with child's reality. Another type of contradiction children faced was that in which the teacher talked or acted in a way that contradicted a child's experience. In the first week of school, Ms. Lane had the kindergarteners practice the fire drill procedure. During the first drill with the whole school present, Kim burst into tears as she went down the stairway. Ms. Lane, who was at the head of the line, did not see the crying incident. By the time Kim got outside, she had been comforted by another child and an adult. When the children returned to the classroom, the teacher proudly announced, "This is the first class ever when nobody cried the first time." Kim did not respond to Ms. Lane, but gave a knowing look to the researcher who had witnessed the crying.

In art class the teacher was showing the class how to draw pumpkins, working through sequential steps. When she was ready to move to the next step, she said, "Raise your hand if your stem is on." All raised their hands except for one child who was still working. The teacher's response was "Good, we're finished," and she proceeded to the next set of instructions, without a word to the child who was not finished. During regular class, the teacher repeated a comment Ned had made so the class could hear it. In the process, however, she repeated it incorrectly. Other instances occurred when Ms. Lane said a child's name wrong: Cindy turned a paper in to Ms. Lane who responded, "Beautiful, Tammi," not realizing her error. A substitute teacher complimented Jamie for standing nicely in line, but called him James. For all of the instances in this category, children were never observed to correct a teacher who had made an error. Instead, they were seen to look confused, make a "funny face," or give a knowing glance to the researcher.

Summary. There were a number of instances in which teacher talk or behavior was inconsistent, one teacher contradicted another, and teacher action was discrepant with a child's reality. Taken in conjunction, these instances may result in youngsters feeling confused and uncertain and having to face a great deal of ambiguity about the student role. This uncertainty and ambiguity need to be reduced for students to feel comfortable in the role.

Dealing publicly with private trauma. This category is comprised of instances in which children were observed to cry. Thus, in the context of this case study, the term "trauma" denotes any event in which a child cried. During the data collection period, 20 traumatic events involving 10 children were observed, primarily during the first month of school. An eleventh child experienced a trauma every day, beginning the second week of school. Although it was sometimes difficult to be certain about causes, traumas seemed to occur as a result of anxiety, embarrassment, or physical discomfort.

Traumas of anxiety. One girl, Katie, had intense feelings of anxiety about starting school and manifested these by crying every morning of the first week as her parent left her in the classroom. She repeatedly said she did not want to go to school, did not want to be left, and physically clung to her parent. Her parents were recently separated and both felt that her anxiety about being left at school was exacerbated by the father's leaving home. By the fifth day of school, she did not cry in the morning, but instead cried when it was time to leave school. The fifth day was actually the first full day for kindergarteners, and Katie was to go to the home of a classmate instead of being picked up by one of her parents. This experience of going to another new environment proved traumatic for her.

Another girl, Joan, cried every day of school, beginning the second week, until the teacher and her parents agreed that she should leave the school. She seemed fine during the first week when the children stayed only for three hours in the morning and engaged primarily in establishing procedures, setting rules, and playing. At the start of the second week, however, with the first all-day session, she cried every day. From observing the child, talking with her and her mother, and talking with the teacher, it seemed that she cried because of anxiety over starting school, anxiety over being separated from her mother, and fear of new tasks. Although the child had an older sister in the school and was reported by the mother to be excited about starting school, she seemed unable to cope with the myriad of new demands as well as the absence of her mother. This child's experiences were the most traumatic and resulted in her withdrawal from school after seven weeks. She was unable to make the transition from home to school, did not construct a student role that was acceptable, and thus did not experience successful socialization into school.

There were also less extended examples of traumas. One incident involved a boy who went to the bathroom by himself for the first time. As he left the classroom, he took the wrong set of stairs and got lost. When Ms. Lane found him he was in tears, apparently bewildered and frightened. The traumas due to anxiety were all incidents in which children were confronted with a new and unfamiliar experience, such as being at school for the first time, being around a large group of older students, being asked to work on new tasks, or getting lost in the new environment. These traumas may be indicators of a high level of student concern about self. It is reasonable to expect that youngsters going to school for the first time would have a great deal of self concern. And instead of expressing these concerns verbally, going to the teacher for reassurance, or going forward in a stoic manner, these children responded by crying.

Traumas of embarrassment. The embarrassing situations that prompted children to cry were ones that occurred in public, that is, in full view either of other children or adults in the environment. Typical situations included wetting pants, falling down on the playground, being reprimanded in front of others, being unable to answer a question asked by the teacher, forgetting to bring lunch from home, and spilling milk in the lunchroom.

Traumas of physical discomfort. Children were also observed to cry when falling down stairs, getting hurt on the playground, having a stomach ache, vomiting, and having a nose bleed. These situations were unremarkable in that most children this age typically cry when experiencing pain or feeling sick.

Children's perceptions and comments about traumas. During the interviews that occurred during the middle of the term, the 10 children who had been observed to cry were asked, "Have you ever cried at school? When? What for? Tell me about it."[5] Five of the children volunteered that they had cried because of physical pain—a stomach ache or a scraped knee. Only two of the five children whose trauma was attributed to embarrassment admitted to having cried; three denied ever having such a trauma. Finally, the two girls who had the daily bouts of crying due to anxiety firmly denied ever crying at all. Even when probed by the researcher and reminded of various incidents, the girls refused to admit the experiences. A conclusion that can be cautiously drawn is that crying at school has a negative connotation for children and is something that they are reluctant to discuss. Physical discomfort is the one cause of crying that seems to be at least somewhat "acceptable" and one to which children will admit.

Additional support for the children's negative perceptions of crying was garnered in the final set of interviews when they were asked, "Why wasn't Joan (the child who withdrew after seven weeks) ready to be in kindergarten?" Fourteen of the 19 children replied that she wasn't ready for kindergarten because she "cried too much," "was crying all the time,"

---

[5] The eleventh crying incident had not occurred at the time of the interview.

"kept on crying," or "always had to cry." Other reasons were offered in addition to crying, but it was the one most frequently mentioned.

Also during the final interview at the end of the term, all children were asked, "What things make kindergarteners cry?" Among the various responses, children identified causes of crying that could be categorized into the previously discussed categories: anxiety (they cry when they are scared, they cry when they want their mom or dad), embarrassment (getting yelled at by the teacher, spilling milk), and physical discomfort (when they fall off the bars at school, when somebody pushes them down). An additional category, hurt feelings, also emerged. This category included such instances as: "they cry when somebody says that they don't like 'em," "when somebody says 'I'm not gonna be your best friend anymore,' " "when nobody plays with them," and "when somebody is not being nice."

Finally, an isolated response of one boy did not cluster with others, but merits mention because it is an example of sex-stereotyped role learning. When asked why kindergarteners cry, Jake replied with a thoughtful look on his face and in a serious tone: "Cause some girls have hormones. They get sad a lot. Their hormones make them cry." When probed by the researcher as to "What exactly are hormones and who told you about them?" he responded: "Things that girls have. My mother told me about them." These children, although somewhat reticent in discussing their own bouts of crying, readily expressed their views as to why others cried.

Question Three: How Do Children Learn the Role of Kindergartener?

Analysis of the data from classroom observations indicates three major sources for role learning. These include the teacher, other classmates, and oneself through experience and experimentation.

Teacher as a source of role learning. Given a teacher's function in the classroom, she or he is an important source of pupil role learning. Ms. Lane provided such information in two major ways: through explicit definitions of what it means to be a kindergartener, and through a variety of ways in which she exercised power.

Teacher definitions of kindergartener. During the first week of class, Ms. Lane made a number of explicit comments defining what it meant to be a kindergartener. In general, she characterized kindergarteners as children who were special ("We're not the smallest in the school. How about we're the specialest?"), smart ("You're all smart. Anybody here not smart?"), and happy ("Nobody leaves without a smile on their face. You can't have a sour puss." "Can you leave here with a smiley face?" "I want to see smiles on your faces."). The tasks of kindergarteners as set forth by the teacher included learning the rules and adhering to them:

"Just like at home, school has rules. If I stood here and told you all of the rules, you'd never remember them. So I'll just tell you a few now." "We need to write the rules down so we don't forget them."

As the school term progressed, defining comments were still offered by the teacher, but less frequently. While the themes of being special, smart, and happy were evident throughout the term, a new theme, relating to work in school, emerged during the seventh week: "Nice and neat. No scribbling. You're in school now." "It's not always easy but you'll be proud when you're finished." "Remember, you are in school to learn things. If you knew everything you wouldn't need school."

Exercise of teacher power. Ms. Lane attempted to guide and struc-ture children into a student role she deemed appropriate through various expressions of her power, including establishing herself as the authority and use of imperatives, rewards, and negative sanctions.

There were two strategies Ms. Lane used for *establishing herself as the authority:* referring to herself in the third person, and issuing direct reminders to students that she was the boss. Repeatedly, when stating a new rule, invoking a known rule, or making an assignment, the teacher referred to herself as Ms. Lane: "Something Ms. Lane forgot to tell you this morning," and "Ms. Lane wants you to get out your crayons and close your box." On occasions when children were trying to take charge of others or be what she considered too directive, Ms. Lane responded: "Who's the boss around here?," or "Who do you think is the teacher?"

There were four types of *teacher imperatives,* each serving a unique function for some task accomplishment, but also serving to display the power of the teacher: (a) content-related ("I'm going to give everybody a paper. Has your name on it, some dots. How many know what tracing is? It means you go over. Then you're going to make your name twice. Understand? When you get your paper you may start. Start at the begin-ning with the first letter. Remember, all names begin with a capital letter and then small letters."); (b) procedure-related ("First thing we do on a Monday is to help me out. I need volunteers to help Ms. Lane." "Will you check the books on the shelves and make sure none are on the floor?" "I need two people to erase the board if it's very messy."); (c) social norm-related ("When you hurt someone you tell them you are sorry."); and (d) restriction of activity, movement, and talk ("Close your workbooks and put them away; you may finish the work later." "You may not go to the water fountain now." "There is to be no talking while you are working.").

Teacher *use of rewards* was manifest in several forms: (a) compliments ("Nice job." "Good work." "I like the people who are raising their hands."); (b) self rewards ("Pat yourself on the back."); (c) concrete rewards ("You may have a sun [paper sun with smiley face] that is yours to take home." "Those who remembered may come up and get a sticker." "Katie, please come up and get an award for listening."); and (d) privileges ("Table 1, you may go to the line first." "Edward, you may be the first to get a drink of water.").

A final way in which the teacher reinforced student role learning was through various types of *negative sanctions:* (a) verbal reprimands ("Cut out the chatter."); (b) requests to return ("Mickey, Jackie, you got your boxes without your names being called. Return yours to the closet and wait until you hear your name." "Angie, get out of the line and go back to your seat and put your chair up on the desk."); (c) loss of privilege ("If you cannot remember the rules, you will miss recess." "You will not get to see the movie with the rest of the class if you continue to talk."); and (d) threat of public display (Ms. Lane had a large dragon drawn on the front chalkboard. One of the rules she established the first week was that an infraction could result in getting one's name in the Dreadful Dragon: "If you cannot get your work done without disturbing your neighbor, I will have to put your name in the Dreadful Dragon.").

In their classic work on power, French and Raven (1959) identify five types of power that can be used in establishing authority: expert—attributed on the basis of knowledge; referent—attributed on the basis of a group's identification with a person as their leader; legitimate—attributed because of the role; reward—attributed on the basis of control of rewards; and coercive—attributed due to ability to punish. There were many instances in which Ms. Lane relied upon legitimate, reward, and coercive power, but few instances of either expert or referent power. Appeals to legitimate power (I'm the boss), reward (You may have a sticker), and negative sanctions (You will miss recess) are overt and direct, while appeals to expert and referent power are more subtle and perhaps too sophisticated for young children.

Through the use of various imperatives, rewards, and negative sanctions, Ms. Lane reduced uncertainty about the academic tasks she wanted students to perform and about the ways she wanted them to behave. By establishing herself as the authority, she reduced any potential ambiguity about the teacher–student status.

Classmates as a source of role learning. A second important source of information about the role of pupil was provided by classmates and occurred as kindergarteners interacted with one another. Two major categories of interaction emerged from observations: child reprimands child, and child imitates child.

Child–child reprimands. This category includes instances in which one child reprimands the behavior of another, either with or without invoking a classroom rule. Incidences of reprimands were not observed until the beginning of the fifth week of the term, after the group had been together for a month. Because issuing a reprimand to a peer is such an assertive action, it is reasonable that children needed to feel secure and fairly confident in the new environment first. The reprimands took two forms, most frequently as verbal comments addressed to an "offender," and less often as nonverbal (physical or visual) actions directed to a classmate.

Verbal reprimands were frequently made to remind other children about rules they had forgotten to implement: "You forgot to push your chair in." "John, put your box away." At the end of one day a child reminded her seat partner to: "Put your chair up" [on top of the desk]. The usual response in these instances was to comply with the reminder.

Other verbal reprimands occurred when one child felt her or his "rights" were being violated by a classmate who was breaking an established rule. A frequent instance related to breaking into a line: "You cutted." A related example occurred as children gathered around the researcher for assistance with a project. As one child approached the group and pushed her way forward, another girl responded angrily: "I was here first." Another common example occurred during the show-and-tell period. The teacher had a rule that the class must be quiet and attentive and must listen when a child was presenting at the front of the class. Toward the end of the term, children preparing to speak began to be assertive in reprimanding others who were not giving their full attention: "I'm looking around." "Waiting for George." "Joanie is coloring." "Rick is laying down." There were various instances when a child touched, hit, or pinched another, thus violating a widely known rule. These transgressions were followed by a call to "Stop!" Immediate compliance was the usual response of the child who had been reprimanded.

Still other reprimands involved chastising another for violating a rule, even when the violation did not infringe upon another child's rights. One day Ms. Lane brought in a goldfish and told the children its name. As they gathered around the fish, one child asked its name. A girl responded: "She told us, you didn't listen." During music class as they were about to begin a song, one child was lying down on the floor and the boy next to him said: "Sit up."

A final type of verbal reprimand occurred, not with respect to rule violations, but when one child did not approve of what another child had said or done. Examples of this type included a wide range of comments: During art class a child was absent-mindedly hitting herself on the head when the girl next to her said: "Stop hitting yourself on the head." During an in-class party, the birthday boy put on a crown that the teacher had made for him. A girl seated in front called out to him: "Wrong way." One morning before Christmas, one boy exclaimed to another: "Happy Christmas, Steve!" A girl standing nearby blurted out: "Merry Christmas, not Happy Christmas."

Nonverbal reprimands occurred with much less frequency than verbal ones and took two forms: physical (pushing) and visual (nasty looks). A common way of reprimanding another for cutting into line was to push or shove the person back out of line. This occurred in the morning before school began as children stood in line waiting for the teacher to come and take them inside. It also occurred during music class in which the children always stood or sat in a circle. Attempts to break into the circle were often thwarted by a shove. Visual reprimands were observed to be given primarily for transgressions such as silliness and giggling, which did not threaten rights or territory. The child would simply give a "dirty look" to another. At times, dirty looks also accompanied pushes and shoves to prevent another from breaking into line.

These instances of verbal and nonverbal child–child reprimands constitute what Goffman (1967) refers to as "challenges" in the corrective interchange. For these kindergarteners, evidences of misconduct were readily challenged and brought to the attention of the offender. Unlike the sequence of moves Goffman describes for reestablishing order, however, the offending child typically complied with the suggested behavior change or ignored the comment altogether. No interactions were observed in which a challenge was followed by an offering, acceptance, and thanks. In contrast to the kindergarteners observed by Hatch (1987), who engaged both in challenges and offerings, the five-year olds described in this chapter engaged in challenges followed by complying or ignoring.

Child imitates child. This category consists of instances in which one child directly imitates the behavior of another. Two types of imitations emerged: those that serve to help a child accomplish a work-related task, and those that illustrate a way to bend, stretch, or test a rule. Work-related imitations occurred from the outset of the school year, while the latter type began to emerge only after the seventh week of the term.

One type of *work-related imitation* occurred during the first week of school and continued throughout the term. Immediately following the morning ritual of group prayer, individual children made special requests in response to the teacher's query of "What do you want to pray for?" A pattern that developed was for children to repeat the prayer of those who preceded them. For example, if the first child asked the class to pray "for my cold," others would follow with the same request. If a child prayed "that nobody gets their name in the Dreadful Dragon," others joined in. There were always a few children who made unique petitions that could not be requested by others ("that my mother comes home soon from her trip"), but the majority of the prayers each day were very similar. From this imitative process, children seemed to learn what sorts of prayers were acceptable to the group and to the teacher, in effect, building a repertoire of acceptable types of petitions.

Children also relied upon imitation of others to generate "correct" answers to questions raised by the teacher. During a religion lesson, Ms. Lane asked students to pretend they lived in a hot climate without much food and asked them what they would need. The first child to respond called out: "fork and knife." Although the answer was not what Ms. Lane had in mind, she nodded anyway. Immediately, others chimed in with similar responses: "maybe a knife," "napkin," "plates." These responses, based on imitation of classmates, continued despite the teacher's efforts to redirect the lesson.

Similarly, children imitated one another in order to complete tasks designated by the teacher. Ms. Lane assigned children to "study" a particular letter each day, asking them to bring an object from home that began with the new letter, not a required task but a voluntary one that was rewarded by a sticker. A pattern developed for those children who forgot to bring in an object but who wanted to receive a sticker. One creative child displayed his hat for the letter "h." Immediately, several other children got up from their seats, went to the coat closet to retrieve their hats, and went to the front of the room to show them. This particular form of imitation occurred repeatedly.

Finally, children imitated one another as a way of being innovative and gaining latitude in their activities. Toward the end of a day in which a substitute teacher was present, she announced that the class had done all of their work and that they could now listen to music. One assertive child asked: "Can I sing a song first? Everybody's heard it, but I want to say it for you." He went to the front of the room and sang his song. Several others then volunteered to sing songs as well.

The *rule-stretching imitation* was a way in which the less daring children learned from the more bold ones ways to deviate from the norms. There were a variety of examples: During music class, children were to sit on the floor and not in the chairs. As one particularly self-confident child sat down on a chair, another less confident one followed suit. In another instance, on the way upstairs to the math room, the class passed by the water fountains which were covered over with cardboard boxes for repair. Several children passed by without seeming to notice. One girl then stopped to lift the lid of the box and have a look. Most of the children following her also lifted the lid and looked, many glancing around to check the whereabouts of the substitute teacher. Another example occurred during the morning song routine in which children formed a large circle around the desks and marched in time to the music. One outspoken girl,

Jane, cut inside the desks instead of following the child in front of her. The girl behind Jane also cut inside, all the while looking to see if she would be reprimanded. Thus, imitation is an important strategy that children use in accomplishing work tasks and testing the limits of established rules and norms.

Self as a source of role learning. Although the first major source of role learning for the new kindergarteners was the teacher, students were by no means passive recipients of teacher socializing talk and behavior. Indeed, students actively carved out their own roles as they interacted with the teacher and with their classmates.

Child reprimands child. This previously discussed category is a strategy whereby peers influence other peers, but it should also be viewed as one children use to structure the role of pupil for themselves. The child who issues a reprimand to shape the behavior of another is also involved in her or his own role construction. "Teaching" the role to another reinforces and enhances the role for the one doing the "teaching."

Child imitates child. For this previously discussed category, although the child doing the imitating is not innovating, she or he is involved actively in role learning as she or he implements a new behavior.

Compliance. A major way in which children learn the role of kindergartener is through compliance. As discussed, the teacher exerted power by establishing herself as the authority, issuing imperatives, dispensing rewards, and administering negative sanctions. From the moment school opened, children began to learn the role by compliance with the teacher in three domains: normative, affective, and cognitive.

The first order of business was to establish norms for appropriate classroom procedure. Some of these were outlined by Ms. Lane; others were negotiated with the children through teacher-led classroom discussion. Once rules had been set, children demonstrated knowledge of them by reciting them when called upon by Ms. Lane. Behavioral compliance with the classroom procedures (e.g., raise your hands, push your chair in every time you get up, line up when we leave the room, sweaters belong on the back of chairs, say a prayer before snack) was the "norm" during the early weeks. Children learned by articulating procedures and by enacting them.

A second domain of the pupil role was the affective or social/relational. In addition to learning surface procedures and routines, on a deeper level children internalized their status with respect to the teacher and to peers. Through compliance with all forms of teacher regulative talk and behavior, children learned that Ms. Lane was the one in charge and that classmates were to be considered as peers. A family metaphor with the teacher as parent and students as siblings was elucidated by Ms. Lane during the first week and was one with which students complied:

We don't say anything bad about anybody else. What's important about that rule? If you call somebody a name will you get upset? Will the person get upset? We are one big happy family. We are like brothers and sisters. We are together every day. We see each other every day. If somebody does something mean, you come to me.

The final aspect of the student role was a cognitive one. Ms. Lane's philosophy was that children must adhere to the classroom norms and must understand the teacher–student relationship in order that the academic goals might be accomplished. Thus, the first weeks of school focused more heavily on normative and affective dimensions than on the cognitive. Initially, children began learning academic tasks by complying with teacher directives. The pattern that developed was for Ms. Lane to announce a task, give instructions to the whole class, then tell students to begin. There were no early instances of children questioning the merit of a given task or asking questions to clarify the task. Instead, children were observed to comply immediately, either attempting a task even though uncertain about what to do or looking over to see how a classmate was executing it. In some instances, a child sat and looked confused, but did not question Ms. Lane. After the third week of school, however, children began to ask questions and be more assertive when an assignment was not clear or when they needed assistance. They were still learning the academic aspects of the student role by compliance with assignments, but having learned some of the normative and affective dimensions, students were better equipped to handle increased teacher–student interaction and negotiation about the tasks.

Noncompliance. Another important strategy by which children experiment with the new role of pupil is that of noncompliance. This category is comprised of instances in which children do not participate in group activity, do not comply with an established rule, or refuse to follow a teacher directive. Through such instances, children test the limits of the explicit rules, assert themselves, and learn another dimension of the role of pupil (i.e., how much of what the teacher says do I really have to do?).

After the first month of school, there were instances in which certain children did not participate fully in the morning routine of singing and marching along with the records. A few put their hands in their pockets instead of making hand movements to accompany the music. Various children did not join in singing the songs, but remained silent. This form of noncompliance also occurred during music class. For particular songs, certain children would lay down on the floor (while others were sitting on the floor) and not join in the singing. Occasionally, individual students would not take part in an academic task. During a group lesson using flash cards to teach sounds, one kindergartener said to the teacher: "I hate this."

The teacher responded that she did not have to participate. Later in the lesson, the girl commented: "I wish I got picked since I didn't do the thing." She apparently changed her mind and decided she wanted to participate.[6]

There were a variety of instances of behavior which were not in compliance with classroom rules or norms. During prayers one morning, two seat partners folded their hands in an upside-down position instead of in the prescribed manner. During roll check, one girl crouched behind her chair that was still on top of her desk and hid from the teacher. Noncompliance in the form of rowdy behavior (behavior that exceeds the acceptable levels established by the regular classroom teacher) was often exhibited when a substitute teacher was present and during music class. Typical out-of-compliance behaviors observed when a substitute teacher was in charge included: frequent getting out of seats, increased acts of physical aggression (hitting) among children, and talk among small groups of children instead of paying attention during show-and-tell time. During music class there was a marked increase in off-task behavior such as playing around on the floor, pretending to sleep, turning somersaults, crawling on all fours, giggling, and writing on the chalkboard. These were all behaviors not permitted by the regular classroom teacher and children were aware that they were breaking rules. In music class, even children who were normally compliant were observed to break rules.

A third, but less frequent, type of noncompliant behavior was one in which children actually refused to follow a teacher directive. One striking example occurred when a boy was in line at the pencil sharpener and also had his supply box with him. Ms. Lane told him to go back to his seat and put the box away. As she then became involved with other children, the boy turned around, looked at the rather long line in back of him, and stayed where he was. The researcher was left with the impression that he decided it was worth the risk not to lose his place in line. Another instance occurred when three boys were writing on the chalkboard and playing with chalk dust as they stood in line in music class. The music teacher told them: "Don't get your fingers on that or your Mama will get mad. You'll get chalk all over you." Although it was clear that the boys heard the teacher, all three continued with their activity.

---

[6] From the very beginning of school there was one girl who had an especially difficult adjustment. Katie cried each morning when one of her parents brought her to class. She did not take part in morning prayers, the pledge, or songs. For her, however, this noncompliance behavior did not seem to serve the same function as for others. She did not participate because she did not want to be a member of the class, whereas for others, it seemed that they felt a part of the group, but were asserting themselves.

Question Four: What Are the Critical Dimensions in the Passage to the Status of Kindergartener?

From a synthesis of the data drawn from classroom observations, student interviews, and teacher interviews, a picture of the status passage emerges. Viewed from the conceptual framework of Glaser and Strauss (1971), entry into kindergarten occurs as a ritualized status passage for most five-year olds in American society. It is a *regular, scheduled* occurrence that many youngsters await with great excitement and anticipation. For others, the prospect is greeted with proverbial fear and trepidation. Becoming a kindergartener is inevitable for most; it may occur earlier for some (as young as four years of age) and later for others (as old as six years), but it does occur for all but the rare exception.

For the kindergarteners discussed in this chapter, the passage was *central* to them and *desirable*. During interviews with them the spring before school began, all children expressed a wish to attend kindergarten. Similarly, after the first week of school, 19 of the 20 indicated that they were glad to be in kindergarten. The one exception was Katie, the girl who cried every morning of the first week. When asked if she was glad to be there, she responded: "Not really. Takes too long to get home." After more questioning of the child, the researcher concluded that she meant too much time was spent at kindergarten and away from home.

Similarly, for most of the kindergarteners, the passage was not *reversible* or *repeatable*. The assumption of the teacher and the parents was that the kindergarteners were progressing steadily toward first grade. There was no classroom discussion even entertaining the possibility that the passage would be reversed or repeated. There were, however, two children for whom these temporal dimensions were salient. One child, Joan, who was discussed previously, cried everyday and never adjusted to the classroom environment. The teacher and her parents agreed that she should withdraw, thus reversing her passage into kindergarten status and necessitating a repeat of the passage the following year. A second child, Edward, was four years old for the first six weeks of school and was admitted with special permission only. His mother was very casual about this and told Ms. Lane throughout the year that she did not mind if he repeated the next year. This was the course of action that was taken ultimately.

Another critical dimension of the socialization into kindergarten is that the children experienced the status passage as a group or *collective*. The kindergarten encounter was a new experience for all of the children, as acknowledged openly by their teachers and by the kindergarteners themselves when asked by the researcher. Because all parties were consciously *aware* of the passage of the whole group, there was a great deal of explicit *communication* in the system about being new kindergarteners. The class was singled out and permitted to attend school for only half a day during the first week, in contrast to all of the other grade levels who remained for a full day. They were given guided tours of the physical facility and formally instructed about school rules. Most of the first week was spent establishing and discussing rules for the class, with the teacher emphasizing the collective and articulating a family metaphor, that is, teacher as parent and pupils as brothers and sisters.

The rules that Ms. Lane permitted the children to generate were designed in part to protect individual rights, but more importantly, to permit the class to function as a group (e.g., "No pushing." "No hitting." "Don't touch people's things." "Don't talk when somebody else talks.").

Finally, the passage to kindergartener can be characterized as one that occurred in this school with a certain degree of *formality* and a particular set of rituals. There was *clarity in the signs of the passage.* For example, the regular classroom teacher, as well as the art and music teachers and the principal, all addressed the children as "kindergarteners." Although individuals were called by name, when the class was addressed as a collective or referred to, the term "kindergarteners" was used much more often than the terms "students" or "children." In addition, various school rituals and routines served to set the kindergarteners apart from the other students. Every morning before school, kindergarteners were required to line up along a fence outside the front entrance. They had to remain standing until Ms. Lane came and escorted them into the building. Children in all of the other grades were permitted to play freely until the bell rang and enter on their own accord. At dismissal time, only the kindergarteners remained supervised outside by Ms. Lane until picked up by a designated adult. The kindergarteners, by school custom, were the first ones to get to the lunchroom daily. During recess, they were allowed to play only with their own classmates, while students in other grades were observed to interact across grade levels. The kindergarteners were fully aware of this "segregation," as were other students in the school. Clearly, there were a number of formal mechanisms and signs of the passage whereby kindergarteners were set apart from students in other grade levels.

DISCUSSION

The results presented in this chapter point clearly to socialization into the student role as an extremely complex and challenging process for children barely into their sixth year of life. Accompanied by a cohort of strangers, these youngsters had to become knowledgeable about academic, social, and procedural tasks, many of which were unfamiliar and even unusual (e.g., what child had ever contemplated the prospect of getting lost on the way to use the bathroom?). That 19 of the 20 students were "successful" in their socialization into kindergarten is really quite remarkable given the complicated nature of the process.[7]

Centrality of Communication in the Socialization Process

Communication was at the center of the socialization process as children learned to be students. From the moment of entry into class, this group of children listened to the teacher's comments about what kindergarteners were like and what kindergarteners should do. They listened to her directives and imperatives and observed the types of behaviors that she rewarded and punished. As children interacted with one another, they learned appropriate procedures and academic tasks by imitating classmates. They also learned from negative sanctions received from one another. By compliance with the teacher, children engaged in appropriate normative, affective, and cognitive dimensions of the student role. By noncompliance with established rules and norms, they began to assert themselves and test the limits of the student role as prescribed by the teacher.

For these new kindergarteners, communication functioned to help them "make sense" of the first school experience and served as the means by which they acquired needed information to reduce their uncertainty about the student role. As they experienced the array of new events and engaged in numerous communication interactions, the children began to learn what was expected of them by others. Along with this increased knowledge came an ability to predict the behavior of the teacher and classmates, as well as the consequences of their own behavior. As the school term progressed, there were more instances of student reprimands to one another and fewer instances of traumatic events. Students became more skilled in deviating from the rules, being careful, for example, to keep a watchful eye out for the teacher when engaging in a questionable act. Overall, they became more sophisticated in integrating "interactional form and academic content" (Mehan, 1980, p. 137) and thus, more competent in the classroom (e.g., students who forgot to bring an object from home that began with a designated letter of the alphabet improvised and used a garment they were wearing, never admitting that they had forgotten the assignment). These findings are consistent with previous correlational

---

[7] At the end of the term, Ms. Lane indicated that she felt all 19 children who remained in the class had settled into a comfortable and appropriate student role.

research indicating that communicative competence is important in kindergarten adjustment (Skarpness & Carson, 1987).

Communication also served to facilitate children's resolution of various self and task concerns. Katie, who cried the first week of school and who expressed concern about how difficult kindergarten would be "cause I don't know anybody," was a well-adjusted student by the end of the first term.[8] When asked by the researcher about her feelings toward kindergarten, she responded several times about having friends and having somebody to play with at recess. For her, making friends and interacting with them was a key to resolving her self concern about not knowing anybody. So too, children resolved concerns about academic and procedural tasks as they engaged in communication with the teacher and with classmates. As discussed, they gained knowledge and were reassured about what to do, thus resolving concerns through interaction with others.

Children as Active Constructors of the Student Role

Consistent with the concepts presented in Chapter One of communication as a transaction, socialization as a dialectical process, and human society as symbolic interaction, these kindergarteners were active in their role enactment. During the first weeks of the school term, compliance with the teacher's regulative communication was the norm. After the first month, however, a variety of instances of noncompliance began to emerge with the regular classroom teacher as well as with a substitute, the art, and music teachers. Children enacted the student role in different ways when interacting with various teachers and classmates. Similar to the descriptions of primary school children offered by Pollard (1985), the student role for these kindergarteners took on variations when they were functioning in the separate domains:

> children's culture develops within an informal social structure of friendship, hierarchy and status. This is very important to children and provides a social context which runs in parallel with that of the official academic and organisational structures of the school. To enjoy their school days to the full children must cope in both spheres at the same time. (p. 49)

Although the school system itself as well as the teacher both function to shape and constrain the student role, the children themselves must also be considered as "initiators and controllers of schooling" (Riseborough, 1985, p. 204).

---

[8] Ms. Lane characterized Katie as well-adjusted and the observation data supported this conclusion.

A Concluding Note

Just as Christopher Robin anticipated an end to his days of doing "Nothing," the children in this study who entered kindergarten experienced a new world filled with academic, social, and procedural activity. Christopher Robin's poignant exchange with Pooh ("I'm not going to do Nothing any more." "Never Again?" "Well, not so much. They don't let you.") is an apt characterization, except for its implication that it is only external agents who prevent children from doing "Nothing." Indeed, the kindergarteners in Ms. Lane's class actively constructed and enacted their own roles as pupils. They have taken the initial steps on their journey through formal schooling and have experienced the first of many status passages.

chapter 3
Learning the Ropes: Third Graders in a New School

Co-authored with Dee Oseroff-Varnell

This chapter is a case study of a single third-grade class in a public elementary school. Unlike the kindergarteners who were experiencing their first taste of formal schooling, these children are veteran newcomers entering a new grade level in a new school building. They have already experienced socialization to the student role in previous years of schooling. What they must do is make sense of the role of third grader in a unique classroom setting with an unfamiliar group of interactants. Individual students bring their own role definitions to the classroom and must fit them with those of other classmates and the teacher in order to come together as a coherent classroom group. Through communication, the teacher and the students establish academic and social norms for the classroom and achieve cohesion.

Ramona Quimby hoped her parents would forget to give her a little talking-to. She did not want anything to spoil this exciting day. "Ha-ha, I get to ride the bus to school all by myself," Ramona bragged to her big sister, Beatrice, at breakfast. Her stomach felt quivery with excitement at the day ahead, a day that would begin with a bus ride just the right length to make her feel a long way from home but not long enough—she hoped—to make her feel car-sick. Ramona was going to ride the bus, because changes had been made in the schools in the Quimby's part of the city during the summer ... which meant Ramona had to go to Cedarhurst Primary School. ... All summer, whenever a grown-up had asked what grade she was in, she felt as if she were fibbing when she answered, "third," because she had not actually started the third grade. Still, she could not say she was in the second grade since she had finished that grade last June. ... Ramona had too many interesting things to think about to let her responsibility worry her as she walked through the autumn sunshine toward her school bus stop, her new eraser in hand, new sandals on her feet, that quivery feeling of excitement in her stomach, and the song about high hopes running through her head. ... Ramona's new room was filled with excitement and confusion. She saw some people she had known at her old school. Others were strangers. Everyone was talking at once, shouting greetings to old friends or looking over those who would soon become new friends, rivals, or enemies.... "My name is Mrs. Whaley," said the teacher, as she printed her name on the blackboard. (Cleary, 1981, pp. 11–12, 19–20, 31–32)

Moving up from second to third grade may not be viewed as a monumental event for those of us who are years removed from elementary school, but to an eight-year old like Ramona, it is an important milestone, marked by "a quivery feeling" of excitement and confusion. Each new grade for a "little kid" symbolizes another step in the slow and sometimes painful process of becoming a "big kid." Each of these steps is accompanied by a host of new situations for the child to process and make sense of: new teachers, more difficult academic work, increasingly complex social relations, different friends, more responsibility, and, for youngsters like Ramona, a first bus ride and a new school environment. Between the increase in status and the high level of uncertainty that accompany the move to the next grade, it is no wonder that children anticipate the first day of the school year with mixed feelings of excitement and trepidation.

This chapter examines a class of third graders who not only began a new grade level, but also moved from their previous primary schools in which they were the "big kids" to a third- through fifth-grade school in which they were once again the "little kids." The focus is on what it means to be a third grader from both the children's and the teacher's perspectives, and how these newcomers "learn the ropes" in a new school after three years of prior experience as students in a different school.

The Mutual Shaping of Roles: Students as Active Participants

The acquisition of new roles is an integral part of being human: "For the sociologist, to be human is to be socialized. To be socialized is to acquire roles" (Mackay, 1974, p. 181). When children enter school, they are entering into a world of prescribed roles. In this world the rules, expectations, social behavior, even the proper time to get a drink of water are all monitored by adults in an attempt to introduce children to the normative roles of students and of citizens in a larger community.

Although it cannot be denied that the schools have hidden agendas that shape children's roles within the school system, children themselves bring to school their own values, norms, and expectations which interact with the nonacademic agendas to create a mutual shaping of the socialized "product." The importance of the children's role in the socialization experience is illustrated in a two-year observation study of two primary school Italian American youngsters in their respective school and home environments (Florio & Shultz, 1979; Shultz, Florio, & Erickson, 1982). In examining the interactional contexts of these children, the researchers found striking functional similarities between the patterns of interaction in the two contexts. The children, however, often experienced problems applying the proper interactional norms in the classroom. For example, the authors cite functional parallels between the preparatory stages of a dinner and the preparatory stages of a math lesson, yet in the former multiple conversations were permissible while in the latter they were not. The children's understanding of the interactional behavior that was appropriate for a functionally similar event at home (preparing dinner) was inappropriate for the event that occurred in the classroom (preparing for a math lesson). The students in their study were engaged actively in the socialization process, organizing the rules of the school structure in ways that made sense to them, and through which they could come to learn the appropriate patterns of action.

Bossert (1979) analyzed four elementary school classrooms and focused on the structure of class activities. He found that differences in types of activities (e.g., recitation or large group task, small group task, individual task) affected classroom interaction patterns: "As teacher and pupils interact within the context of recurrent classroom activities, patterns of interaction emerge and particular social relationships develop" (p.1). His analysis viewed students as active agents who, in conjunction with the teacher, define the situation that delineates rules and norms for appropriate classroom behavior.

These studies indicate a reciprocal process of influence occurring between teachers and students. And, in fact:

> There is no doubt that students are influenced and modified by adults; but equally as important, students structure and modify their environments, just as they are structured and modified by it. That is, the student, the teacher, and the world are mutually constituting the classroom environment. (Mehan, 1982, p. 80)

Student and Teacher Perceptions of the Socialization Process

With the recognized emphasis on the interactive nature of the school socialization process, it is particularly important to consider both children and teachers as important sources of input into this process. Mackay (1974) posits that children are "competent interpreters of the social world and that they possess a separate culture(s)" from that of adults (p. 184). His analysis of interviews with first graders supports the view of children as competent interpreters of a culture that they create, and suggests the value of their interpretations because of their distinction from adult perspectives.

Weinstein (1983), in discussing student perceptions of schooling, suggests that researchers begin to interrelate "student views of classroom phenomena with those of teachers and outside observers" (p. 305). She cites research to support the importance of student perspectives:

> The literature on social cognition suggests that children are active interpreters of classroom reality and that they draw inferences about the causes and effects of behavior ... these studies also indicate that such inferences are not always rational and that children's views and adults' views of classroom reality may not necessarily be synonymous. Such disparity in views may actually hinder communication. (p. 288)

The Socialization Process in the Initial Days of School

The process of socialization is not demarcated by finite time boundaries; the secondary socialization that occurs in the school affects an individual's roles and social behavior throughout her or his student life. There is a heightened awareness of the negotiation of roles, rules, and procedures that occurs in early experiences in initial classroom encounters, however, that makes the first days and weeks of school particularly important for the participants. The socialization process in initial classroom experiences has been examined by various researchers (e.g., Ball, 1980; Galton & Delamont, 1980; Willes, 1983).

Ball (1980) collected participant observation and interview data in a British primary school, and outlined a series of negotiations that he termed the "process of establishment" in the new classroom. He defines this as "an exploratory interaction process involving teacher and pupils during their initial encounters in the classroom through which a more or less permanent, repeated and highly predictable pattern of relationships and interactions emerges" (p. 142). Ball found evidence that the students and teacher negotiated an intricate set of "testing out" procedures that identified the parameters of the teacher's control and her or his power to enforce that control. He suggests that students used these initial classroom experiences to establish a repertoire "of relevant and/or acceptable strategies" that could be used to determine appropriate rules and behaviors in other classroom situations (p. 152).

Willes (1983) also examined initial classroom experiences and analyzed the way first graders learned the rules and norms of classroom procedures through discourse on the first day of school. She found that the socialization experience focused on the negotiation of what it meant for the children to be students. They learned the rules and norms of the classroom system through a dialogic process between the teacher's cues (behaviors and discourse) and their own trials and errors.

Summary

Previous research attests to the importance of socialization into the student role and has underscored the need for additional study of student and teacher perceptions of the process. Consistent with the assumptions of this chapter, some related research has focused on the negotiation between teacher and students that occurs during the initial days of school. This chapter responds to the call for an investigation of student and teacher perceptions and provides an examination of student socialization as it occurs from the first day of class to the end of the first term.

PURPOSE OF THE CHAPTER

The focus of this chapter is on the socialization process by which third graders in a new school make sense of the transition into a new grade and a new school experience. The chapter addresses four research questions:

1. What does it mean to be a third grader?
2. What are the ways in which the teacher creates group cohesion?
3. What is the nature of the process by which children learn the academic and social norms?
4. What are the critical dimensions that children face in the passage to their new status?

METHOD

Research Setting

The participants of the case study in this chapter were a class of third graders in a third- through fifth-grade public school (the school also offered a kindergarten class and a Head Start program) during the 1986 autumn term. The school was located in a middle- to lower-middle class neighborhood in a large, West coast city. Many of the school's minority population (blacks, native Americans, Alaskan natives, Hispanics, and Pacific Islanders) were bused in from another district, and the school also accomodated two temporary housing shelters. Enrollment was 150 students; of these an estimated

41–50 percent were from low-income families of less than $15,000 annual income. The racial ratio was approximately 50 percent white and 50 percent minority students. The school had a retention rate of 3–5 percent per year. In the particular third-grade class there were four retainees. The school population was transitory by nature, with one teacher reporting as many as 21 new students during the academic year.

The third-grade class observed for this chapter was comprised of approximately 20 students and their teacher.[1] Eleven of these children had come from the same primary school, while the remainder were from various schools throughout the district. The four retainees had attended the present school the previous year. The third-grade teacher, Ms. King, was an Asian female with nine years of teaching experience, three of which were in the present school.

Procedures for Data Collection

The first source of data for this chapter was approximately 60 hours of observation, conducted primarily in the classroom and on the school playground. During the first two weeks of school one of the researchers observed daily. Observations were made twice weekly for the remainder of the autumn term.[2] Observations took place in the same class except for occasional visits to accompany the children to their various reading classes. Three "special events" that were observed included a field trip to a nearby high school, a musical assembly, and a videotape viewing of a television show on which some of the children appeared. The researchers were primarily participant observers. Occasionally, when the teacher was occupied with a student or reading group, she directed the children to address their questions to the researcher present. At other times, the teacher asked the researchers to participate in such activities as helping out with classroom procedures (e.g., issuing textbooks), assisting a new student, or monitoring the class if she had to leave briefly.

The second source of data was a series of three interviews with approximately half of the children in the class. Only those who volunteered were interviewed. These interviews, at the beginning, middle, and end of the term, were held to obtain the children's perspective on being third graders and to determine how they learned the norms at a new school. They were

---

[1] This number is approximate because of the numerous children who transferred in or out of the class during the term.

[2] After the first two weeks of class, the majority of the observations were conducted by only one of the researchers. All interviews with the children were conducted by both researchers.

conducted on the playground or in the gym, either before school or during recess, and were from five to 10 minutes in duration.

The third data base included two, scheduled 20-minute interviews with Ms. King that focused on her perspectives concerning (a) the academic and social goals for the third graders, and (b) the extent to which the class was meeting the goals. Informal talks with her were conducted on numerous occasions and much of the background information about the children and the school was obtained during those conversations.

The final source of data was demographic information about the school furnished by the principal.

Procedures for Data Analysis

The methods for analyzing data paralleled those employed in Chapter Two, and thus will be described only briefly in this chapter. Observation as well as interview data were analyzed in stages according to analytic induction procedures detailed by Goetz and LeCompte (1981).

For the observation data, handwritten field notes were typed daily, with reflections recorded. Summary sheets with emergent categories were prepared at the end of each week. Categories were continually refined at intervals throughout the data collection period, with final analysis after the school term concluded. Similarly, teacher and student interview data were analyzed inductively, question by question, by openly coding responses of all participants to each specific question. Categories were allowed to emerge rather than being predetermined by the researchers.

RESULTS

Question One: What Does It Mean To Be A Third Grader?

Drawing from the various data bases, this question was addressed from the perspectives of the third graders themselves and from their teacher.

Children's perspectives. During the first interview in September and the final interview in December, the children were asked directly: "What does it mean to be a third grader?" and "What do third graders do?" Three dimensions of meaning emerged.

Academic dimension. Their responses, both at the entry phase of socialization and at the end of the term, three months later, reflected a primary emphasis on the academic demands of their new role. With respect to the academic category that emerged in September, to be a third grader meant "to be a good learner, a good student," and "to learn more things to get into the fourth grade, to get up higher." The academic tasks third graders do included "a lot of writing," "they read books first thing in the morning," "they mostly do math and numbers," "they color and do work," "math, reading, spelling; we work on the alphabet, do math solving worksheets," and "make lots of pictures, do art projects." The children's perspective of what it meant to be a third grader did not change during the three-month period, but on the whole the youngsters elaborated more at the end of the term than they did at the beginning of school, and were more specific about their school activities: "You do minuses where you have to borrow," "You get to do lots of things like science and art, language, go to reading class—lots of things." Occasionally the children offered commentary on the academic demands of third grade: "You have to do hard work every day. On vacation, most of the teachers make you do three pages of your math. It will kill an elephant."

Social dimension. The children were also aware that being a third grader had a social, or nonacademic dimension. Their responses related either to engaging in enjoyable activities ("It's fun. It's nice—you can play outside.") or to rules for deportment ("If you be bad you do four pages in the back of the book. If you make noises, she'll say 'stay in at recess and make noises,' " "You get in trouble for chasing boys."). Although not as frequent as comments about the academic tasks of third graders, the children's responses about "having fun" seemed to be an integral part of what it meant to be a third grader. In contrast, although they were cognizant of many of the rules that comprised Ms. King's nonacademic agenda ("When she's talking you're supposed to listen to her and not talk to the others," "Not to fight, no hitting, no kicking, no punching, no killing anyone else," "Keep your hands to yourself," "Behave when you're in class"), they did not express these expectations as part of their role as new third graders. Rules for the youngsters were rules—they were made by the teacher and/or the principal, and were important to follow "so people won't get hurt," "so you won't get in trouble," and "so it isn't like a forest with wild animals." For the students, however, these rules did not constitute their definition of being a third grader.

To encourage children to elaborate further on their perspectives about being third graders, they were asked at the beginning and the end of the first term what they liked most. Although most of their defining comments depicted third graders as children who did hard academic work, their favorite activities were fairly evenly divided between academic and nonacademic. Academic responses included: "Work is easy. I like it. I get to take work home, like homework," "You get to learn different things," "Math. I like it because it's kinda fun, but not when there's too much or you have to stay in to finish it or take it home," "Science—we get to use computers." Some of the favorite nonacademic activities were: "Coloring picures,"

"The most fun is recess," "We get to paint and make cookies," "We get to do popcorn on strings and then we put glitter on toilet rolls. We made pumpkin cookies."

Status dimension. Finally, almost all of the children recognized a difference between second and third grade, and could articulate at least general reasons for this difference. Some of the responses included: "Third graders know better than second graders. You feel smarter," "You feel older," "You get to ride the bus," "It's a lot different than second grade and fun too. It feels interesting to change into a different school and grade," and the frequent comment: "It's 'funner' than second grade." Many of the children acknowledged three specific differences as important in the transition from a second-grade primary school to the new third-grade school: (a) new teachers ("some are nice and some are mean"), (b) the playground ("[the old school] had a big slide that went around and around. Here they have tire swings and bridges"), and (c) the larger, two-story building ("You kinda get lost in the halls. Once I went to the wrong classroom."). Some also expressed an awareness of being in a school with older grades: "It's just like there are some big people walking around,"and "It's different with older kids, there is more teasing kinda like because they are older and 'ha-ha.' "

Teacher's perspective. From classroom observations and interviews with Ms. King, four dimensions of meaning emerged for being a new third grader.

Being responsible. The first dimension was that a third grader was "responsible." Ms. King expressed this both explicitly ("It's your responsibility to make sure that it's done. . . . You need to be responsible and make sure that you finish.") and implicitly ("When that bell rings, I want you in here . . . your parents want you in here . . . just remember those of you who are grounded you just better show up at recess."). Responsibility included remembering rules and procedures ("Yesterday you showed responsibility by bringing your pencil in. Now if I give you one today how are you going to show me that you're responsible tomorrow?"), doing one's work without being told ("Oh, I like what I see. [Children are on task.] Some real responsible citizens."), finishing one's work ("So if you're not done, you lost it, you better come in at recess. You're not going home until it is done . . . correctly. It's called responsibility, gang."), and remembering to take care of one's own business ("It's your responsibility to make sure you can see. . . . Those of you who forgot [to put permission slip in Ms. Kings's mailbox] it's your responsibility to get it after recess and put it in my mailbox. I'm looking for people who are responsible.").

In talking with one of the researchers, Ms. King indicated that an important teaching goal was for the third graders to learn "responsibility, to do things out of responsibility." These "things" included social skills such as getting along, working well together, and being careful of others. Responsibilities associated with their academic work included completing assignments, doing neat work, rewriting incorrect assignments, and so on. She also expected the children to accept responsibility for their own actions (or failure to act), as illustrated by the exclusion of two children from the field trip to Bigley High School because they forgot to bring in their signed parental consent forms. Although for legal reasons Ms. King could not take the children off campus for a field trip without written parental consent, she emphasized to the two youngsters and to the class that they were being punished for their irresponsibility because they repeatedly forgot or lost their consent slips.

Despite her strong emphasis on teaching the children responsibility, Ms. King indicated in one interview that "telling them [to be responsible] and applying it are two different things," because on the playground "they still hit each other and fight, no matter how much you try to teach them." As she explained: "You try as much as you can to teach them to be responsible citizens.... Academically they are coming along but some of them still don't apply themselves. They really need support at home."[3] She described Joshua's situation to illustrate her point:

> Right now I'm having a personality conflict with Joshua. I don't know what to do with him.... He's always down at the arcade, you know, on State Street? He has older brothers who are always in trouble with the juvenile hall, and he models them, I think. So they're always going down to the arcade and finding him and bringing him into school.

Following directions. A second quality of a third grader was the ability to "follow directions." This was a key issue in the classroom, and Ms. King made a point of having the children work through both social and academic procedures step by step. For example, on the first day of school she took her class on a tour of the school building and grounds. After a brief walk across the playground, she instructed the children as they reentered the building:

> Hold the door for the person in back of you. Just for the person in back of you. (Jeremy stopped to hold the door for the others.) No, don't wait for

---

[3] In an informal interview with Ms. King, she offered specific examples of some of the home situations of the children. For example, Matt had been having discipline problems that Ms. King attributed to an unstable home environment in which his father was alternately "in and out of the picture." Molly lived with one illiterate parent and was given little encouragement from home to perform well in school. Joshua's disinterested attitude was related to uninvolved parents, who didn't "even care to call" when they were informed that he had to repeat the third grade. Samuel's parents took him out of school for five weeks to go to Puerto Rico; they failed to notify the school or Ms. King of his absence.

everyone. (demonstrating) Just hold the door this way for the person coming in behind you. Then he can hold the door open for the next one. (Ms. King remained by the door while two other children passed to make sure that they were proceeding as told.)

In addition to paying attention to social procedures, it was particularly important for the youngsters in Ms. King's class to follow directions for academic procedures. When giving directions for classwork or assignments, Ms. King was always explicit and repetitious: "Start left to right. You do not skip around, you have to go in order. Can you skip around everyone? ... You do this first, this first, this first, then this. Got it?" She sharply reprimanded children who violated the given sequential order of events, as illustrated in the following examples: "Tony, we're not down there yet. Erase that!.... Yvonne! Follow directions!" Serious offenders of the rule for following directions were required to stay in at recess and write 50 to 100 times: "I will listen and follow directions."

Working independently. A third observed dimension of what it meant to be a third grader included the ability to work "independently." Ms. King introduced this word in the third week of class, and from that day on repeatedly encouraged, as well as cajoled and mildly threatened, each child to do her or his own work: "We have to learn to be independent. Do work by yourselves.... You've got to do your own thinking.... Read #1 to yourself. This is more and more on your own. Kathy, on your own!" This independence included thinking for oneself ("Cover your answers ... you've got to do your own thinking") as well as thinking in general: "Those gears have to be working every day in third grade to go to fourth."[4]

Although the theme of independence was predominant in Ms. King's classroom, there existed an ambiguous tension between her desire for the children to work alone and her encouragement that they seek assistance if necessary from each other and/or the teacher. On most occasions, she insisted that the youngsters learn to work alone, as indicated in the above examples. But she also frequently directed the children to ask her for help ("If there's something you don't understand you ask me and tell me what part you don't understand") or to rely on fellow students for assistance ("If you don't know what to do, look at your neighbor. It's okay to look at your neighbor sometimes."). These double messages were further con-

---

[4] Ms. King's individual emphasis was not characteristic of all of the children's classes, however. In three of the other four reading groups observed and in the children's science class, there was much greater flexibility in the classroom structure, allowing for increased child–child interaction and opportunity for group work.

founded by the fact that at no time during the observations did Ms. King indicate when or under what circumstances it was acceptable or appropriate for the youngsters to seek help, particularly from one another.

Demonstrating a higher level of academic performance. A final important aspect of being a third grader was displaying a "higher level of academic performance." From the first day Ms. King demanded that the children read more than they had been reading in the second grade ("I want you to read books with lots of writing, not just look at the pictures"), and by the second week that they turn in neater work: "This week I will start making you do things over if it's not your best. That's your warning." Toward the end of the term she had them try to read cursive writing, commenting: "After vacation we're going to learn to write in cursive, and you're going to have to learn to read it, too." Although certainly the academic demands of being a third grader were a focus of teacher socializing talk, Ms. King placed less emphasis on them than on the social expectations in the classroom.

Comparison of perspectives. Comparison of teacher and student perspectives highlights the disparate conceptions of what it meant to be a third grader. Ms. King emphasized the social demands of third grade, while from the children's viewpoint the academic dimension of third grade was more salient. Although the youngsters were aware of and acknowledged the social expectations of the teacher, they did not explicitly articulate them as goals to be achieved in third grade.

Question Two: What are the Ways in which the Teacher Creates Group Cohesion?

For children to become members of the classroom group was an important social goal of Ms. King. From her perspective, what they needed in order to become members was a strong sense of class cohesion. She used both explicit and implicit strategies to create group cohesion within her classroom. One of her explicit means was to tell the children on the first day of school that "We're going to be a big family of friends here, so we need to know about each other." She then instructed the children to get to know someone new during recess. On occasions throughout the term when a new student joined the class, she assigned one of the "veteran" students to be a buddy for the newcomer and help her or him feel a part of the group. An implicit way Ms. King fostered class cohesion was through frequent use of the term "we" in response to an individual act: "I know we're tired. We need to yawn more quietly." At the end of the term the researchers asked the children if they felt like "one big family." Almost half of the children responded "yes," offering such reasons as: "I know everybody in the class," "Ms. King's nice," "Cause almost everybody likes each other." The other children interviewed responded negatively, focusing on the differences in the classroom: "Cause there's blacks and whites, and I don't have blacks and whites in my family,".... "Cause everybody likes something and some like something else,".... and "I hate Walter."

In an interview session Ms. King verbalized her conscious effort to create class cohesion by increasing the children's awareness of their classmates, particularly with respect to the ethnic groups represented in the class. During the first few weeks of school, Ms. King encouraged the youngsters to participate in activities, discussions, and games "to learn to be careful of other kids.... Sometimes we do group things like human relations in a group activity, learning about different ethnic groups that are represented in the class, just to learn about other people." Ms. King also reinforced her desire to create social awareness in her classroom through more implicit means, such as calling attention to absent members. For example, during attendance-taking, she would ask the children to account for those who were absent: "Did Dennis come on the bus? How about Deanna?" On one occasion when many of the children were absent, she remarked, "Gee, I feel kinda lonesome today. Where is everybody?" She also had the children remove the absentees' chairs from their desktops if they had been placed there for floor cleaning the night before. She further encouraged awareness of others through sharing (e.g., when the children were bringing in empty milk cartons for art projects or using glitter to decorate Christmas cards, Ms. King encouraged them to bring in an extra carton or to wait to see if there was enough glitter for everyone before decorating a second card). She also facilitated awareness of classmates by having children respond in unison to her questions or read aloud in unison.

Although Ms. King's emphasis in the classroom was on individual academic work, on occasion she allowed the children to work as "partners." Usually these partners were also "neighbors," and served as handy references for instrumental help ("Need a little help, Hon? Help her out, Daniel?"), checking procedures ("If you forgot where to put your nametag, see where your neighbor put theirs."), and practicing recitation ("Tell your neighbor how to find out the main idea of a story."). On two occasions during observations she allowed the children to select partners for work, once for spelling, and once for reading practice. She also had the children pair up to walk as partners during the field trip to the high school.

Another way that Ms. King promoted group cohesion was through the use of group rewards and punishments. She granted permission to line up first for lunch or recess to the row who showed her that they were "ready" by putting their work materials away, sitting quietly, and straightening their desks. Likewise, she also disciplined row members jointly, as in the following example: "Walter's row, when it is recess time I want you to come in and read. This row rumbles when you read. I want you to come in and practice reading. Without rumbling." Ms. King also exercised exclusion from the group as a form of punishment, as in the case of Tina and Connie whose desks were separated from their rows by a space of about 18 inches because they were "disruptive" (normally the children's desks were lined up end to end). Often she reprimanded the entire class, as in the case of a fire drill the second week of school. Because Ms. King was displeased with the amount of talking that went on during the exercise, she punished the group by making them repeat the fire drill, threatening to take away their lunch and recess time if they did not practice without talking. Her intent in these collective rewards and punishments was to promote a sense of class cohesion and social responsiblity, thus having children be a part of the classroom group.

Question Three: What is the Nature of the Process by which Children Learn the Academic and Social Norms?

Academic norms. Ms. King had four general methods by which she taught and enforced the academic norms of her classroom: (a) giving explicit directions (and repeating them when necessary), (b) reprimanding violations, (c) asking questions, and (d) praising work properly done. She often accompanied these strategies with an explanation of the resulting consequences ("If you don't put your name on your paper, will I know whose it is?"), or a threat of impending punishment if the procedure was not completed properly ("Joshua, will you finish up yesterday's paper right now? You're almost done. Then you won't have to stay in at recess."). When these strategies failed, or when she wanted to make a procedure specific for the benefit of a newcomer, Ms. King would repeat explicit directions. All of these methods were apparent during classroom observations and were mentioned by Ms. King during the interviews as well. A final, less important, way children learned the academic norms was through peer influence.

Giving explicit directions. The primary method, particularly in the first few weeks of school and when the children were engaging in new activities, was for Ms. King to give explicit directions: "Put your name on the top—just your first name".... "Everyone put your finger where it says 'Directions.' " She would often repeat these instructions two or three times, either verbatim or with slight modifications, to make sure that the children were following her directions step by step: "Okay, read question number one. Don't write, just read to yourself. Don't do anything. Now do number one and I'll come around and check ... Now read number two.

No writing, just think about what it says." Ms. King's explicit directions helped to decrease the children's uncertainty about academic procedures. By having students follow step-by-step directions and by emphasizing procedurally correct work, she taught and enforced certain academic norms in the classroom.

Even after the initial few weeks of class, there were occasions in which Ms. King would explicitly repeat rules for academic procedures. She seemed to use the repeat strategy to benefit a newcomer or to remind multiple offenders of a previously stated rule: "Remember, no doodling or drawing. Just your name," and "People in Reading Group A be sure you correct your mistakes." As she said in an interview, "At first you teach them the rules, and then I sometimes ask them the rules, ask them to write them down, model it, role playing, practice."

Reprimanding violations. Ms. King's second method of teaching the academic norms to her class was through reprimands of violations of specific directions or procedures. For example, after instructing the children to put their names on the tops of their papers, two youngsters were late in getting their materials out of their desks. Rather than delay the entire class, Ms. King reprimanded them: "If you haven't put your name on it by now it's too late. Put your pencil down." In classroom work she would reprimand the children for proceeding out of sequence, particularly as a result of not listening: "Number two. No, underneath the picture. I'm not on number three I'm on number two".... "This is how I check for who's listening. You've got to listen! That's what you're here for!" This strategy served to reduce the students' uncertainty not only about academic expectations, but also about the consequences of violating the classroom academic norms.

Asking questions. A third strategy for teaching academic norms was that of questioning the children. Often Ms. King used questions to test their memory of previously stated rules or procedures, as in the following examples:

Ms. King:	When we look at the main idea in your reading groups, what are you going to do everybody? (silence) I think we're lost. What did Deanna say?
Child:	Look at the picture.
Ms. K.:	Then what do you do?
C:	Find the main idea.
Ms. K:	Okay, but what are you going to do to find the main idea?
C:	Look at the words underneath the picture.
Ms. K.:	And what are you going to do with the words?
C:	Read them.
Ms. King:	If you finish early, what are you going to do? Tony?
Tony:	Read a book.

Ms. K.:	No, what can you do?
Child:	Check it over.
Ms. K.:	Yes, check it over.

Praising. A fourth strategy was to use praise as positive reinforcement to illustrate desirable work habits or academic procedures to the class. To accomplish this, Ms. King often referred to "good" children who were following directions as models for the others:

> I like the way some of you are already reading, getting ready to be fourth graders. Remember I look for good third graders who are good and they can go you-know-where [to fourth grade].... When I say get ready to correct your math papers, you'll have your book open, your papers ready, and a crayon out so that you can correct papers. I like the way Joshua is practicing even though he doesn't have a paper so that the next time he'll know how.

Peer influence. Ms. King's control of child-to-child interactions was strict; therefore, the children did not rely much on one another to learn the academic norms in the classroom. On a few occasions she allowed the children to check with "their neighbors" if they were uncertain about how to do something that she had explained: "If you're not sure what to do, look at your neighbor's." Except for a few whispered instructions and comparisons behind the teacher's back, the only other times the youngsters participated in "teaching" one another the academic norms occurred when Ms. King was out of the classroom during recess or lunchtime. Recess was a time for makeup work; Ms. King often left the children on their own or with one of the researchers as she attended to other business outside of the classroom. During these "independent study" times, the children frequently took on the teacher's role for enforcing on-task behavior:

Deanna:	I'm finished.
Molly:	No you're not. You have to make problems [math computations]. (Ms. King had left the room, and a few children were talking among themselves, trying to decide what they were supposed to do.)
Walter:	She said to look in that blue box, and if you guys can't find it [the assignment] you gotta wait till she makes some more. And you can't go home until you're finished.

Social norms. As indicated previously, Ms. King stressed the social demands of third grade. This emphasis is consistent with Denzin's (1977) view that "Instruction cannot be separated from social interaction, and teachers spend a large amount of time teaching students how to be proper social participants" (p. 197). Ms. King taught and enforced the social norms in her class in the same way as the academic norms. She often used the four verbal strategies discussed previously for academic procedures, with a fifth category, "repeating rules," emerging as a distinct strategy:

1. Giving explicit directions: Please sit up. Put your chest next to the desk and a little bit of room in front so that your tummy isn't next to the desk.... We share—nobody is to hog the ball all day long.
2. Reprimanding violations: You do not speak that way in my room. Is that clear sir? ... You do not speak that way in my room.... Johnny, you may go back and walk. Try it again.
3. Asking questions: Ms. King: And what should the person do who gets their desk bumped? Should he go [slam!] "You bumped my desk!"? Children: NO! Ms. K.: What should you do?.... Stop. Do we laugh at others who try?
4. Using praise: I like the way you girls are standing with your chairs all pushed in.... I like the way that people who are done are waiting patiently and quietly.[5]
5. Repeating rules: Remember our signal, remember our three rules. If you don't follow the rules you have to stay in at recess and say it a bunch of times or write it. All you have to do is look this way.

In addition to these five strategies, Ms. King frequently used nonverbal signals, such as finger snapping, disapproving facial expressions, or staring to get attention if a child was overtly violating a rule. Another nonverbal strategy was the use of a particular tone of voice in the phrase "excuse me" to indicate disapproval, such as when a child interrupted her or was talking out of turn: "Excuse me. I'm talking to Cindy right now." She also used hand or arm gestures, such as pointing or motioning, rather than speaking out or repeating a rule. For example, Ms. King did not permit the children to go behind one another when leaving their seats; she instructed them to go around the outside of the row rather than disturbing their row mates. If a child violated this rule, Ms. King would point and make a circular motion with her arm to indicate "Go back and go around the outside of the row." Thus, she expressed and enforced the social norms of the classroom both verbally and nonverbally.

The children disciplined one another in the social realm of the classroom much more frequently than they interacted to teach and enforce the academic norms. This was often accomplished through verbal interac-

---

[5] The use of praise to introduce social norms was more prevalent in the initial few weeks of class, after which the use of questioning and repetition became more frequent.

tions: "You better put it back—if Ms. King sees it she gonna think you took it and be mad!".... "Shut up, Tony-pony." On other occasions the use of nonverbal messages would suffice, as was the case with an ongoing conflict between Walter and Deanna. In this interaction, every time Deanna got out of her seat to get supplies from the back of the room, Walter pushed his chair back so that she was unable to pass behind, thereby reinforcing the rule to go around the outside of the row. These examples of "peer discipline," similar to those displayed by the kindergarteners described in Chapter Two, were ways in which children engaged in role construction. Such instances increased as the term progressed, and most frequently occurred behind Ms. King's back or when she was out of the room.

Another way in which students actively learned classroom procedural norms was to challenge rules to see if they could be bent. The rules in Ms. King's class were strict, and she clearly defined and enforced procedures (both academic and social). Yet despite her inflexibility with the rules, the children began to test her in an attempt to stretch the limits of classroom policies. For example, Ms. King had a mailbox in which she required all notes from home, written assignments, or special flyers (such as the field trip consent forms) to be placed before school. Although this was a firm rule in her class, almost daily a child would try to hand her a note or homework assignment before school. The following interaction occurred on the 33rd day of class:

Ms. King:	[Roger tries to hand her a piece of paper.] Where do you put things for me?
Roger:	I don't know.
Ms. K.:	You don't know? Think. What are you supposed to do with things for me? Think, Roger.
R:	I don't know. [He is still trying to hand her the paper.] In your mailbox?
Ms. K.:	Good!

On day 48 of the term, the children were still testing Ms. King's rules, and this scenario was almost a daily routine for Connie:

Connie:	Here. [Tries to hand her a piece of paper.]
Ms. King:	Put it in my mailbox.
C.:	Which one?
Ms. K.:	In my mailbox.
C.:	The yellow one?
Ms. K.:	In my mailbox.
C.:	The blue one?
Ms. K.:	In my mailbox.
C.:	Oh.

As the term progressed, the children began also to test the researchers to see if our "rules" were as stringent as Ms. King's. One of Ms. King's procedures prohibited the children from interrupting her if she was working with another child or group: "Tina, I can't talk to you now, I'm talking to Daniel." On one occasion when the observing researcher was assisting Walter with vocabulary words, another student approached her with a question. In keeping with the classroom rules, the researcher told the disgruntled youngster, "I can't talk to you right now, I'm working with Walter. I'll come help you at your seat when I'm finished."[6]

Stretching and testing rules can be characterized as a process of "learning the ropes" in a new environment. Unlike kindergarteners who were learning classroom norms and procedures for the very first time, these third graders had three previous years of rule learning. This familiarity with a general set of classroom rules may have facilitated their willingness to try and bend particular rules.

Question Four: What are the Critical Dimensions That Children Face in the Passage to Their New Status?

From observing and talking with the children, it was apparent that the third-grade status was highly *desirable*, particularly because it prepared them for the fourth grade. As one youngster said about being a third grader: "You do harder work to get ready for fourth." There were a few specific references to indicate what was desirable about the subsequent passages, such as being able to put a padlock on their lockers in fifth grade and taking shop in high school. Generally, however, the desirability and *centrality* of the status passage seemed to be the inherent progress toward becoming a "big kid."

Although the passage into third grade was considered an *inevitable*, *regular*, *scheduled* event, Ms. King frequently reiterated that it could be *repeated* if the children failed. Implicit in these comments were the signs that identified the passage: "You need to get out of this reading book to get to fourth grade ... You need to get your work done. It should be neat, with nice writing. You don't come to school with your work not done. Unless you're planning on repeating."

There was little *formality* associated with the passage into third grade.

---

[6] The above response from the researcher was the exception; normally the researchers tried not to interfere with the classroom dynamics or to take on the teacher's role unless it was specifically requested. For the most part the researchers remained nonjudgmental and did not reprimand the youngsters. As a result the children seemed to lose their inhibitions, displaying blatant violations of classroom rules in Ms. King's absence.

Although Ms. King clearly articulated many of the *signs* of third-grade status, others seemed to be ambiguous for the children. One implicit assumption of the teacher discussed above was that the youngsters knew when it was acceptable to "share" with their neighbors and when they were expected to work independently. She also assumed that the children understood and could differentiate among the rules and expectations of her classroom and those of the science teacher, the music teacher, and their respective reading teachers. For example, Ms. King strongly emphasized independent work, while Ms. Wolf and Ms. Ball deemphasized it in their reading classes. In Ms. Wolf's class the children rarely worked alone; she stressed cooperative learning both in the informal structure of her classroom and in her comments: "You're doing a pretty good job of learning together but once in a while . . . (puts fingers to lips, her signal for be quiet) . . . I hear that in some classrooms when people talk too much they aren't allowed to work together." Ms. Ball reiterated this theme in her classroom by a banner across the side board which read: "WORKING TOGETHER = SUCCESS."

Other dimensions centered around the procedures for the passage. Although Ms. King implied an element of *choice* in the passage ("If you just sit there, are you going to learn? I'm real pleased with you. If you don't want to learn, I can't help you."), for all practical purposes she and the principal were ultimately in *control* of and had to legitimate the status passage. The social aspect of this *legitimation* of the passage added another dimension; retainees often vacillated between social acceptance by their former classmates and agemates and their new peers. As Ms. King expressed in an interview, the children were often cruelly aware of their ability to illegitimate the status passage for children who were repeating a grade: "But it's the fourth and fifth graders who know the kids and they'll ask what grade they're in. Like for instance some of the fourth graders asked what grade Richard and Molly are in, and I just said I didn't know. Let the kids handle it themselves." Molly, who was repeating third grade, articulated that the passage to third grade status actually had occurred and went on to offer her perspective of the social legitimation:

Interviewer:	Tell me what it's like to be a third grader.
Molly:	It's okay. I'm not in third grade, though. I'm in fourth.
I:	You're in fourth? But now you're in the third.
M:	Well, I was in Mrs. Sanders' class but there were too many kids so they put me in third grade. . . .
I:	Where did you make most of your friends?
M:	With the other kids in the class.
I:	Do you have most of your friends in the third grade or the fourth?
M:	In the fourth.

Finally, the *collective* nature of the passage into third grade was an important dimension. The majority of the children entered the class as a group and experienced the passage into third grade as a collective. Newcomers throughout the term assimilated quickly into the group, and there seemed to be no evidence that they were ostracized because of their late arrival to the class. The differing emphases in the classrooms discussed above created varied levels of *communication* with others in the collective, from a low peer interaction classroom like Ms. King's to a high interaction atmosphere like Ms. Wolf's. As noted previously, regardless of the amount of peer interaction permitted during class time, all of the teachers encouraged at least some degree of social *awareness*. Interestingly, when questioned about what they talked about with their friends, the children rarely said that they talked about school or school-related things, as illustrated in the following interview:

> *Interviewer:* What do you talk about with the other kids?
> *Hanna:* (shrug)
> *I:* Do you talk about school, your homework? Maybe what happens in class?
> *H:* We don't talk about school. Maybe after school sometimes we do [talk about school]. Mostly we talk about when we're going to get together and play.

This was consistent with the researchers' observations, which revealed infrequent occasions of comparison with others' work or progress, and rarely (if ever) any specific conversations focusing on the class or school-related activities.

DISCUSSION

For some of the youngsters observed, the passage into third grade was marked with uncertainty like Ramona Quimby's first experiences. When asked by a researcher, "Were you scared to come to this school the first day?" responses included:

> *Hanna:* Yeah, it was kinda scary except that I had Amber and I knew her since I was a real little baby. So I stuck with her the most.
> *Alice:* The first day I was scared, but now I'm not.
> *Interviewer:* Why were you scared?
> *A:* Just scared. Changing to a new school. I never rode the bus. Now it's just like one of the facts of my life. We can sit where we want and there are seatbelts.

Other new third graders reported no "quivery feelings" about the passage to the new school and new grade, and if they did experience anxiety, it was quickly abated:

> *Interviewer:* How did it feel when you first came to this school?
> *Jeremy:* It felt nice.
> *I:* Nice? Was it scary?
> *J:* No, I liked it.
> *I:* Did it take a while to learn about this school?
> *J:* No.
> *I:* You knew all about it right away?
> *J:* Yeah, I knew it all right away.

> *Interviewer:* How long did it take you to find everything in this school?
> *Kathleen:* It took a whole day to find my way around. Almost a whole day.
> *I:* Was it hard to learn about this new school?
> *K:* No ... well, kind of.

> *Interviewer:* If you were going to tell someone new about this school, what would you tell them?
> *Hanna:* That it was a good, good school.
> *I:* What might they need to know coming to this school?
> *H:* They don't really need to know anything because they will be here and can learn for themselves.
> *I:* How long did it take you?
> *H:* A couple days.

Regardless of their initial response to attending a new school, the majority of the children recognized that the new school was different from their previous one and that third grade was distinct from second.

Differences in Concerns of Students and Teacher

Of foremost interest in these findings was the indication that the concerns of the youngsters differed from those of their teacher. While Ms. King expressed concern predominantly with the social dimensions of third grade and the socialization process by which the children became responsible, independent, hard-working students, the children articulated more concern with the academic demands of third grade. To the students, their social responsibility was not an important aspect of the new school or grade. The children seemed to focus on the tangible dimensions of third grade such as the physical aspects of the school and the academic demands of the grade level, while their teacher emphasized the social experience of being third graders in a new school. The learning of roles for the students was more a matter of accomplishing increasingly difficult schoolwork, while for Ms. King the socialization experience was more globally focused on learning social responsibility, developing good work habits, and demonstrating attentive listening. The method for establishing the rules or norms of the classroom and school was recognized equally by both students and teacher, although the implications of these rules were construed differently. For example, both the students and Ms. King acknowledged that they learned/taught the rules by being explicity told and/ or having them written down, yet Ms. King's reason for having the children learn to keep their hands to themselves was to promote social responsibility, while from the children's perspective it was to "keep someone from getting hurt."

A second area of teacher–student differences was in the emphasis on the motivation to complete the passage through the grades. Although Ms. King stressed the need to be "good" third graders so that they could move up to fourth, the threat of repeating the grade did not intimidate the children or cause them great concern. Even the retainees did not seem motivated by social pressures or status concerns to work harder to ensure moving up to fourth grade. The children seemed impressed with the high schoolers on their field trip to Bigley High School and expressed enthusiasm for being in high school, but appeared not to question that they would one day advance to ninth grade. The natural progression through the school system seemed inevitable for the youngsters, who acknowledged that fourth grade would "be harder, so you'd learn better" without questioning their own abilities to do harder work.

Third, Ms. King was conscientious about integrating children from different schools to facilitate friendship formation and peer awareness, yet the transition to the new school appeared to be fairly rapid and relatively smooth, even for the latecomers who quickly made friends in the group.[7] One newcomer related the following event with a tone of disgust rather than apprehension: "And all the kids kept turning around and staring at me and I asked, 'What's wrong with these people?' And the girl next to me said, 'Oh, it's just because you're new.' " Helping the children fit socially into the group was a conscious concern for Ms. King, and some of them recognized her efforts to integrate the class: "Our teacher says 'pick a friend and learn something about them,' " "Ms. King had a buddy take care of me the first few days. She introduced me to her friends." For most of

---

[7] The strong possiblity must be noted, however, that the transition into the new school was a relatively smooth one *because* of the efforts of Ms. King.

the youngsters, however, making friends came quite naturally: "You just tell 'em 'hi' and ask 'em their name and they ask you yours and you become friends."

A Concluding Note

The socialization process observed in Ms. King's classroom clearly reflected the mutual influence of both the students and the teacher in learning the third-grade role. The lack of complete congruence between the perspectives of third-grade students and their teacher highlights the need for educators to address the concerns and expectations of the students and teachers alike in future research and in teacher education. The process of socialization was an ongoing, evolving experience for the children, who brought their own knowledge, beliefs, and feelings to the new school situation. For the teacher it was also an emergent process, one in which she played an instrumental role. Ms. King described the nature of the socialization experience as a parent–child relationship. When asked how long it took for the children to settle into the new classroom she responded:

About two to three weeks.... They get adjusted and get to know you—they get to know me, get to the point where I'm like their mom or dad. Some of them even call me "Mom" sometimes, and after the first couple of weeks they start talking back, start talking like they do at home, and you can feel that they are more comfortable ... the way they talk to you.

chapter 4
Becoming a Middle School Student

Co-authored with Dee Oseroff-Varnell

This chapter presents results from observations and interviews of some 100 new sixth graders in two public middle schools. The focus is not on what happens in a single classroom experience, as in Chapters Two and Three, but on the information needed by the youngsters as they make sense of middle school and the communication strategies they utilize to acquire the information. The youngsters actively seek information about such aspects as procedures, course content, and the people with whom they came in contact. They employ communication strategies that range from highly direct and face threatening to indirect and face saving. The sixth graders feel the move to middle school is accompanied by greater academic and social responsibilities and that they have a new identity as adolescents.

The bus pulled into the rear of the school. Everyone scattered in all directions. I was mixed up. On orientation day we had gone in the front doors! It took me fifteen minutes to find the auditorium where the new students were meeting. (I also found the gym, the boys' locker room, and the cafeteria in my search.) Ruffner is sure a lot bigger than Meadowbrook. In the auditorium, I sat down next to a chubby girl who looked almost as upset as I felt. A man who looked like a movie star came on stage and introduced himself as our new principal, Mr. Zale. He said he was new at Ruffner too. We'd learn the ropes together.... Mr. Zale gave the same orientation speech we'd heard last spring. I craned my neck to find Becca or some of the kids I knew from Meadowbrook. I only saw a few. I guess that's not too unusual. There are over two hundred of us from five elementary schools. Mr. Zale began introducing our teachers. They called out the names of the students in their homerooms. When your name was called you stood and followed that teacher out of the auditorium. I was in the second group with Mrs. Page. So was Chubby. "Your shoe's untied," she whispered as we filed out. I ignored her. I sure wasn't going to stop and tie my shoelace and risk getting lost again.... I looked around the room. There were only a few kids from Meadowbrook. I didn't know any of them very well. My heart sank to the bottom of my stomach. Where were my pals? Other kids were looking around just like I was. I sighed. We'd been tossed together like a salad in a big bowl called middle school. I think we all felt lost. (Kassem, 1987, pp. 17–18)

Graduating from elementary school to middle school is an event often accompanied by mixed feelings for young students. Although they may feel older, more grown up, and more responsible, they may also feel the kinds of fears and misgivings about a new school that are expressed by the student in the passage above. Thrust into an unfamiliar school that seems like an endless maze of hallways and classrooms, the newcomers often experience an adjustment process which can be overwhelming. Yet, despite the first day fears and concerns, the threat of middle school quickly diminishes as the newcomers explore the new building, meet new friends, and learn the "ins and outs" of the new school.

This chapter reports on the transition into middle school of sixth graders in two schools. Through classroom observations and interviews conducted during the autumn term, the sixth graders are followed as they socialize into the new middle school environment and their new student role.

The Middle School Experience

As a child progresses through the educational system, each year marks the passage into a higher grade level and often a new school environment. By the time children have reached the middle school level, they have achieved a certain degree of socialization into the school culture, which means an understanding of the roles they must assume as students and a knowledge of how the school system functions (Mehan, 1980; Rothstein, 1979; Spencer-Hall, 1981). Yet the process of socialization continues as youngsters enter middle school. Incoming middle school students must become competent members of a new school "society," one in which there is a unique set of rules and expectations, a variety of teachers and classes, and a larger and often more heterogeneous student population. New middle schoolers must also meet more challenging academic demands, be responsible for increased homework assignments, and make use of more opportunities for independent study. In addition, middle school students are coping with the physical, social, and psychological changes that occur in the preteen years.

Thornberg (1980) acknowledges the varied developmental changes of the "transescent" (Eichhorn, 1966) or "in-between-ager" (Alexander & George, 1981), referring to those youngsters who are between childhood and adolescence (approximately ages 10 through 13). He offers the following list of "developmental tasks" that the youngsters must achieve as they progress through middle school: (a) becoming aware of increased physical changes, (b) organizing knowledge and concepts into problem-solving strategies, (c) learning new social/sex roles, (d) recognizing their identification with stereotypes, (e) developing friendships with others, (f) gaining a sense of independence, and (g) developing a sense of morality and values. It is from the understanding that youngsters face unique developmental tasks at the middle school age that the idea of designing a special school to meet the needs of preadolescents was conceived and tested in this country around 1950.

Middle schools were introduced into the American educational system with the intention that they would act as "bridges" to ease the transition from elementary school to secondary school (Noblit, 1987). The goal of the middle school was to provide an environment that would promote learning and instruction, yet allow the youngsters to develop their growing sense of autonomy while preparing them for the high school system. As Alexander and George (1981) note: their "interests are many but short-lived, and the school is challenged to provide a variety of worthwhile activities to stimulate each child to explore and latch on to an interest that is desirable and persistent" (p. 8).

At the middle school age youngsters are developing an increasing sense of independence and freedom from adult authority and greater reliance on their peers. They are also developing physically, and sex-role differences begin to take on new interest and meaning to the budding preadolescents. The middle school is an environment in which the youngsters can experiment with different activities, new social roles, and varied friendships as well as increased academic expectations that come with the higher grade level. Thus, as youngsters socialize into the middle school environment they are faced with managing the various physical, social, emotional, and intellectual changes that accompany this age group.

School values and the socialization process. One of the many challenges facing educators concerns the maintenance of the balance between the academic and social demands of the classroom. Middle school youngsters need to learn and develop academic skills that they will need in their future education (academic agenda). They also must assimilate various social and cultural rules, norms, and expectations which they will need in order to become active members of the larger society (hidden curriculum). Gordon (1984), in his analysis of the hidden curriculum in the schools, comments that the structure of the system teaches youngsters beyond the epistemic function of the school to the inculcative function. Gordon (1983) discusses the importance of the school in teaching students about the very nature of rules:

Schools are clearly organisations in which rules are very pervasive. The variety of these rules, the insistence of the school staff that rules be obeyed, the range of school activities for which rules are relevant, all suggest that pupils may learn in school not only specific rules but also a great deal about rules in general. (p. 207)

While the school structure and hidden agenda of the school system function as socializing agents for the students, there is a tension between the degree to which the school and teachers act to socialize the students, and to which the students reciprocate and mutually influence the socialization process. Researchers have argued for conceptualizing socialization as a more bidirectional or reciprocal process in which students actively participate as they interact with persons of authority at school and at home (Apple, 1980; Peters, 1985; Weinstein, 1983).

Peer influence in the socialization process. The pre- and early adolescent experiences an increased reliance on her or his peers in a variety of arenas. In the friendly context of one-on-one friendships with "chums" (Sullivan, 1953), or in the more extended peer group "gang" or "clique," the youngster can try out her or his changing social and sex roles, practice communication strategies, and receive emotional and instrumental support. Some comprehensive functions of the peer group have been summarized by Savin-Williams (1980): (a) it [the peer group] facilitates the transition from the nuclear family to a peer orientation, (b) it provides various models for experimenting with identity, ideology, and value orientation, (c) it enhances a clearer sense of self by providing feedback, (d) it provides a variety of experiences which allow the individual to practice social and interpersonal skills, (e) it socializes the expression of aggression and sexual attitudes and behaviors, allowing for the development of more mature relationships, (f) it assists in interpreting verbal and nonverbal cues concerning the youngster's position and power, (g) it fills an emotional and social void, and (h) it offers a way of regulating social norms and acts as a proving ground for attitudes and aspirations. In middle school the concerns of the youngster are expressed not only in the identity question of "Who am I?" but also in the social acceptance question of "Who do you think I am?" (Alexander & George, 1981).

In a three-year study of Little League baseball, Fine (1981) examined the influence of the peer group on socialization. He found the peer group in the preadolescent period to be important in such specific functions as mastering impression management techniques, developing social competency in rule negotiation, exploring modes of expressing sexual attitudes, aggression, and attitudes toward school and work. Peers also facilitated learning about topic areas that young people generally do not learn about from adults (e.g., sexual practices, the informal rules of institutions, the art of insulting, and how to have excitement and adventure through pranks, mischief, illegal behavior). He concludes:

> Socialization does not consist of rote learning of behaviors or of an encyclopedia of practical knowledge. Socialization can best be considered instruction in dealing with situations ... The child needs to learn the process by which social meanings are constructed, ways of knowing the expectations of others, and methods of determining their likely actions. ... The friendship group, by placing the child in such situations in a supportive environment, provides the opportunity to acquire and refine skills that are necessary for interaction with others. (p. 47)

Summary

A review of research on socialization and the middle school experience reveals a variety of factors that should be considered in order to gain an understanding of the socialization process. These factors include an examination of the students' perspective, a look at the hidden curriculum of the school (as expressed by teachers and administrators in their communication), and an analysis of peer influence on the new students. This chapter analyzes the socialization process from the perspective of the new middle schoolers, with an examination of teacher classroom communication. Friendships and social relationships from the perspective of the new students are also considered.

PURPOSE OF THE CHAPTER

This chapter focuses on students' perceptions of the role and expectations of a middle schooler, and the communication process by which the transition to middle school is accomplished. Four research questions are addressed:

1. What does it mean to be a middle school student?
2. What is the nature of the information youngsters seek as they socialize into middle school?
3. What is the nature of the process by which youngsters socialize into middle school and what communication strategies are employed?
4. What are the critical dimensions in the passage to the status of middle school student?

METHOD

Research Setting

The data for this chapter were collected during the 1987 autumn term at two public middle schools in a large, West coast city. Both middle schools (Everhart and Harrison) contained students in the sixth through the eighth grade. Children from approximately six "feeder" elementary schools formed each sixth-grade class. Harrison also housed a group of gifted sixth graders who had been transferred as a class from one elementary school. Everhart's total student population was 886, with 243 sixth graders; Harrison had a total of 639, 200 of whom were sixth graders. The schools were located in middle-class residential neighborhoods accessible by school buses and public transportation. Both schools were integrated through busing, with minority populations of approximately 40 percent at Harrison and 50 percent at Everhart. Black, Asian, Hispanic, and native American (in descending order of frequency) comprised the minority groups represented at both schools.

The two schools were selected for data collection because the researchers considered them to be representative of the public school district in size, ethnic distribution, school philosophy, and curriculum. They were also schools in which the incoming sixth graders were moving from elementary to middle school, many of them leaving their neighborhood schools for the first time. The principals, vice principals, and teachers at both schools were willing participants in this project, allowing for easy access to the classes for observations and to the children for the interviews.

Procedures for Data Collection

There were three data bases for the chapter. In order to identify the nature of the information sought by newcomers and the communication strategies employed in the socialization process, the researchers observed approximately 40 hours in the sixth-grade classrooms during the first five weeks of school in the autumn term. Intensive observations were made every day by at least one of the researchers during the first two weeks. Time during the next three weeks was directed toward observing the children in at least one of each of the basic sixth-grade classes.[1] Observations

---

[1] The researchers observed at least one of each of the sixth graders' required (core) courses. An effort was made not only to vary the courses observed, but also to observe different teachers and varied groups of students.

were also made during lunch, assemblies, and in the hallways before school and between classes. In addition, the researchers attended a special orientation session, prior to the opening of school, for the youngsters and parents from one elementary school. The researchers were participant observers, yet had only occasional interactions with the students when approached with a question or concern (e.g., assisting with opening lockers the first day, helping to find classrooms). Casual conversations with the teachers and administrators also occurred throughout the observation period. Field notes were taken during classes and assemblies, and summaries of conversations with students and teachers/administrators were written following each interaction.

The second data base drew upon the children's perspectives, and served to supplement the observational data as well as to elicit information about specific strategies that could not be easily observed (e.g., observing other students' behavior or asking questions of family members). This data base consisted of a set of two interviews with 96 volunteers (51 males, 45 females; 69 Caucasian, 27 minority, primarily black, Asian, and Hispanic), and an open-ended letter (letter data) that the youngsters were asked to write.[2] The first interviews were conducted by the researchers and two trained interviewers within the first few weeks of school, and the second round of interviews was conducted after the tenth week of school. Interviews took place in the hallway outside the children's homeroom classes, and were from 10 to 15 minutes in duration. The letters to prospective sixth graders were written by the students during the last two weeks of the term.

The third data base consisted of demographic and general school information. Documents were obtained from the principals and/or counselors at each school.

Procedures for Data Analysis

Field notes were taken daily during the observations, with complete notes typed at the end of the day by the observer. The field notes were scanned weekly by the two researchers independently and, utilizing the analytic

---

[2] The students were given a sheet of paper on which the following directions were written: *In the space below, please write a letter to an imaginary 5th grader named "Chris" who will be a new 6th grader at this school next fall. In the letter, please say everything that Chris will need to know in order to do well and be happy at this school. Please give as much advice as you can about what is important to know, who is important to know, what to do, and how to do things here. Do not worry about making mistakes in writing or spelling. I just want to see what you have to say.* **Dear Chris,**

induction method (Goetz & LeCompte, 1981), categories emerged from the data. Weekly summary sheets were then prepared from the field notes.

The responses for both interviews were unitized according to question, with summary sheets of each set of interviews prepared after reading through the responses to each question individually. Notes were made of the most frequently repeated responses, as well as those responses which were particularly eloquent or poignant. Categories from the interviews and letter data were gleaned from the data using the analytic induction method.

An initial reading of the letter data revealed that the students' comments addressed themes and issues which overlapped with those which emerged from the interviews. Thus, the letters were used to supplement the youngsters' interview comments in an attempt to capture the spontaneous character of the new middle schoolers as they expressed their experiences in the "letter of advice" context.

RESULTS

Question One: What Does it Mean to be a Middle School Student?

Students' perspectives. The question of "What does it mean to be a middle school student?" was asked of the interviewees twice during the term. Additional responses were derived from questions asking the children to articulate the differences between elementary and middle school, what they liked most and least about middle school, and if they had made new friends. The students' responses to these questions changed slightly over the duration of the term, with earlier responses reflecting an awareness of some of the physical changes in the environment (e.g., having lockers), as well personal developmental changes (e.g., "feels older"), status changes ("You get pushed around 'cause we're the youngest"), and changes in responsibilities ("more work, more responsiblity"). The youngsters' later responses focused more on the responsibility and social dimensions of middle school, with less emphasis on the physical environment. Generally, for the students, to be a middle school student meant to be in a new and different physical and social *environment*, to have a new *identity*, and to have new *responsibilities* (both academic and social).

To be a middle school student means to be in a new and different physical and social environment. Early in the term, many of the children's interview responses focused on the physical, structural (referring to the structure of the school procedures, e.g., changing classes, showering after gym), and social differences in their new environment. They noted such physical and structural changes as: "It's a huge school, the other's real small," "Classes are bigger," "Have to walk around a lot," "There's a cafeteria with trays," "They have two gyms, an auditorium, and a lunchroom on the stage," "[It's] new. We never had combination locks before. It's like going to another century, into the future," and "[There are] vending machines in the lunchroom." Some youngsters initially claimed that to be a middle school student was almost like being an elementary school student, yet their responses expressed some crucial differences: "It feels just as it would in elementary except that you have to move from class to class and stop at your locker to get your books and put stuff back," and "Ain't nuttin' really different 'cept you walk through a whole lot more children, there are a lot more teachers." There was also the frequent comment that "There's no recess," which was often accompanied by a wistful look on some of the faces.

Although the physical and structural changes in middle school were less predominant in the children's second interview responses, the theme surfaced again as an important one in the letter data. Many of the students offered comments concerning the physical aspects of the new school, both in the form of encouragement and practical matters: "There are lots of rooms and lockers but don't worry you get a schedule and a locker number. Your schedule gives room numbers and teachers' names. The lunchroom, office, counselor, nurse, and auditorium [are] located on the first floor. There are three boys' bathrooms located on the first, second, and third floor," and "Everhart will probably seem very big, in students and in size. I know I thought it was huge ... Just remember the 100's are on the first floor and the 200's are on the second floor." Although by the end of the term the students had gained confidence with their lockers and the school layout, they remembered their initial fears concerning the new physical and structural changes that they had encountered in middle school.

The social environment was also a notable change for the youngsters, and added another dimension to the meaning of being a middle school student. Along with being a middle schooler came new teachers and students, and the youngsters recognized the difference this made in their social environment: "The teachers are different because in middle school everybody's sort of bad ... lots of people goof off," "There's a lot of older kids around," "You can beat up on elementary school kids," "I'm not too crazy about boys, [the other girls are] always talking about what they do with their boyfriends," "Mr. Whitney is too old, has a hearing aid. You can talk without him noticing," and "The girls are cuter." One youngster expressed his fascination with the different social environment created by the integration of various ethnic groups in middle school: "It's neat cause you learn about—there are a lot of just plain American kids in my neighborhood [predominantly white, middle-class neighborhood near the school]. Here you meet a lot of Chinese and stuff."

In the letters, many of the students offered advice in the social realm, as their focus changed from the physical and academic demands of sixth grade to the social aspects of making friends and being liked. Their responses included general encouragement ("As far as friends go, don't worry! I made a lot of new friends, very soon too.") as well as specific strategies for making friends: "Try to make friends and don't think that you're the best or you will get beat up," "If you want to have friends give them your neatest respect and try to help others," and "Talk to people [and] be yourself, don't try to be anyone else. They should still like you."

To be a middle school student means to have a new status and identity. As the children entered middle school, they were aware of an age-related change in their identities. They often expressed ambivalence between liking the new and higher status, yet disliking the fact that they were "little kids" who often got "picked on" by the older students. Some of their responses reflecting the identity issue were: "It makes me feel like a big shot ... I feel kind of like a baby 'cause we're in the lowest grade," "It's hard because when I came from fifth grade being the oldest and here I'm the youngest," and "I'm more like an adult." The older students were perceived as a threat to many of the youngsters throughout the first term as they expressed various concerns about the seventh and eighth graders: "You get pushed around by the seventh and eighth graders, they call you 'little sixth graders,' bump into you in the hall, don't do anything to go out of their way for you," "Sometimes the seventh or eighth graders mouth you off or bump into you," and "You will have to expect that some of the seventh and eighth graders will pick on you."

Some advice to new sixth graders from the letter data included strategies for dealing with the older students: "The first thing you need to know is never to mess with anyone," and "If a seventh grader picks on you, you come and see the house administrator and he will solve your problem right away." One youngster noted racial tension that erupted in an assault on a sixth grader at one of the schools the week before the letter data were collected: "You see fights but I'd never pick on anyone 'cause they might have friends, especially if they're black."

A second dimension of the children's new identity as middle school students included an increasing sense of maturity and volition to make their own decisions. This dimension was reflected in some of the youngsters' comments: "It makes me feel older," "[I like] having some choice in the classes you take," "Teachers don't always talk to you as a little kid," "They treat you older," "[I like] making your own choice of which class to go to," and "It means that you have to act more mature 'cause we are growing up and becoming young adults."

To be a middle school student means to have new academic and social responsibilities. The youngsters noted the increased academic responsibilities and expectations that accompanied their new status as middle school students. Not only were they expected to do harder work and to demonstrate a higher level of academic competence, they also perceived a growing sense of pressure to take responsibility for working independently and accounting for their own actions. Examples of these perceptions are expressed in the following comments: "It's more work, more independence, responsibility," "I like it because it's a challenge," "More homework," "You have to pay attention or you miss out. You could miss a day in elementary school but now if you miss a day you get behind and have to make up work from all your classes," "[We] have more things like foreign language and drama," and "You have to rely on yourself to do everything. The teachers in fifth grade help you through the year—they went around with you. In sixth grade they just said, 'Go.' "

In addition to the academic expectations, there were social responsibilities that the youngsters articulated which focused both on deportment and autonomy: "They're really strict on notices and being late—everything has to be with the rules. You have to be on time a lot," "When you get in trouble you have to go to detention," "[There are] more responsibilities ... in fifth grade, the teacher does stuff for you but in sixth grade you do it on your own ... [Like what?] Take you to lunch, get to class, not talk in class, help you with your work ... there are too many kids here for them to do that," "More privileges—you get out earlier even though you start earlier."

The responses of the youngsters in the second interview reflected an increased sense of responsibility as middle schoolers. Some of their later responses included: "[It means to be] more grown up, more responsibility, like you can be trusted with things like a locker combination and getting to class," and "They don't watch you, don't have to walk in lines, get to do stuff on your own, but I also don't like that because if you mess up it's all your fault."

Teachers' perspectives. From the teachers' perspectives, to be a middle school student meant primarily to meet a set of *expectations*, both academic/procedural and social. The expectations were addressed at the school, classroom, and individual levels. They were often explicitly expressed by teachers and administrators in classroom talk, during assemblies, and in the class rules posted in the classrooms. To be a middle school student also meant to deal with *physical changes*, both in the school environment and in the youngsters' growing bodies. Finally, teachers viewed middle school students as having a new *identity*.

To be a middle school student means to meet certain academic/ procedural and social expectations. The observational data revealed a strong emphasis in the teachers' classroom talk on academic/procedural expectations. These expectations concerned specific academic content or procedures for completing a classroom task, and included such comments as: "Do your pencil planning on your own paper first. On the pennant use pencil and soft, soft strokes. I won't give you any more handouts. I will give you time on Monday. Then if you don't finish you may take it home," "Stop. Take out a fresh sheet of paper. Put a proper heading on it. Copy down today's notes," "Write in pen, not pencil. Homework is due at the beginning of class. Homework time will help, but don't wait or leave everything till then," and "Make sure you put your name, date, and this is period five." Often the teachers' expectations were not verbalized but instead were posted somewhere in the classroom (usually the front of the room). These class rules included academic/procedural expectations: "Follow directions the first time they are given. Come to class prepared with completed assignments and proper materials: three ring binder, white paper, pen (blue or black ink), pencil, dividers, reading book, appropriate texts, colored markers ... Must have due date and grade on assignments ... Pencil—No papers in ink! NO CREDIT!!"

The second domain of expectations was social, expressed both proactively and reactively. Proactive social expectations were expressed frequently during the first two weeks of school, with increasingly more instances of negative sanctions for infractions as the term progressed. Some of the proactive expectations included comments at the classroom level: "That's elementary school stuff. We don't do that here," "We're going to work on behavior modification first. Then, maybe if I see you mature, you can work in a group," and "Class rules: Be seated and wait at station before the bell rings and while roll is being taken. There will be no horseplay, loud talk, or running in shop.... Ask to leave your seat ... be considerate ... BE IN YOUR SEAT when the bell rings. Be polite and considerate to all persons."

At the school level, the principals and vice principals expressed social expectations during assemblies that were held for the sixth graders during the first two weeks of school: "If there's a problem, I need to know about it. With 900 kids you will end up having a problem with someone. Maybe you will, maybe you won't. If you do, contact the counselor or me. The last thing we want are fights, yelling, or shouting in the halls. You will go home, or get in-house suspension," "Disruptive conduct is the most common infraction [of school rules]. The school is a learning environment and disruption is not acceptable. Horseplay, being loud, being disrespectful [is punishable by] parent notification, noon detention, lunch duty, after school detention, suspension," and "Verbal abuse—some was tolerated in the past, but we will be strict this year. Verbal abuse is not allowed in your homes and we have the same standards here."

There were a few occasions in which the teachers reactively expressed social expectations during the first week of school. These expressions occurred in response to an infraction of a rule that the children should have been aware of, even during the first week: "No foot resting on desks," and "You're interrupting. I'm in the middle of a sentence. . . . I don't appreciate competition when I'm calling roll. When you are talking that is competition." The attitude of most of the teachers the first week, however, was a forgiving one: "I shouldn't have to tell you. Next week I will get tougher. You should be on time."

By the second week, the teachers employed more verbal reprimands in reaction to violations of class rules, particularly rules of conduct such as class disruptions: "Um, you have to stop talking," "Now, what are we saying? Why are you sitting here with all of those pencils and your papers are empty?," [Teacher tries to regain order] "Gentlemen and ladies. Gentlemen and ladies. Gentlemen and ladies. Gentlemen and ladies. Gentlemen and ladies. BE QUIET is what I am trying to tell you," "Get out. I'm tired of that. Go out of here until you're not bored," "This is not a talking time . . . wait, wait. Rob, please put your chair down flat. Carl we're waiting for you to come back with us. . . . This is not a talking time, this is a working time." Teachers' reactive comments to social infractions often included a statement (or repetition) of a class rule: "When discussion goes on when I'm passing out papers, it really uses up time. So I'd like you to get in the habit of doing it quietly," "No, no [you may not go to the bathroom]. You just had first lunch, second lunch, 20 minute recess—you have to learn to stop playing around with your friends," "Please don't talk out from this point on," "No [you may not go to your locker]. You're just going to have to remember to bring it [your textbook] to class. We're in the third week of school and I can't be letting you go back to your locker," and "Jeremy, you cannot talk out during the test. Remember what happens to your paper if you talk out and disturb other people during class?"

To be a middle school student means to deal with physical changes. A second category which addressed the teachers' perspective of what it means to be a middle school student was concerned with the physical changes that the middle schoolers were experiencing, both in managing the new physical environment and in dealing with the physical changes within their own bodies. In the classroom and during assemblies, teachers directly addressed these physical changes as important ones, particularly environmental changes to which the students had to adapt during the first few days: "Ask any adult. Ask Mr. J. [to help open your locker]. Feel free to ask any of us questions. We know it's been an adjustment for you and are happy to help you," "Anybody having trouble with your locker? Anybody having schedule problems? Anybody lose a copy of their schedule? Everybody know where your bus is?," and "You are savvy and quick to adapt. You follow directions well. The week seems to be going well. How many of you like changing classes?. . . . I know it's different from elementary school where you had one place to store your things and you didn't have to pack up at the end of each hour."

The references to bodily changes that the youngsters were experiencing were not as frequent, but nevertheless did emerge in the teachers' talk to the new middle schoolers: "At this time in your lives you are showing interest in the opposite sex. My body is my personal being and your body is your personal being. If anybody violates that, we [the staff] need to know," and "In chapter one we're talking about changing and growing, and I'm trying to help you understand it in terms of your own experiences since you are at an age when you are doing a lot of changing and growing. These are the difficult stages, and one of the hardest ones."

To be a middle school student means to be identified as sixth graders and middle school students in the teachers' talk. A final dimension of the meaning of middle school student included direct references to the youngsters as sixth graders and middle schoolers. Many of these comments referred to changes the children were experiencing, new responsibilities which they were facing, and/or the teachers' expectations of them (both academic and social) within this new role. Some examples of these comments include the following: "You're middle school students now. Along with being middle school students comes a number of expectations," "Remember I told you last week when you were in elementary school you were told it was right or wrong. I'm interested in the process. I will always ask you why or what process you went through to get there," "You are not fifth graders, you are in sixth grade now. Older and more mature," and "The sixth graders have to show the other grade levels that they have a lot of team spirit. . . . It's great to see how a grade level can make a difference as you move up through grades."

Summary. The findings reveal both similarities and differences in the perspectives of students and teachers in response to the question: "What does it mean to be a middle school student?" From the students' perspective, to be a middle school student means to be in a new and different environment, to have a new identity and status change, both as a sixth grader and as a "little kid" again, and to have new academic and social responsibilities. The youngsters' responses in the first interviews suggested a strong emphasis on the environmental aspect of being a sixth grader, with the identity and status change as less salient issues, and social and academic responsibilities a third component of their definition. Their second interview responses focused more heavily on the responsibilities of middle schoolers, as well as the social aspect of the school and their new status as older and more mature yet still subject to harrassment by the older students.

From the teachers' perspective as revealed in their classroom talk, to be a middle school student means primarily to meet academic and social expectations as identified at the school and classroom levels. Their class-room talk also included references to the environmental changes in the school and bodily changes within students. A third dimension of what it means to be a middle school student from the teachers' perspective is to have a new identity as a sixth grader and a middle school student. Inter-twined with this new identity is a set of responsibilities and expectations that were implicitly or explicitly expressed by the teachers. The teachers' talk addressing this new identity did not reveal the perceptions expressed by the students, namely that accompanying the entrance into the new grade and the new school was a dramatic change in the youngsters' social status.

Question Two: What is the Nature of the Information Youngsters Seek as They Socialize into Middle School?

The data that addressed this question are categorized into two domains: (a) information actively sought by youngsters, and (b) information pro-vided by teachers without solicitation by students. These two dimensions of the question are important because they address not only the informa-tion gained through the youngsters' information seeking behaviors, but also information which the teachers provided either before questions could arise, or in response to previous questions or concerns which arose in their other classes. It is presumed that both kinds of information are critical in order for the students to become competent members of the school community.

Information actively sought by youngsters. The first few weeks of school were filled with various efforts by the students to obtain information about the school and about their new roles. The interview data coupled with classroom observations provided two rich sources in response to Question Two. While there was some correspondence between the two data sources, there were also differences that will be highlighted in the discussion below.

Procedural information. The first type of information that the new middle schoolers sought was procedural clarification: how to do an assign-ment, where to go, what to do. These examples were drawn primarily from the observational data, as incidents of question asking were easily identifi-able in the classrooms and occurred frequently during the first few weeks of school: "When is it due?" "Can we use scratch paper?" "My seat is sticky. What should I do?" "Where should I sit? There's no place to sit and I don't know anyone," "How are you supposed to check it [a book] out?" "Can I go to my locker?" "Is that the side we're supposed to write it on?" and "I was wondering, you said first quarter is done in November? When in November? So you get your report card that day? If you are moving, do you get your report card before?"

The need for procedural information also emerged from the interview data, but was primarily focused on opening lockers and finding classes, especially in the early weeks of school. Most of the youngsters recognized the need to seek assistance from friends, siblings, teachers, and school staff to open their lockers ("My friends—they've been helpful, helped me if I'm lost or can't get my locker open," "Mr. N. helps you with your locker, helps you get used to the other kids,") or to find their classes ("My sister helped me find my homeroom," "The teachers also help with homework, show you around if you're lost."). A few youngsters recognized the need for special information, such as how to find the right bus or how to meet people: "Mrs. L. [helped me], she's in charge of buses, needed to give me a bus card at first because I didn't have transportation home, she let me call my mom to talk to her," "Teachers help, if you don't have friends, the next person down the hall they introduce you to and then they're your friend," "Charles, the Filipino kid with the flat top [helped me]. His sister went here and I got to look in their yearbook and learn people's names."

Content information. A second type of information sought by the sixth graders was content information, particularly concerning homework or class assignments. Content information was solicited from teachers, friends, and family members, and emerged from both classroom observations and the interview data. Some examples from the classroom include: "What do we write about?" "How do you spell 'unless'?" "If you were rounding to the nearest 1000th would you go 005? Round to the nearest whole number means nearest to the decimal?" and Girl: "Do we have to do that [assignment] now?" Boy: "No." Girl: "Do we have to do that for homework?" Other examples are drawn from the interviews, and reflect the various sources of information the children utilized: "My parents, they read with me, help me with my homework. When it's completed they go over it, make sure it's right," "My sister, she came here last year and the year before. She helps me with my homework," "Ms. K., my first period teacher. She can help if you don't understand the work," and "My friends help me with my homework sometimes, we study together."

General information. There were occasions observed in which the new sixth graders sought general information about the school or the classroom: "Is this fourth period? How long is your sixth period? What time is this over?" and "Do you have a wastebasket here?"

Identification. The youngsters also frequently asked identification questions of the teachers: "Are you from New York or New Jersey?" and "Who taught you [American Sign Language]?" They also questioned the researchers, inquiring about who they were, what they were doing, and other personal information: "What are you writing? Are you a mother?"

"You a new teacher? Is that [the teacher] your husband?" "Are you the woman who's observing the sixth grade?" and "How old are you?"[3]

Reassurance and comparison. A fifth type of information that surfaced primarily in the interview data was the newcomers' need for reassurance that middle school would be fun, that they would do well, that they would get used to it. Often this type of information came in the form of a comparison of experiences, either with friends, siblings, or parents. Family members provided most of the reassurance: "My mom [helped me]. I was worried and I talked to her, she told me to listen to my sister [who was reassurring], there's nothing to worry about," "I couldn't get all my assignments in and they just said, 'Keep trying,'" Child: "My grandparents, they would, if I need anything, they would help me 'cause they live right down the street." Researcher: "Have you ever needed to call them for something?" Child: "No, but it's good to know that they are right there just in case," "I always thought middle school would be real hard and mean. My dad said it would be a good school, he said, 'Don't worry.'" "Whenever I ask him [my dad] a question, he got it all figured out with the office. I didn't want shop and he had the class changed." In some cases the reassurance occurred through a comparison of experiences: "My mom and dad told me how it was for them," "My sister and brother, they went here, kept saying it's really nice, it's gonna be fun," and "On the first day I was scared, I didn't want to go. My dad gave me a pep talk because he went here for junior high."

Information provided by teachers. The type of information offered by teachers without active solicitation from the students was determined from the classroom observations. The most predominant type of information was teacher or school expectatations (academic/procedural and social), yet other information included general information, encouragement and praise, and identification of other students and teachers.

Expectations. The types of expectations expressed by the teachers were discussed previously. Additional examples include: "Today we will do a paragraph about how to organize yourself when you get home from school. First let's review a paragraph," "I would like to hear a 'here' from you when I call your name," "Hey! Watch your language. Watch your language," "I know it's hard. But you need to sit down when that bell rings and stop talking. And don't get out of your seat until I say so." (See Question One for elaboration.)

General information. During the homeroom period, there were numerous occasions when the teachers informed the students of school pol-

---

[3] Only on one occasion did the teacher introduce the observing researcher to the class. The other teachers often acknowledged the researcher but did not introduce her or attempt to explain her presence to the youngsters.

icy or special events. There was a daily bulletin of announcements read to the students that informed them of the lunch menu, assemblies, or upcoming events such as dances and field trips. There were also occasions during the first few weeks when the teachers overviewed certain policies or procedures for the newcomers: "I've neglected to talk about fire drill procedures in this class. Use your good judgment about time and the stairs that are closest. Have a partner, then get two others and go down the stairs four at a time. The third floor is most likely to be trapped. I know it's unlikely there will be a fire, but try to take it seriously," and "Once again I want to remind you that this room is very hot—you have to dress in layers. Pretend you're on a survival camping trip and dress in layers."

Encouragement and praise. This category parallelled the students' category of seeking reassurance, and focused on the students' success in their new school. General praise for positive behaviors was also included in this domain. Examples from classroom observations include: "Welcome—this is the most popular school of its kind in the city. We have more requests to transfer to this school than any other school in the state. That's because you are here," "Most of you are doing a super job," and "See Greg, wasting not a minute. He's reading. It's just so lovely to see."

Identification of teachers and students. The final category of unsolicited information provided by teachers was that of identification. During the first few days of school there were numerous occasions for the teachers and administrators to introduce themselves to students, as well as introduce other students to their classmates. Some examples of this type of information include the following: "I failed to introduce myself. I am Mr. N.," "I'm Mrs. H., the sixth-grade team leader and I will be the Language Arts teacher for many of you," "Let's each take a turn [introducing ourselves]. Stand by your desk, let your heart beat fast, tell us your name and one thing from the data sheet," and "Ernie is a new student who arrived yesterday from Alaska."

Summary. The type of information needed by youngsters as they socialized into middle school was analyzed from three sources: (a) questions raised by the students during classes, (b) information obtained during student interviews, and (c) information provided by the teachers during class without solicitation from the students. It appeared that the students were concerned with many of the same issues that the teachers' talk reflected, primarily academic and social procedures, general information, reassurance, and identification of unknown persons. The students' comments also reflected a desire for content information, comparison of middle school experiences, and identification of adults, while the teachers' comments included social expectations and identification of students and teachers.

Question Three: What is the Nature of the Process by Which Youngsters Socialize into Middle School and What Communication Strategies are Employed?

The communication strategies employed by the youngsters in the process of socialization were varied. They ranged from highly direct and face-threatening strategies which included interactions with others (e.g., asking questions), to more indirect, face saving strategies, which often included minimal or no contact with others (e.g., observing). These strategies will be discussed in order of their placement on a direct-indirect continuum.

Overt means. This strategy was described by Miller and Jablin (1987) as a type of information seeking in which questions were asked directly of target persons who had needed information. The target persons in the school setting were teachers, administrators, friends, older students, or any individual (including the researchers) whom the newcomer thought would be a knowledgeable source of information. The youngsters were frequently observed asking direct questions: "Where can we buy the book?" "What if your locker is real hard to turn?" "What time does this [class] end?" "How do you put it on, Mr. V.?" and "Ms. H.? Why are you being so nice?" The students confirmed the use of this overt strategy in their interviews, as many indicated that they asked questions to find out about the school or to receive help: "On the first day, I was crying, she [the counselor] found me someone to eat lunch with," "My neighbor is in seventh grade, we walk to school together, I ask her about things," and "If you're lost, you can ask a teacher and they will help you." Despite the frequent use of friends and older siblings as resources, one youngster gave the following warning: "If you need help go to a teacher or any grown up but you should usually never go to a fellow student."

Being Interpersonal. This category emerged from the interview data and included behaviors that focused on youngsters making friends with their classmates and with their teachers. Many of the middle schoolers responded that they learned things about the school and became more comfortable in the school in various ways: "Getting to know people, getting to know teachers and stuff," "I try to get along with people, try to be friends with the teacher and be good in class," "I've tried to be helpful and remind the teachers what my name is. I've turned in all of my assignments," and "I just try to be happy—just try to go along with everybody."

The letter data also pointed to an emphasis on utilizing interpersonal strategies in order to do well and be happy in middle school. The youngsters' responses were often quite revealing, indicating direct strategies for making friends or for getting along with the teachers: "Do not try and make friends with seventh and eighth graders, but if you're sitting next to someone you think you will like, start a conversation and that's how I made friends," "Pretty soon you will get to know your classmates better and most of them will like you but you have to be nice to them because if you don't they will not like you," and "Some teachers like you to do certain things, and if you do you might get a better grade. The band teacher, Mr. C., likes you to laugh at his jokes and not drop stuff. The social studies teacher, Mr. W., likes you not to talk and always raise your hand. The science teacher, Mr. S., hates talking. The rest I haven't figured out yet."

Indirect and rhetorical questions. While question-asking was an overt means described above, Miller and Jablin (1987) distinguished indirect questions as those which might be noninterrogative and/or implied. The youngsters employed indirect questions as a means of checking their progress against others in the class without directly asking the teacher for assistance. Some of the questions were noninterrogative or implied (e.g., "It's gone! Mine is gone!," "I can't cut these out," "I didn't do anything exciting this summer.").

Rhetorical questions were another way of asking questions without directly addressing the target person. These questions seemed to allow the students to express confusion or concerns without expecting a response. Indeed, teachers and fellow students did not respond to most of these types of questions. Examples included: "Can I sit here?. . . . Where do I go? Where do I go?," "I'm giving up right now. . . . Do we have to do this?," and Child 1: "Hey, this is chalk!" Child 2: "I know, I got chalk too. Are we supposed to use chalk?"

Testing limits. This strategy, also called "Garfinkeling" by Miller and Jablin (1987), involved the deliberate transgression of a rule in order to discover the importance of the rules to the newcomers and the circumstances under which they would be enforced (Garfinkel, 1967). Testing limits seemed to be employed more frequently as the term progressed, with few occasions of rule violations in the first week of observations, and increasingly more instances of rule violation or direct challenge of the teachers in subsequent weeks. Some examples of this strategy are evidenced in the following teachers' comments: "No foot resting on desks," "Next time, raise your hand," and "You're interrupting. I'm in the middle of a sentence." On some occasions the rule violation was unintentional, as reported by the following youngsters in interviews:

Child:	Once I went to the library at the wrong time, and I had to learn the right time when we can go to the library.
Interviewer:	How do you learn that?
Child:	People tell you, other kids. No one told me [not to go on the] second and third floor during lunch. I got yelled at by one of the teachers who watches the halls.

After the first week the youngsters sometimes challenged the teachers when reprimanded: Teacher: "Kurt, what did I just say?" Kurt: "I'm gettin' my notebook!" Teacher: "Come and see me at 11:20." Girl: "I have to eat lunch then." Teacher: "I don't care. I'll be in the lunchroom ... wiping tables. What you're going to join me in doing."

Observing targets' behavior. This strategy, as presented by Miller and Jablin (1987) included observations of the target person(s) (primarily other students) without direct interaction with that person(s). This strategy was difficult for the researchers to see and record, but many of the students responded in interviews that they "learned the ropes" in their new school by observing others, particularly other students: "Look at some of the other people who seem to fit in, take what they do and add what I know—see what they don't do," and "[I needed to know] what you should wear, how to treat people. [I learned] by watching other people, got a lot of friends who were eighth graders."[4]

Getting around in the school. Another important strategy was figuring out how to get around in the new school building. This strategy included gaining familiarity and confidence with the physical layout of the school. In the interviews, the students remarked that they felt comfortable in their new school when they learned "where to go ... know where the bathrooms are, where the lunchroom is." Although many newcomers directly asked teachers or classmates for assistance, others found their own way around, wandering the halls until they figured out the system and found their way to their various classes: "I use landmarks: the billboard by my locker, the gym and the boys' restroom are by my homeroom," "I learned to go to the right rooms without looking at my schedule," "[I had to learn] where my rooms were. I sort of searched for them," and "After school sometimes I walk to my dad's or take a bus to my mom's. When I walk I can figure [my] way around easier 'cause there's not so many people in the hall—between classes it's like trying to swim upstream."

"Hanging loose." This strategy was employed by several students who seemed to take a more passive approach than even those who learned by observing others. These students expressed a "gestalt" type of approach in which they became comfortable in middle school by letting things happen and trying to get a "feel" for their new school. Their responses included such tactics as: "Just been myself," "Going with the flow," and

---

[4] It was interesting to note that while many of the youngsters expressed concern with the older students and disliked being pushed around and treated like "little sixth graders," they did not address this issue with specific strategies for dealing with the seventh and eighth graders or for obtaining information about them. The older students were viewed as knowledgeable authorities from the perspective of information seeking.

"Sitting down, looking around, feeling everything. Looking at everything, getting to feel the school."

Summary. The newcomers employed various strategies that facilitated the socialization process. Some were directed towards seeking information about the school and about their roles within the school, and ranged from overt behaviors such as asking questions to more discreet strategies such as observing others. Additional strategies involved familiarizing themselves with the new school by finding their way around and getting a feeling for the school.

Question Four: What Are the Critical Dimensions in the Passage to the Status of Middle School Student?

The status passage from elementary to middle school was an important one for the youngsters. With respect to temporal dimensions, the youngsters viewed the passage into middle school as *inevitable, regular,* and *scheduled.*[5] The impression that the students gave of their fifth-grade year was that they had been prepared psychologically and academically for sixth grade: "My fifth-grade teacher had us work on sixth-grade stuff," "My favorite teachers at my old school, they taught me stuff, taught us things to get ready for sixth grade," and "Last year they got us in shape for sixth grade, they'd say things like, 'This is how it will be in the sixth grade.' " The fifth graders were also given a tour of the middle school during the spring of the previous year in anticipation of their arrival in the autumn.

Other salient aspects of the passage into middle school addressed the *desirability* of the move and the *centrality* or importance of it in the youngsters' lives. Although the transition to middle school was desirable in the way that growing up is desirable intrinsically to 11-year olds, many of the students interviewed expressed some uncertainties about the new school and about being "little sixth graders": "At first it was scary, there were big kids around and we were the littlest ones . . . in grade school we were the oldest class." In general, however, there was consensus that the move to middle school was a positive step and marked an important milestone: "It means like I'm growing up. Kind of like a birthday," "It means I'm closer to high school, kind of in between. I like it," and "I been waiting all my life for middle school, Junior High. It feels like I'm really high in my education, I've come a long way."

---

[5] The researchers acknowledge the inherent bias of the youngsters interviewed, who had all passed the fifth grade. We were unable to note if there were different expectations concerning the inevitability of the passage that were expressed by those youngsters who repeated the fifth grade.

The *signs of the status passage* were both explicitly and implicitly apparent. Explicit signs of the passage included: (a) the new school environment, (b) the assignment of combination lockers, (c) lunchroom "luxuries" such as a vending machine and choice of menu, and (d) changing classes. These signs explicitly marked the passage from elementary school to middle school for the new sixth graders. A fifth sign, that of special orientation assemblies for sixth graders, was an indication that the passage was considered a *formal* one in the student career. Other signs of the status passage included more implicit markers such as the responsibilities outlined to the students in the orientation assemblies and the structure of their gym classes (sixth, seventh, and eighth graders combined). The expectations expressed in the orientation assemblies emphasized the youngsters' responsibilities to the school as well as to the community, implicitly referencing their growing maturity in their new status as middle schoolers. The combined gym classes emphasized the acceptance of the sixth graders as middle schoolers from the teachers' perspective, as the sixth graders received the same treatment as the seventh and eighth graders during gym class.

The final dimensions of the status passage that emerged from the data centered around the *collective* experience. The passage to middle school was a collective one as most youngsters moved from their respective schools en masse to the new middle school. There was a sense of cameraderie among the sixth graders, who were sharing similar experiences in the new school as they struggled to open combination lockers, meet people to sit with at lunch, find their way through the halls, and learn the rules and procedures of middle school. The teachers' references to the newcomers as "new sixth graders" and singling the sixth-grade class out for special assemblies also reinforced the sense of the collective and the *awareness* of the collective. The occasions when students were paired, introduced to others, or allowed to work together were other means that the teachers had of reinforcing a group awareness. The strong emphasis on social responsibilities expressed orally by the teachers and administrators, or written as class rules, also served to promote a sense of awareness of the collective, both as sixth graders and as middle schoolers.[6]

Finally, the degree to which the youngsters *communicated with one another* during the passage was important. As discussed previously, com-

---

[6] From the students' perspective, however, it must be noted that the passage to middle school often seemed like a solitary endeavor, particularly if there were unfamiliar faces in the children's individual classes. Until the students found at least one "buddy" with whom to share the experience, many of the youngsters interviewed expressed concern and uncertainty about being on their own in the new school.

munication with peers and siblings was of primary importance in the socialization process. Communication with others during the transition period served not only to reduce uncertainty about the new school and the
newcomers' roles within the school, but also to provide emotional support
to reassure students and resolve their concerns during the passage from
elementary school to middle school.

DISCUSSION

There were several important conclusions emerging from the results of
this chapter. These related to the ease of the passage, the nature of the
academic concerns, and the importance of the social concerns.

Ease of the Passage

First, it appeared that despite the fears and nervous stomachs reported by
the youngsters in anticipation of sixth grade, the passage from elementary
school to middle school was relatively easy for most of the students. The
majority of the youngsters interviewed said that they felt comfortable and
liked middle school within the first few days or weeks. Although many
had negative expectations of the school, most of these fears were quickly
allayed: "Don't worry about sixth grade. It's really not as hard as you might
think!.... I thought I'd get a bunch of white slips for being late, or forget
my [gym] basket combo or locker combo, not being able to find my
classes, etc. I was pleasantly surprised, however, everything went just
great," and "As soon as you come to Harrison, everything will look VERY
big. Everyone looks almost like giants.... On the second [day] everything
is easy and the bigger kids sort of shrink."

The uncertainty about what to expect in the new school was much
more troublesome upon first entry than later in the term. Judging from
the changes in their responses from the first to the second interview, it
appeared that the newcomers adapted easily to the new school system
and responsibilities of sixth grade, and enjoyed the status of middle school
student with all of the privileges that it allowed. In the first interview,
there were a number of ambivalent or negative responses to being a middle school student: "It's weird—I'm not used to going to different classes,"
"It feels scary at the beginning—gonna be big kids who beat you up," and
"It's not very fun, it's okay but you have six classes, you have to keep your
work together." By the middle of the term, however, only a few of the
students still held negative or ambivalent feelings about the school. Generally, by the tenth week of school, the sixth graders had enthusiastic re-

sponses to being middle school students. Except for the status change from being a "big kid" in elementary school to a "little sixth grader" in middle school, the move to the new school was a positive experience for most of the youngsters interviewed.

There are two most likely explanations for the relatively easy and smooth passage from elementary to middle school, and the generally positive responses to middle school. One consideration is that the rapid transition was due to the availability of information to the newcomers. From the researchers' observations and the youngsters' comments, it appeared that the teachers and administrators made themselves available to the new sixth graders by standing in the hallways in front of the classrooms to direct traffic and answer questions, encouraging the students to talk to them about any problems they had, and in general being visible and readily approached. Their attempt to reduce the newcomers' uncertainty about where to go, what to do, and what was expected of them was reflected in the comment: "If you have a question, ask someone." This theme also surfaced in the youngsters' comments: "I made friends with the teachers so they knew who I was if I needed help." The teachers gave explicit instructions during class, repeating directions and answering questions that arose concerning academic, procedural, content, or general concerns: "The teachers are helpful ... getting to classes. There's less homework at first, they explained how things would be run, talked about rules like if you were tardy."

Thus, both teachers and students focused on increasing the newcomers' confidence by reducing their uncertainty about procedures, assignments, expectations, and the physical layout of the school. In addition, the students exhibited multiple strategies for obtaining information about the school and about their roles in the school. They employed a variety of direct and indirect tactics in order to obtain information about their new environment, and to socialize into the new school and their role as middle schoolers. The youngsters also expressed a heavy reliance on friends, family, and school personnel to answer questions and/or to provide reassurance. It is encouraging that many of the students found that the mechanisms employed by the school (e.g., assemblies, a tour of the middle school while the youngsters were in fifth grade) were effective in helping them socialize into middle school: "Ms. J., my fifth-grade teacher, she took us to the middle school and looked at it and told us how it was gonna be, made it like it wasn't as bad—usually when you go to a new school it's horrible," and "The teachers here, they tell you everything you need to know, they don't leave anything out. They keep you informed all the time."

Another explanation for the relative ease of the passage from elementary school to middle school may be the sharp contrast between their expectations of negative experiences and the actual reality: "Nobody messed with me—I thought they were going to beat up on you," "I expected in each class the teachers would be mean—I heard stories from people and people were just trying to be mean," "I thought it was gonna be really hard and I thought I was gonna have so many books that I couldn't carry them home," and "I also thought the teachers would have low rim glasses and have their desks in front and center and have our desks in straight rows." It may be that upon their arrival to middle school, the youngsters' relief that "the worst" did not happen to them may have eased the transition into the new school and made for a more positive experience.[7]

Nature of the Academic Concerns

A second conclusion was that although the coursework in middle school was more difficult than in elementary school, the students' academic concerns were centered more on the responsibility aspect of doing homework and handing assignments in on time rather than on the level of academic performance expected of them. It appeared that for these youngsters the most difficult aspect of sixth grade was not the academic work, but the increasing responsibilities that accompanied the passage to middle school. Although some of the youngsters interviewed admitted that "the problems are a little harder," the following response sums up the academic concerns of many of the new sixth graders interviewed: "They expect you to be— to act older. In elementary school they kept track of your papers. Here you have to do it yourself, keep track by yourself. They just say, " 'Okay, hand in your papers.' "

Importance of the Social Concerns

A third conclusion was that it appeared that both students' and teachers'/ administrators' comments reflected the social aspect of middle school as the primary concern of the newcomers. The definition of the "social dimension" of school, however, differed slightly for the students and the school personnel. From the students' perspective, their major efforts in middle school (even during the initial days of finding classes and opening lockers) were directed towards making friends and getting along with oth-

---

[7] A third possible explanation, a methodological one, for the relatively smooth passage from elementary to middle school must be considered. The total sixth-grade enrollment in the two middle schools was 443. Ninety-six of these students volunteered to be interviewed. It may be that the volunteer sample consisted primarily of students who were experiencing an easy passage.

ers. In the confusion of the first few days, finding a friend they knew from the previous year or making new friends with classmates was a welcome consolation: "I relied on people I knew, they have the same thoughts, we got through it together. I have classes with them, we talk, help each other, tell you where the room is," "All my friends are here, I have a friend in every class so it's not like you're alone," and "The first day I was kinda 'freaked,' I didn't know what to do and stuff. I found some people from my old school and they were 'freaked' too. So it was okay."

From the teachers'/administrators' perspective, although it was important for the youngsters to make friends, be happy, and "get involved" in the school activities ("We want you to feel comfortable, to learn how to participate so you will know how to join in and participate when you go to ninth grade"), their social emphasis was more directed towards keeping peace among the students and avoiding conflicts and confrontations. As the vice principal warned in the introductory assembly at Harrison:

> It is always wrong to strike another person. . . . Even if someone says something bad about you—you're not very pretty, your face, about your mother—it's wrong to hit. You're learning here how to get along. We have to call the police if you break the laws. But most of you don't break the laws, just the school rules. The two school rules are: do not disrupt class, and do not disobey teachers.

Thus, the social dimension of middle school had a more far-reaching emphasis from the perspective of the school personnel, as they impressed upon the youngsters that they not only had to be good students in school, they were also responsible for being good citizens in society.

A Concluding Note

Socialization into middle school was a complicated process in which communication played a major role. As the youngsters negotiated their first few weeks in the "salad bowl" of middle school, the use of communication by both students and teachers was seen as the means through which socialization occurred. Teachers expressed their expectations for the newcomers regarding school norms in their comments during class. The new sixth graders also utilized communication to resolve concern and reduce their uncertainty about school procedures, expectations, and their role as middle school students as they gained information about the new environment and the social implications of their new role. The newcomers employed various communication strategies in order to obtain information during the socialization process. They utilized these strategies with different people, not only to solve first-day problems such as locating the auditorium or identifying their homeroom teacher, but also to continue to verify their experiences, to make friends, and to obtain reassurance from others. Thus, the transition to middle school was accomplished with relative ease.

chapter 5
Becoming a High School Freshman

This chapter, similar to Chapter Four, presents perspectives of several hundred new ninth graders in four different high schools (three public and one private) during their first term. The students articulate what it means to them to be high school freshmen, their concerns during the entry phase, and the ways in which communication facilitates their socialization into high school. They seek and acquire information from friends, siblings, and teachers about academics, school policies, and procedures. They begin to feel a part of the new school and comfortable in the new role of freshman through communication that meets their emotional needs and helps them to make friends.

> I checked my school map at the door of the commons. If I went straight through and out to the courtyard, I should be facing the building with the home ec rooms. I put my map in my Pee Chee so I wouldn't look like a freshman, and I'd started weaving my way past the crowd around the Coke machines when someone yelled. . . . I had to think a minute. Which class was next? Geometry? Geometry, room 36. Right. I bumped into the back of a letter jacket as I burrowed my way down the hall. I let the crowd surge ahead of me so the boy wouldn't know who had hit him when he looked around. . . . I had lunch with Jenny, and then my last two classes were the usual school downers, especially social studies. The teacher started off sourly with a bunch of rules about getting papers in on time, not losing the assignment dittos or the textbooks, and showing up for every test or else. She acted like she expected half of us to mess up, and by the equally sour look on the kids' faces I guessed her expectations would come true. I stopped in the girls' lavatory before I went to P.E. I found the gym easily enough by following my map of the campus. I knew I was a little late; still I wasn't so late the door would be locked. I gave the knob a third yank and heard the class bell ring inside. I *was* locked out. Now what was I supposed to do? I stood there, hoping I wasn't sweating my new sweater. It was too hot to be wearing a sweater. But you can never tell about weather on September mornings. (DeClements, 1983, pp. 1, 7–8)

Entry into high school involves finding one's way in a new and unfamiliar building, learning to make sense of the expectations of different teachers, and trying desperately to project an image of one who is not a newcomer. The character of Elsie in the fictional *How Do You Lose Those Ninth Grade Blues?* is not vastly different from actual high school freshmen on the first day of school. Demands on the newcomer are varied, including the social dimension of trying to appear "cool" and one of the crowd, the physical dimension of locating classrooms, and the academic dimension of surviving the classroom learning experiences.

The High School Experience

Since the early 1970s, a number of studies have emerged which describe and analyze the high school experience. One of the first of these was Lacey's (1970) *Hightown Grammar*, a detailed case study of a British secondary school for boys. In a participant observation study, Cusick (1973) examined the nature of student activity as it evolved over an extended time period. Peshkin (1978) analyzed life in a small town American high school and the relationship between the school and the community. In his study of three American high schools, Cusick (1983) provided descriptions of curricular and extracurricular activities and developed a model of the common school structure with its commitment to an egalitarian ideal. Perrone and associates (1983) described 13 public high schools across the United States in order to "gain a significant understanding of the schools, their principal motifs, and the issues that confronted them" (p. 2). In a related study, Lightfoot (1983) described six high schools that were selected for excellence in order to "capture the culture of these schools, their essential features, their generic character, the values that define their curricular goals and institutional structures, and their individual styles and rituals" (p. 6).

The mid-1980s saw the publication of several volumes focusing on high schools in America. In *Horace's Compromise*, Sizer (1984) discussed the usual routines of schooling and ways these could be changed productively. Powell, Farrar, and Cohen (1985), through observations and interviews in 15 schools, examined the American high school from the perspective of a "shopping mall in terms of variety, choice, and neutrality" (p. 7). In *The Last Little Citadel*, Hampel (1986) charted changes in the American high school since 1940 and analyzed its present commitment to equality. And although not limited to the high school years, Peshkin's (1986) case study of the Bethany Baptist Academy, *God's Choice: The Total World of a Fundamentalist Christian School*, provided an in-depth view of one group of fundamentalist high school students in their church school.

Each of these books provides extensive description and analysis of high school life and student activity in American society. Although not always stated explicitly, the implicit assumption upon which each rests is that the high school experience is a major one in the life of the American adolescent. Since school can be considered a full time occupation for most teenagers (Fasick, 1984; Hamilton, 1984), it is an important point of analysis.

School Structure and Student Culture

Other studies of high schools have focused more specifically on school structure and the student culture. In his study of suburban youth culture in the 1970s, Larkin (1979) analyzed the social structure of Utopia High, with its formal and informal hierarchies and accompanying subcultures. Shimahara (1983) found patterns of polarized socialization in a black–white urban high school in which racial separation was common. Page (1987) described the chaotic climate of a lower-track classroom and how it was differentiated from the overall environment of the college-preparatory high school in which it was situated. Gamoran and Berends (1987) reviewed literature which suggested that tracking in American high schools or streaming in British schools affected students' friendship patterns.

Additional studies have shed light on the varied activities in which students engage and the importance of the peer group. Cusick, Martin, and Palonsky (1976), in a comparison of three high schools, concluded that "the students spent most of their school time, and probably much of their adolescent energy, hanging around with one another in small, informal groups" (p. 4). Several researchers have given considerable attention to the study of cliques in high school—their composition, student awareness of their existence, and their function (Canaan, 1987; Cohen, 1979; Savin-Williams, 1980; Varenne, 1982). It has been posited that interaction with peers is the primary attraction of high school: "Many teens come to school not because their driving force is to learn but because school belongs to them as a place to meet and to be with friends" (Eggert, 1984, p. 32).

The Transition to High School

Although there have been few empirical examinations of the ways in which students make the transition to high school, the process itself has been viewed as important. Salmon (1979) identifies the transition period as significant:

> The transition to secondary school ... must also alter peer group relationships. It seems likely that where other children from the same junior school are present in the secondary school class, the friendship group will for a time consist of this little group. Nevertheless, adjustment must, even in these

cases, be made to new children, and ultimately a new set of peer group relationships will have to be made. (p. 104)

In a study of some 300 students in the United Kingdom, Bryan (1980) described pupil perceptions of transfer from middle school into high school. With data derived from student essays written prior to entry into high school ("My Thoughts on Changing Schools") and again several months later ("My Thoughts on my New School"), he identified four categories of concern for students: material resources, friendship, status, and regulation of time and dress. Additional studies are needed to elucidate the process by which students make the transition to high school.

Summary

Previous research has examined the high school experience and the structure of the school and student culture. Limited attention has been accorded the process by which youngsters make the transition from middle school or junior high to high school. This chapter responds to the need for empirical research on socialization into high school.

PURPOSE OF THE CHAPTER

This chapter provides an understanding of the perspectives of high school freshmen as they enter a new grade level, a new school building, and a new structural arrangement. The chapter addresses four research questions:

1. What does it mean to be a high school freshman?
2. What are the concerns of new freshmen as they socialize into high school?
3. How does communication function in the socialization of high school freshmen?
4. What are the critical dimensions in the passage to the status of high school freshman?

METHOD

Research Setting

The primary participants of the study were approximately 300 high school freshmen enrolled during autumn of 1986, in two inner-city public high schools in a large, West coast city. Both schools were racially integrated, with 63 percent white and 37 percent minority in one school, and 52 percent white and 48 percent minority in the other school. All freshmen in both schools were invited to participate. Enrollment in the first school was 1380, 390 of whom were freshmen. Of these, 185 were participants. In the other school enrollment was 1045, with 233 being classified as freshmen. There were 128 participants from the second school.

The freshman classes of two additional schools wrote responses to the initial question of "What does it mean to be a freshman?" One of the schools was a suburban, public school with an enrollment of 1150 students, 230 being freshmen. During autumn of 1985, 210 of these freshmen described what it meant to them to be a freshman. Minority population of the school was less than 14 percent. The other school was a private, religious high school with a total enrollment of 950 students, 255 of whom were freshmen. During autumn of 1986, 241 of these students responded to the question. Minority population of this school was less than 23 percent. Thus, a total of over 750 freshmen were participants.

Procedures for Data Collection

The major source of data for this chapter was student responses to two, open-ended questionnaires administered during the autumn term of the 1986–87 school year. Students completed the first questionnaire at the end of the second week of class; they wrote responses to the second questionnaire during the eighth week of the term. All questionnaires were submitted anonymously (with the only demographic data solicited being the gender identification of the participant). Both schools required a course for new freshmen which dealt with the transition to high school. Teachers of this course administered the questionnaires to students during class time. Participation was voluntary and over 300 students returned the questionnaires.

A second source of data was a set of letters written by these same freshmen during the last two weeks of the term. They were asked to write a letter to a hypothetical eighth grader who would be attending their school the next year. They were directed to tell the prospective freshman everything she or he would need to know about the school or need to do in order to make a successful transition.

A third data source included: (a) a set of four open-ended questionnaires completed by eight students at the private high school, and (b) the responses of these students during a 15-minute interview conducted midway through the 1986 autumn term. This data source, although collected from only a few students, provided an in-depth view of the socialization experience from the students' perspectives.

Procedures for Data Analysis

The responses to the two open-ended questionnaires were read question by question and analyzed inductively according to the procedures of Goetz and LeCompte (1981). The questionnaires were sorted by school, then by sex. Responses to each question were listed individually, then analyzed and placed into categories according to frequency.

The letter data were analyzed in a similar fashion, inductively and with notations made of the responses of girls and boys from the various schools. The categories that emerged from these data overlapped with the categories resulting from analysis of the questionnaires, and therefore functioned to provide elaboration rather than new themes.

Finally, the questionnaire and interview responses of the eight students at the private school were analyzed inductively. Since only one new category emerged from this analysis, the data served primarily to supplement the written responses of the larger groups of students. Although not providing many distinct issues, this source of data was important in that the students' written and oral comments were rich and detailed.

RESULTS

Question One: What Does it Mean to be a High School Freshman?

The high school freshmen were asked twice during the term to respond to the question, "What does it mean to be a high school student?" In addition, data were derived from student responses to questions about differences between high school and middle school, highlights of the freshman experience, and feelings about missing the former school. Five dimensions of meaning emerged: (a) to experience a new and different physical environment, (b) to experience changes in status, (c) to experience new academic expectations, (d) to experience a new beginning, and (e) to experience a transition period. The definition of "freshman" according to the physical environment was predominant early in the term, but was not a defining aspect by mid-term when the second set of questions was asked. The other four dimensions seemed to be stable, defining characteristics throughout the first school term. A sixth dimension emerged from analysis of data from the private school: to be a representative of the high school. This was not a component of the meaning of being a freshman for students at the three public high schools.

To experience a new and different physical environment. Early in the school term, students defined themselves as high school freshmen by focusing on physical aspects of the new school (e.g., size, the greater number of people) and structural differences (e.g., being able to leave campus, having a smoking area). Regarding the physical and structural differences, they noted such aspects as: "The school is so much bigger so instead of finding your own way around you have to go around asking directions," "It just means being in a new building and learning new rules," "A lot bigger and a lot more people," "Being a freshman at _____ is like being a sardine in a can. There are so many other kids and we are all packed into this one school," "More people. More floors. More teachers," "High school has a bigger gym, swimming pool, they have milk shakes, 8th grade doesn't," "Now I can smoke at school, go off school campus and take many different classes," "Going to gym and being able to go off campus at lunch," and "Is different changing classes. And lunches. And we have telephones in the halls." These sorts of physical differences were prominent at the beginning of the school term as the adolescents offered definitions of themselves with respect to the new environment.

To experience changes in status. Another dimension of the meaning of being a high school freshman related to changes in status, both positive and negative. At the beginning of the term, positive changes were noted by the students: "It means to work harder and little kids will look up to me. Yesterday I was walking home and some little kids said, 'Look! Teenagers!' and that made me feel good," "It's something for me to look up at my brother and cousins and say 'Hey, I'm in high school too,' " and "A step up." The emphasis in many of these types of comments was on being older and having greater responsibility: "I think being in high school is a privilege because it states that you are mature and no longer 'kids,' " "Makes me feel much maturer," "Means I'm grown up and people expect me to be responsible," "I get a chance to make most of my own decisions," "It means more freedom and more fun but it's a lot more serious than middle school so I have to work hard for my future," "You feel older and more sophisticated," and "Freshmen have more privileges. They treat freshmen as an adult."

A number of other responses, made both early in the term and at the end, were negative in tone and focused on the drawbacks of being the youngest in the school: "Means being the underdog of a high school," "In 8th grade we ruled the school. Now it's like we're the baby of our school," "It means you're on the bottom of the stack. Everyone in a higher grade looks down on you," "You're the youngest one and the people who don't know what's going on. The people who get lost all the time. The victims," and "As an 8th grader you're on top of the pile, one summer passes and you're quickly pushed to the bottom. It will take four years to pull and push your way to the top again." The freshmen articulated an array of colorful metaphors about the lowering of their student status: "You're the pip squeaks of the school," "Bottom of the bucket," Feel like a pebble instead of a rock," "A sand on a beach," "Being a little fish in a big pond," "Like an unimportant blob floating on the surface of a pond," "Feel like a cat in a new alley," "Miss being at the head of the pack," "I feel like a newborned baby," and "Means you are at the bottom of the stair while the senior is on the top." It appears that although the students were positive about the new freedom and responsibility accorded them because they were older, they felt their status within the student hierarchy was low because they were the youngest in the school.

To experience new academic expectations. Throughout the first term the ninth graders also associated being a freshman with increased expectations for academic performance and a consciousness that academics "really count." Various comments supported their view of more rigorous academic expectations: "It means that you must do good in all your classes. This is not middle school," "To be starting the beginning of my education SERIOUSLY. To be in harder classes and working hard," "The classes are so much harder. The teachers expect more out of you," "More homework," and "That it is harder than 8th grade." Coupled with the view of harder work is the notion of academics being more important now than previously: "I have to try harder because this four years of grades WILL go on my record," "You have to be more serious about your work 'cause every minute counts and you need all the credits you can get," "From this year the grades will count for the real GPA," "I've got to be a good student and through the years to prepare for college," and "I feel it's more important to get good grades here because now they really count."

To experience a new beginning. Another important aspect of being a new high school freshman was viewing it as a new beginning, both in school and in life: "It means that you've just started high school," "It means a new start, and meeting new people," "Feels like I'm going into a new life," "Means a new beginning and a fresh new start. Just like the first day of kindergarten," "It also means starting to look at life and make my own decisions," "It means a beginning. A 'start' for the rest of my life. Here's where things start counting," "The beginning of some of the best times of my life. New friendships, relationships, and seeing and doing stuff you've never done before," "The start of a whole new life of freedom to be treated as an adult," and "It means I've got a big challenge ahead of me, and I'm starting something new." Throughout the first term, the youngsters continued to feel that being a freshman was a new beginning, in school and towards adult life.

To experience a transition period. A related, but distinct, concept is the notion of high school as a time of transition. Many adolescents considered being a high school freshman as a means to an end: "Being in high school is the last step before moving on, either college or a profession," "Getting closer to graduation," "One more step to being a man so I can drink more,"

"You have to get education first so you can get a job," "Another grade and four more steps to graduating," "It's pretty nice to know you only have three more grades till you can decide and get to college, a job, or married," "One step closer to being grown up," "I think of it as another step towards college also," and "It means I'm out of middle school and moving up in the world." The view of high school as a transition period included getting closer to achieving such diverse goals as being a senior, going to college, getting a job, and getting married.

To be a representative of the high school. A final dimension that emerged for the ninth graders at the private school was that of being a representative of their institution. Students expressed a strong sense of pride at being a part of this new school and a responsibility for living up to its high standards and representing it well in the larger community. There were numerous examples: "You must behave in public for you are a representative of _____ in and outside the school," "It means you get to carry on the tradition of being at _____ , " "It means that you are part of the best school in _____ state," "It means I'm an official 'papoose' of the _____ community," and "I'm proud to be a freshman student at _____ because I'm a part of _____ ." Students considered it an honor to be members of this school community, and accepted the responsibility that accompanied the membership.

Summary. With respect to their perspectives on being high school freshmen, the ninth graders articulated five major dimensions related to: the physical environment, the status change, the new academic expectations, the new beginning, and the transition. A sixth aspect was important for freshmen at the private school: being a representative of the school. A view emerges of the freshman experience as "the real thing," a serious time of new challenges and expectations.

Question Two: What are the Concerns of New Freshmen as They Socialize into High School?

The concerns of the new freshmen were identified through an analysis of their responses to questions about difficulties at the new school and adjustments which had to be made. Their concerns were grouped into four categories: social, status, environmental, and academic.

Social concerns. The most prevalent category of concern consisted of comments about the social aspects of high school life. These included concerns about being alone and the difficulty of making friends as well as concerns about fitting in with others and insecurity. Being alone and not knowing others in the school were important concerns for many: "I just don't have anyone to talk to or eat lunch with," "I don't know that many people," "I am no longer surrounded with the friends I've known forever and ever," "Most of my friends go to a new school," "Probably the first couple of weeks were the worst because I was new and hardly knew anyone," and "The worst part has been feeling alone." Related to concern about being alone was concern about having to make new friends: "Making friends is hard because you're new," "I don't really have real friends. The girls that I have been hanging out with are my sister's friends," "Leaving my old friends and having to find new friends," "It's hard to know who to make friends with," "The people are mean. Making new friends. Everyone stays with themselves," and "I just moved here and it is like everyone has their 'groups' picked and they don't want anyone else. I didn't know very many people so I couldn't really talk to a lot of people."

Fitting in with others and feeling a part of the new school comprised another type of social concern: "I was lost. And it seemed like I didn't fit in," "It's just that the popular kids think they're on top of the world and they make my life like 'hell.' They are always in groups laughing and when you pass them, they'd laugh probably because I'm not popular or anything," "Trying to fit in socially. It's hard to have 'the popular crowd' like you," "Trying to blend in with everybody," "Sometimes in classes where teachers put you with all the nerds and you don't want to talk to them," "There are many cliques and it gets really old when someone won't let you in their group just because you dress a certain way or listen to a certain type of music," and "Sometimes different people don't like you because you dress better or look different than they do." For some students, this concern was coupled with feelings of insecurity: "I dislike many of the new people I've met and the feeling of insecurity," and "I do not feel comfortable here."

Status concerns. A second category of concern dealt with the issue of freshman status in the school. Many students felt that upperclassmen looked down on them: "People call you names," "Put downs by the older kids," "The teasing," "I hate when the seniors call us 'little freshmen,' " "The seniors think they're pretty cool and look down on us," and "Seniors and jocks giving me a bad time." Another type of status concern related to anxiety about or fear of physical harm: "Being pushed in the halls," "The worst part about the first two months of high school is that some of the upperclassmen treat me badly," "The threats of higher classmen," "Almost getting beat up," "Getting froshed," "Getting pushed around by the seniors," "Getting picked on, money taken, beat up," and "Just being shoved around." Although both boys and girls expressed concern about physical violence, the comments of the girls were much milder than those of the boys. It appeared that actual physical threat was of greater concern to the boys than to the girls. Similarly, concern about "getting froshed" was expressed only by boys. Most of the girls were aware of the phenomenon, but did not express personal concern about it. And a few girls were oblivious to this type of harrassment: "I'm just as puzzled as you are about 'getting froshed.' I've never heard of the saying," and "I was never 'froshed' so I wouldn't know [what it means.]"

Environmental concerns. A set of concerns which was predominant at the beginning of the school term was that which dealt with the new physical environment. Not knowing their way around the larger building was a concern articulated by many students: "Getting lost and bumped around in the halls," "I spent most of my lunch time trying to find my locker and my classes," "Not knowing where anything is," "Three school floors," and "I'm still having trouble with knowing where there is a girl's bathroom that is near my class." Other concerns dealt with adjusting to new procedures and using the various facilities: "The lockers are smaller," "Getting used to the lunches," "Keep forgetting to get my books from my locker," "Getting to classes on time and using my locker and the aroma of the school lunch. Yech!," and "Adjusting to the new atmosphere."

Academic concerns. A final category of concern dealt with the academic demands of high school. Students expressed three types of academic concern: about a greater quantity of homework, about more difficult academic work, and about boredom. Increased homework was a salient concern for many students: "Too much homework. I hate doing it. It damages my brain," "There is homework every night. In middle school, some days you had work, and others you didn't, but in high school I've had homework every day since I started," and "Homework (is the worst thing) because my math teacher pours it on and I hardly have any time for it because of volleyball."

Greater teacher expectations and a more difficult level of academics constituted a second type of concern: "The teachers expect so much more from you and the work is harder," "You have to write a lot faster and pay attention a lot more," "The long essays and reports and being in classes with older people," "The extreme amount of work and the pressure of getting it done and trying to get a good grade," "Schoolwork is the hardest because I'm used to slacking off and not doing the work, but in high school you can't do that," "Schoolwork, most of the teachers just expect you to know the stuff and if you don't they give you a bad time about it," and "All the schoolwork. The teachers act like we don't have life beyond the school."

A final type of academic concern dealt with boredom. This concern was evident at the outset of the school term and was articulated by a few students who did not consider the academic work to be challenging: "My algebra class is boring," "The teachers were boring us to death by telling us the rules and regulations," and "It was boring in some of the classes 'cause they weren't giving any work to us. All they were doing was telling us about school and class rules." This concern was voiced with respect to the first week of the term during which the content of most classes consisted either of review or overview of rules and regulations. For some students, this constituted a "slow" start and seemed boring to them. The concern was not articulated later in the term.

Summary. Freshmen expressed concern across four categories: social, status, environmental, and academic. The social and status categories of concern related to *self*—feeling alone and insecure, and being anxious about the older students in the school. The environmental and academic categories related to *task*—how to find one's way in an unfamiliar, large building, and how to handle a greater quantity of more difficult work.

Question Three: How Does Communication Function in the Socialization of High School Freshmen?

To determine the role of communication in the socialization process, students were asked to discuss the importance of communication in helping them adjust to high school. They were also asked to respond to questions about: the people who had been most helpful to them, their sense of belonging, and what they did in order to feel a part of the school. These responses provided data for an analysis of the functions communication served for the freshmen and the communication strategies they used.

From the perspectives of the students, communication served primarily two functions in the socialization process. First, communication was the means by which information about the new school situation was sought and acquired. Second, it was the means of integration into the school, that is, it served emotional needs and was a tool for making friends and developing a sense of belonging.

Informative function. An important function of communication in socialization was the simple exchange of needed information about the school, primarily procedural but also academic. Communication was the means by which students learned their way around the school building: "Communication is important because I would still be lost otherwise," "For finding my way around the building," "To find my classes, certain places, office," and "Asking people where things are located and getting help."

Communication was also the mechanism for learning about school regulations and procedures: "Help me open my locker, understand rules better," "Helps you get in touch with the school," "It is important so you can understand more about the school," and "If you talk to people then you can ask questions about things that you don't know about the school and the work and things like that." For the freshmen, communication about school regulations and procedures served primarily an informative function. Occasionally, however, the talk that was reported about school policies served a regulative function.

Communication was also important in the exchange of information about academics: "Well, it's hard to keep track of all the work we have to do, so I have to ask friends," "Helping friends who need help with homework and vice versa," "Communication has been very important because otherwise I would be totally lost in my classes," and "Teachers explain and give directions." Although this informative function of communication was articulated by students throughout the first term, no specific communication strategies were identified.

With respect to the people who were most important in providing information, students identified friends, siblings, and teachers. Friends provided instrumental support: "My friends helped me learn my combination, find rooms, and which line in the lunchroom to go in for the kind of food I wanted," "My friend—he helped me register," "My friends. They helped me when I was confused," "My older friends. They told me which girls were easy," and "My friends have helped by telling me what teachers not to take." Teachers were also primary sources of information: "The teachers wear these little pins that say 'ask me' and they don't make you feel stupid when you say something like 'Where's the bathroom?'," "My teachers were nicer since we were new and they spent a lot of time telling us what this school has to offer," "My teachers have been helpful because they showed me the work I didn't know how to do," "My teachers help me find my way around," and "My metal shop teacher has helped me a lot by telling me how the school works." Older siblings who attended the school also provided informational and instrumental assistance: "My sister was really helpful in showing me my classes," "My sister. She told me what to do, what not to do, and what mistakes not to make," and "My sister helps a lot because she knows the way around."

Integrative function. Students responded in greatest detail about communication as it functioned to integrate them into the new school and the new student role. Specifically, there were two integrative functions described by the freshmen: communication served to meet emotional needs (e.g., moral support) and served to help students make friends and gain a sense of belonging.

To meet emotional needs. Friends, family members, and teachers were all identified as being helpful in providing emotional/moral support for the new freshmen. The communication of emotional support was a critical aspect contributing to students' feelings of integration into the new school. Friends were mentioned most frequently: "Talking to my friends helps me get used to high school when I'm nervous," "One of my friends.

She helped by being there to talk to. I don't feel alone because she is here," "My friends—they've stuck to me and saw me through the first week of school," "Friends because you get a feeling that you aren't in this alone," "My friends, 'cause we just stick together through the hard times," and "When we talk about school we aren't so scared about it any more."

Students also reported receiving moral support in the form of reassurance from their parents: "My parents—they told me I would be ok and do fine," "My parents, by telling me to act like I always have," and "Mom and Dad saying that it would be all right and I would get used to it."

In addition, teachers were a source of emotional support: "The teachers . . . when I need help or need something to get out of your mind she would listen," "My teachers have been very helpful giving support," and "Two teachers made me feel I'm worth being here."

To help make friends and gain a sense of belonging. The second integrative function of communication was to help the new freshmen make friends, thus facilitating their sense of feeling a part of the school. Students articulated this function in various ways: "Communication is very important. If you didn't have communication you wouldn't have friends and then you wouldn't like school," "Communication is very important because if you walk down the hall with a snotty look on your face, people don't want to get to know you. But if you smile, and are eager to get to know one another you'll make a lot of friends," "Communication is important because it's made me feel I belong with people and not just an outcast," "If you don't get out there and talk to people you aren't going to have any friends," and "Communicating has got me to understand where I fit in at this school!"

In addition to discussing communication as being important in integrating them to the new school, the freshmen identified specific communication strategies for making friends and developing a sense of belonging. The five strategies that emerged included: participating in school activities, being interpersonal, being myself, being introduced by common friends, and impression management.

The strategy of *participating in school activities* encompassed the joining of clubs and playing of sports, as well as merely being involved in classes. Most students articulated that participation made them feel a part of the school: "Yes, [I feel a part of the school] because I am in the color guard and it represents the school," "I try to participate in lots of activities and I make friends easily," "I've joined the flag team. I'm also going to try out for the swim team," "Participating in group projects, participating in class discussions," "I'm joining the basketball team. I've went to our school dances, I've went to our football games," "Took one month to feel belonging. Joining volleyball, elected to be a natural helper, being an honor student, just getting involved," and "Get out of my shell. Answer questions in class instead of holding back. Eating with people instead of being by myself."

Participation in sports was a reason given for a sense of belonging more often by boys than by girls: "Yes, because I'm on the football team and I know many people in the school," "I'm participating in school athletics, football and soon wrestling," and "About two weeks to feel like I belonged. That's when I started being recognized for being a running back for football. I also got involved with school activities and school spirit."

A second communication strategy for making friends was most aptly described by students as *being interpersonal*. This strategy included being nice to people, talking to others, and generally being kind and helpful: "Being nice to people and smile every day," "Smile, kindness, comfort, don't make fun," "Being considerate, good attitude, no put downs," "I was friendly, open, kind, understanding and happy to everyone," "Be friendly," "I talk to people, I'm nice to them, I just fit in I guess," "I started talking to a lot of people and they are now my friends," "Being nice, talk to them, help them with a difficult assignment," and "Talk, talk, talk, talk."

A third strategy, *being myself*, was described by students as simple and straightforward. The important aspect was to communicate oneself to others: "What I did was just be myself," "I socialized with a lot of junior, sophomore, and freshmen friends. And I got accepted as myself," "But there aren't really people and things that make you feel 'belonged.' It's really yourself," "It didn't take me long. Just acted normal," "I made a lot of new friends, mostly girls because they think I'm so fine and cute. I can't help that," and "All I did was give the other kids a chance to know me and eventually we became friends." For one girl in particular, being accepted for herself was a positive dimension of high school:

> The way I made myself feel belonged was just being me! I'm the type that is a hippo in a giraffe world. I'm overweight so it makes things even harder to find friends. But I've discovered it really doesn't matter around here anymore. People are more friendly and mature. I like that.

Being introduced by an old friend to a new friend was a fourth strategy for making friends. Some students reported asking their friends to make introductions, while others simply commented that new acquaintances were made through old friends: "Asking current friends to introduce me to their friends," "Making friends with my old friends' friends," "Some of my old friends knew them and introduced me," "Met people through other people," and "You make friends from your friends."

A fifth way of making friends and feeling a part of the school was through *impression management*. This nonverbal communication strategy involved looking nice and dressing well so as to be considered "cool." Student comments included: "Dressing up like other people I feel a lot more positive about high school," "Look and dress nice," and "Wear cool clothes."

One final dimension, *having upperclassmen friends*, was not a communication strategy, but was articulated as being an important factor in making the freshmen feel as if they belonged. Knowing upperclassmen and getting along with them was helpful to many of the freshmen: "Upperclass friends helped me feel a little more comfortable," "It took about two weeks to feel I belonged. All the older kids say 'hi' to me. My boyfriend is a junior and is on the football team. My best friend is a senior," "Yes I feel I belong because I have been able to get along with the older kids," "Most of my friends are older than I so I just jumped into everything," "I met some new friends that are in higher grades than me. They can tell me more about the school so I can know," and "Yes, [I feel a sense of belonging] 'cause I know a lot of people, not only freshmen, seniors, juniors, sophomores." Finally, one student reported a single exchange with an upperclassman as an important event in his sense of belonging: "Being able to talk to a senior. He said 'hey, come here.' So I did. He said 'Where did you learn that song?' I told him and showed him how to play. He got excited and said 'thanx.' Then we bullshitted for the rest of the period. IT WAS GREAT!!"

Although by the middle of the first term the majority of students responded that they felt a sense of belonging, there were some students who did not feel integrated. Those who did not gave reasons which included: (a) that they did not participate in school activities—"No, no feeling of belonging. I don't like to participate in school activities, like I said I'm not an outgoing person," and "No because I haven't joined an activity," (b) that they did not talk to others—"I don't know if I'm belonged or anything because I don't talk to many people," "No. I don't know anyone here so I feel sort of left out," and "No because I'm more of a loner," (c) that they did not have friends—"I don't feel like I belong here. Everyone's got their special little groups of friends and I don't. I don't seem to fit in anywhere," and "No because I haven't been here long enough to know a lot of people," (d) that they were generally not accepted—"No. I've never really been a part of any school I went to before. The kids don't like the way I dress or the way I talk of books. Kids think I'm either crazy or knocked in the head when I do get involved. They make me feel like I'm never going to be a part of any school," and (e) that they did not know or get along with upperclassmen—"No, the juniors are trying to be tuff," and "No, because everytime I walk down the hall I hear 'freshman!' and all the seniors act like they own the school."

It is not surprising that participation in school activities was an important socialization strategy and that a lack of participation was reported as a foremost reason that students did not feel integrated. In their review of participation in extracurricular activities (athletic and nonathletic) in secondary schools, Holland and Andre (1987) found that participation was positively correlated with high levels of self-esteem and with a variety of desirable personality and social traits. Since participation is associated with positive self characteristics, it is reasonable that it would also be important to a student's sense of belonging. Indeed, extracurricular activities have been referred to as "socializing agents" (Brown, 1988, p. 110).

Summary. Communication served as the mechanism for information exchange and for integration into the school. The new freshmen sought and acquired information from friends, siblings, and teachers about academics, policies, and procedures. Students accomplished integration into the new school and the freshman role through communication that met their emotional needs and helped them to make friends.

Question Four: What are the Critical Dimensions in the Passage to the Status of High School Freshman?

With respect to the temporal dimensions, the passage can be considered *regular, scheduled,* and *inevitable.* Moving into high school was a fully anticipated event for these students, complete with a visit to the new school the prior spring and an orientation during the previous summer. From the perspective of the school administration, the passage and adjustment to the new status occurred throughout the *duration* of the first semester. Both of the inner-city public high schools had a specially designated course required for all freshmen during the first semester. Although the emphases differed slightly, both courses were designed to serve an orientation function for the new students. The school staff felt that this adjustment to high school was a process that took a full semester.

The orientation course for new freshmen was also an indication of the *clarity of the signs* of the passage. The course was a *formal* mechanism by which students were introduced to high school life—the academic, procedural, and social expectations. Student awareness of major distinctions between middle and high school also pointed to the formality of the passage and the clarity of the signposts. They considered the passage to be a formal one, as did the school personnel. Their repeated references to the new physical environment and the different structure of the school exemplified their recognition of the signs of the passage.

A key dimension of the passage was its *centrality* to the students themselves. As indicated in their definitions of what it means to be high school freshmen, the students internalized the new status. Numerous responses (e.g., "Means I'm grown up and people expect me to be responsible") show that being a high school student is not just something one does while at school, but instead is an integral part of the person. The centrality of the passage also emerged in a variety of student comments about high school as a new beginning of their lives (e.g., "Feels like I'm going into a new life").

Although the passage was viewed by most students as a central one, there were contradictory feelings expressed about the *desirability* of it. The status of being a high school freshman was positive in that it was accompanied by new freedom, new responsibility, and a new sophistication and respect (e.g., "I love being treated my age. Taking responsibility for my own actions," "The start of a whole new life of freedom to be treated as an adult," and "Higher privileges"). There was a negative aspect expressed, however, relating to being the youngest in the school (e.g., "You are at the bottom again, and you don't really know anyone yet except your friends from eighth grade," "Means being the underdog of a high school," and "You're no longer the top guns anymore. You're nothing but some scared little kid"). For most students it seemed that there were genuinely ambivalent feelings about the new status. Sometimes the positive aspects were most dominant and at other times the negative dimensions were foremost.

The social dimensions of the passage were also important in understanding the process of socialization. It was clear that these students experienced the passage as a *collective* and were *aware of the collective*. All of the freshmen at each school constituted a group, the freshmen student body. They were referred to by school staff as "the freshman class" and they referred to themselves as "freshmen" or "freshmans," distinct from upperclassmen or sophomores, juniors, or seniors. Their awareness of the collective also manifested itself in the form of comments about shared feelings, as evidenced in advice written by one freshman girl to a hypothetical newcomer:

> I know you may be scared or nervous about going to high school. Don't worry about it. I was a little nervous my registration day, but I put on a happy face and what do you know, I made a friend just waiting in line. An important thing to remember—YOU ARE NOT THE ONLY NERVOUS FRESHMAN. I realized this while talking to the girl in line.

Another student commented: "When you first get here you're gonna get lost. Don't worry, everybody does."

A final, critical dimension is that the students experiencing the passage *communicated with one another.* As discussed in Question Three, communication served two major functions in the socialization process: informative and integrative. It was through communication with peers (as well as with parents and teachers) that students exchanged needed information about academics and school procedures. Based on the frequency of responses, it was clear that communication with other students helped them to meet their emotional needs, make new friends, and develop a sense of belonging to the school. Communication facilitated the passage to the status of high school freshman. It was the means by which students acquired needed information, accomplished procedural tasks, and integrated socially with one another into the new school.

DISCUSSION

Socialization into high school emerged as a multifaceted process accomplished through communication with a variety of people. The experience did not differ dramatically for girls and boys.

Socialization as a Multifaceted Process

A first conclusion was that the socialization of high school freshmen was complex and multifaceted. As previously indicated, what it means to be a freshman has several dimensions, and the concerns expressed by freshmen were varied. The advice the freshmen gave in their letters to prospective newcomers verified the wide range of aspects involved during socialization.

Social advice. Socially oriented advice was predominant and dealt with such aspects as peer relations and behavior. It was important to project an appropriate image: "First and most importantly don't act like a fool. Ninnies are not highly regarded by anyone," "Don't be a nerd," and "I think if you're one of these macho guys don't act that way, and if you're a girl don't act all stuck up." Advice was also directed towards being oneself: "Be yourself and don't try to please the higher class. Don't try to dress and impress," "Don't be uptight. Act yourself," and "Be yourself and don't try to be like everyone else to fit in." Students encouraged newcomers to feel positively about themselves: "You have to feel good about yourself. Don't put yourself down. If you consider yourself a dumb jerk or a nerd then you will be a dumb jerk or a nerd," and "The best advice is to have a positive attitude. If you think you'll make friends and have fun then you will. But if you go into high school thinking about how awful it will be it probably will be awful."

Status advice. Another important dimension of the socialization process about which the freshmen offered advice was in the realm of status.

Information was given concerning the reality that freshmen were the "lowest" in the school: "When you come to high school—you're the lowest of the school and usually—you don't have your crowd." Both boys and girls advised about how to avoid getting into trouble with the upperclassmen: "Don't back talk to the upperclassmen or you get beat up," and "Don't hang out in the A.C., the bathrooms, or at sport events. That's when you'll get it." Along with this advice were comments expressing fear for the newcomers: "I pray that nothing happens to you here. As long as you don't make fun of any upperclassmen, then you're okay. But be careful, you could do nothing and be thrown in the creek, have your head flushed in a toilet, or something else," and "You probably will get froshed within the first few weeks, but don't go and tell the principal. If you do, you'll get froshed again." An additional, somewhat contradictory bit of advice related to the status of freshman was for them to stand up for themselves: "The first thing to learn is not to let yourself be pushed around. Everyone looks down on you. Make a stand and push back," and "Don't be shy or ashamed to be a freshman, stand up for yourself and don't lie about your age, it wouldn't do any good, they'll soon find out anyhow."

Academic advice. Although not as prevalent as comments about social and status dimensions, the freshmen proffered advice about the importance of the academic component. Specifically, they urged prospective students to make good grades: "Start off school with good grades, then you'll have a back-up for the classes you don't do well in," and "Get good grades and hope for the best." The freshmen also encouraged the newcomers to get along with their teachers: "Get along with the teachers," "Be good to your teachers," and "Be sure to get to know teachers because they'll make it easy for you if they like you."

General informational/environmental advice. A final type of advice was related to general information about the school environment and procedures. Most of these comments dealt with the first days of school: "First you have to register before school starts if you want good classes," "Try to get a locker on the second floor," "You don't need a lot of school supplies, just the basics," and "DO NOT eat the school lunches. Either starve yourself or go buy lunch at _____ ."

The Communication Network

A second conclusion was that the new freshmen relied on a variety of people as they made the transition to high school. Students needed information ranging from academic content to procedural rules and regulations to social rituals. Conversation with various people in their communication network (e.g., other students, teachers, and family members) provided this information. Students also needed to feel integrated into the school, to establish a network of friends, and to develop a sense of belonging. Verbal and nonverbal communication strategies were the means by which students made new friends and came to feel a part of the new school. As previously reported, students were able to articulate the value of communication.

One somewhat surprising finding relates to parental reassurance and the extent to which the freshmen found such support helpful. Despite a widely held view of adolescence as a time of turmoil and rebellion against parental authority (Coleman, 1961, 1979), the ninth graders discussed in this chapter relied heavily on their parents for information about "what high school will be like" and for moral support that they would fit in and be successful. This finding, while disparate with some previous research on the generation gap, is consistent with other research in which parents and youngsters have mutually compatible views and positive relations (Goslin, 1969; Hollingshead, 1975; Vangelisti, 1988).

The Socialization Process is Similar for Girls and Boys

A third conclusion was that the socialization process did not differ much for girls and for boys. Although data for the research questions were analyzed separately for female and male students, the results were generally similar and did not warrant separate reporting.

Only three minor differences emerged in the results. First, with regard to their status concerns, boys seemed to have some real fear or anxiety about physical violence being inflicted on them. Girls were aware of possible threats (e.g., getting froshed), but seldom expressed concern for their own safety. A second, very subtle, difference related to the status concern about violence. In the letters written to prospective freshmen, it was primarily the boys who advised how to keep out of trouble with the upperclassmen. The girls, conversely, were the ones who encouraged newcomers to stand up for themselves and not to be ashamed of being a freshman. Third, boys commented more frequently than girls that participating in sports gave them a sense of belonging. This finding is not surprising in that the schools provided more opportunity for boys than for girls to play organized sports, especially the high-status sport of football.

A Concluding Note

Just as the fictional Elsie in *How Do You Lose Those Ninth Grade Blues?* had to find her way around in an unfamiliar school building crowded with

new and older faces, so did the several hundred freshmen who participated in the study reported in this chapter. The process of socialization
into the role of high school freshman and into a new school environment
was multidimensional and occurred through communication with peers,
teachers, and family members.

chapter 6
The Transfer Student Phenomenon
Co-authored with P. Daniel Cavanaugh, Jr.

This chapter describes the first term experiences and perspectives of 15 tenth, eleventh, and twelfth graders who transferred into the same new high school. The chapter provides a look at the process by which these students attempt to move from being social outsiders at the beginning of the school year to being insiders who feel a part of the new school. Those students who meet with success are able to make friends, become involved in school activities, and learn the norms. Those who do not report success are generally unable to make many friends or get involved in school activities. The transfer students articulate a variety of communication strategies for making sense of the academic and social domains in the new school.

"Say, Pop," I said. "How're you going to get from Jersey City to Queens everyday?" That was the part I understood.

"I'm not going to, Tony," my father said.

"You're not?"

"Nope."

"Well then, what?" I asked.

"I'm going to get from Rosemont to Queens."

"What's Rosemont?" I asked.

"It's a town in Long Island."

"You're going to live there?"

"We're going to live there!" my father said.

"We are?" I asked.

"That's right!"

"All of us?"

"All of us!"

Goodbye Jersey City, I thought.

Goodbye basketball at the Y.

Goodbye Little Joe and Big Joe.

Goodbye Frankie and Billy.

Goodbye Jersey Journal paper route....

I don't cry any more. I'm too old for that baby stuff, which is why I ran for the bathroom and locked myself in. I cried really quiet. (Blume, 1971, pp. 17–18)

Like Tony, children of all ages are frequently on the move as a consequence of the mobility of parents, breakup of marriages, and myriad other reasons. For some, it becomes a routine activity after several moves. For others, those who have put down roots and have known only one home, the move may be anything but routine. Whether routine or not, all young persons who move face similar problems as they transfer from one school to another. Regardless of the other complicating forces in her or his life outside of the school, each transfer student must master the new environment into which she or he has been thrust, most often without choice or desire. The vast majority are the trailers in a moveable society, following along behind the mobile force of parents. It is rarely they, but usually others, who make the decisions about the where, why, and when of their transitions.

High school represents the final stage of a young person's compulsory career as student, the goal reached at the end of a long road which had begun some 12 years before. For the first time since she or he took that first step into kindergarten, the student realizes that in the near future, the choice must be made again whether she or he will do the "Nothing" about which Christopher Robin laments the loss. Graduation from high school usually marks the passage from required schoolwork to additional elective schooling or to the "workplace." This chapter describes one aspect of the high school student career, the socialization process as students transfer from one high school to another.

Student Mobility

In an effort to understand the transfer student phenomenon, some researchers have focused on mobility among students with an emphasis on the effect that changing schools has on academic achievement (Bollenbacher, 1963; Cramer & Dorsey, 1979; Falik, 1969; Frazier, 1970; Mankowitz, 1970; Samson, 1966; Snipes, 1970; Wise, 1971). Whalen and Fried (1973) report that the results of such research are far too inconclusive and inconsistent to be of much value in determining if mobility has any impact on academic achievement.

Other researchers have indicated that geographic relocation and the ensuing isolation from friends may provoke social withdrawal on the part of young people (Stubblefield, 1955; Tooley, 1970). A number of additional studies, however, contradict these findings (Barret & Noble, 1973; Kantor, 1965; Kroger, 1980; Ziller & Behringer, 1961).

Anderson, Haller, and Smorodin (1976) hinted at an interaction effect among a student's mobility, achievment, and social status. They found a link between mobility and academic aspirations when they discovered that students have a greater likelihood of switching academic tracks as a result of moving between schools. They found that a student's level of aspiration was lowered if she or he was placed in a lower track. They claim that such an action "may have the double-barreled effect of telling the student that he is academically competent or incompetent and exposing him to a set of peers whose aspirations and performance positively or negatively affect his own" (p. 350). These results are consistent with those of Schwartz (1981) who determined that academic tracking in high school resulted in higher track students receiving peer support and encouragement, while students in lower tracks were discouraged by their peers who subverted the learning in the classroom.

Taken in conjunction, these results indicate that the impact of relocation on the student who transfers is a complicated issue in need of additional study. Transfer into a new school may affect student success and satisfaction both in academic and social domains.

Differences in Student and Teacher Perspectives

One of the complexities of the transfer issue is that the perspectives about schooling, and what is most important in the adjustment to it, differ between students and teachers. As John Dewey (1964) observed, "the individual to be educated is a social individual, and . . . the school is a primarily social institution" (p. 430). Although many would agree, there is some research suggesting that adults and students view the school environment in different ways with respect to its social nature (Everhart, 1978; Kapferer, 1981; Peshkin, 1978; Ritter, 1979). For students, schools are primarily social institutions where they interact with their friends, while teachers and administrators view the school as a place where young people come together to learn academic subject matter. In observations and interviews in a junior high school, Everhart (1978) noted that school personnel typically described the school in terms of academics, learning, and teaching, while students deemphasized the academic aspect and considered the school as a place where they met their friends and gathered in their groups. Peshkin (1978) provided additional support for these findings from student diaries and interviews about their perceptions of high school. There were few, if any, references to the academic aspect of their school experiences. The emphasis was on friendships, extracurricular activities, and other nonscholastic involvement.

School Orientation Programs

Perhaps because students and teachers have different perspectives about school, orientation programs often do not seem to meet the needs of the transfer students. In a nationwide survey of schools, Cornille, Bayer, and Smith (1983) found that some schools recognize the needs of new students (78 percent social, 22 percent academic) and try to meet those needs through buddy systems and loans of past yearbooks to familiarize new students with school dress norms, activities, clubs, and athletic programs. Although their results show that some schools have formal mechanisms in place, the services provided are usually focused primarily on meeting the functional and procedural requirements of the school. Substantially less attention is given to easing the integration of students into the social network.

Summary

Although previous research has been important in describing the social nature of the school and the activities in which students engage, there is limited information concerning the mechanisms involved in the socialization of students into school. This chapter describes what that passage is like for students who transfer between schools at some point during the high school career.

PURPOSE OF THE CHAPTER

This chapter examines how high school students socialize into a new school environment and the role communication takes in that process. In order to determine how this status passage occurs, four research questions are addressed:

1.   What does it mean to be a transfer student?
2.   What are the concerns of transfer students as they socialize into a new high school?
3.   What is the nature of the process by which transfer students socialize into a new high school?
4.   What are the critical dimensions in the passage from the status of transfer student to insider?

METHOD

Research Setting

The study reported in this chapter was conducted during autumn 1985, in a suburban public high school in a large, West coast city. The student population was approximately 1150, composed primarily of white students from mixed socioeconomic backgrounds, resulting from the expansion of suburban housing developments within the school district. Only 13 percent of the student body was minority, including blacks, Hispanics, and Asians. The participants were drawn from a pool of students who had transferred into the school for individual rather than systemic reasons. Systemic reasons include the natural movement resulting from grade advancement (middle school to high school) as well as mandated busing and school district reconfiguration.

Fifteen students agreed to participate in the study. The sample, although small, is considered representative. Of the 15 participants, seven were male, eight were female, three were seniors, three were juniors, nine were sophomores. Some had moved a great deal; others had moved only once or twice.

Procedures for Data Collection

There were three data bases for the chapter: open-ended questionnaires, interviews with students, and participant observation. Students completed an initial questionnaire when school began, a questionnaire each week for the first six weeks, and one every other week for the eight remaining weeks of the academic term. Students were asked how they "felt" about the school, to whom they spoke during the week, what they talked about, in what activities they engaged, and with whom they "hung around." The questionnaires required about 15 to 20 minutes to complete.

Students were interviewed on three occasions—at the beginning, middle, and end of the semester. Interviews ranged from 15 to 60 minutes in duration.

Six of the students (one senior, two juniors, and three sophomores) were selected to be observed. Each student, with one exception, was observed on two occasions during which time detailed notes were made. Students were observed during classes, during free time between classes, and during lunch time in gathering areas such as the cafeteria and student union. The observations served primarily to confirm and provide elaboration of the self-report data (LeCompte & Goetz, 1982).

Procedures for Data Analysis

Data were analyzed in three stages. First, a framework of four categories was constructed into which the data could be roughly placed. The categories were drawn from a framework developed by Hymes (1972), suggest-

Table 6.1.   Topics of Conversation (communication)

A.   Orienting talk (academic & social/nonacademic)
   1. introductions
   2. how to do work (in class)
   3. how to become a teacher's aide
   4. how to get into driver's education
   5. where to find things/people
   6. determining sports eligibility
   7. how to get class changed
   8. how to become involved in clubs/sports
   9. learning who is who in the school (students)
B.   Problem-solving talk (academic & social/nonacademic)
   1. straighten out schedule
   2. determining missing school work
   3. concern about others use of drugs
   4. rectify grade mistakes
   5. having lunch stolen
   6. having locker ripped off
C.   Activity related talk (social/nonacademic)
   1. ask out on a date
   2. going to movies
   3. social contacts
   4. regular things
   5. haunted house
   6. prom
   7. homecoming
   8. out-of-school sporting events
   9. jokes
   10. helping new kids
   11. stuff and school
D.   School/Class talk (academic)
   1. subjects
   2. answering questions posed by teacher
   3. assignment instructions
   4. school records
      a. grades
      b. classes taken
      c. where to go to college
      d. tests taken
E.   Personal history talk (social/nonacademic)
   1. what school come from
   2. how many times moved
   3. personal narratives, stories
F.   Current events talk (social/nonacademic)
   1. the deficit
   2. GNP of 3rd world countries
   3. the weather

ing that in the process of socialization there are certain types of *people* engaged in various types of *behavior* in different types of *settings* to achieve particular types of *goals*. Second, a scheme was created for codes which were not content-specific but rather pointed to the general domains in which codes could be inductively developed (Lofland, 1971). The domains were derived from the categories suggested by the Hymes framework. Third, having decided on the general categories which needed to be elaborated, the data were then subjected to the process of analytic induction (Goetz & LeCompte, 1981).

The general categories involved in the socialization process were determined to be new students, individual student variables, context variables, communication/topics of conversation, agents/types of persons with whom the student is involved, and avenues/activities (forums in which the interaction takes place). Each category included various subcategories which were arranged in a hierarchy. (For examples, see Tables 6.1 and 6.2.) Thus, the general categories represent the process by which the new students came into contact with agents (that is, people with whom the student must learn to relate socially), within certain avenues (that is, the forums in which the relationships are established), using communication

Table 6.2.   Kinds of Activities/Avenues

A. Organized
   1. In school
      a. academic
         i. class work
         ii. writing papers
         iii. answering
            questions
      b. social/nonacademic
         i. pep assemblies
         ii. school newspaper
         iii. band
   2. Out of school
      a. academic
         ex. honor society
      b. social
         i. prom committee
         ii. sports
         iii. gamer's club
         iv. homecoming week
         v. dances (prom,
           homecoming)
         vi. bonfire (homecoming)

B. Unorganized
   1. In school
      a. academic
         i. study period
         ii. library time
      b. social/nonacademic
         i. lunch
         ii. hanging out
   2. Out of school
      a. academic
         ex. homework
      b. social
         i. movies
         ii. shopping
         iii. hanging out
            Dairy Queen
         iv. cruising
            (in a car)

as the means of initiating and carrying on those relationships. Impinging upon the process are the individual and context variables.

The advantage of this framework was that the *process* began to emerge. It appeared that students entered a new environment which was comprised of two domains, the social and the academic. The student was then faced with a task more complicated than was initially assumed. If the school environment was comprised of these two domains, then this naturally led to the question of how one accomplished the two ends of: (a) friendship formation, and (b) understanding school rules and teacher expectations. It was this question which led to an understanding of the strategies in which the students engaged to socialize into the new school. This new framework was then used to determine if there were any reports of student strategies which were explicit or implied. There were, in fact, a number of strategies for socialization into the academic and social domains. Subsequent analysis focused on how successful students were in

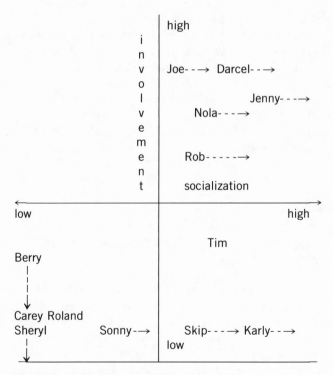

Figure 6.1.   Plot of position of student according to degree of socialization vs. degree of involvement indicating direction of movement.

their socialization efforts (that is, did those who were successful use strategies similar to, or different from, those who were unsuccessful?).

Additionally, were the students at different stages in their socialization? In order to represent the stages in which each student could be placed, a scatterplot was developed (see Figure 6.1). The students were clustered on the scatterplot and the data reexamined to discover similarities and differences. This final framework rounded out the description of the process of socialization.

RESULTS

Question One: What Does it Mean to be a Transfer Student?

To address this question it was necessary to determine students' perspectives of themselves as transfer students in the new school. The major dimension of being a transfer student was to be an outsider.

Initial scanning of the questionnaire data indicated students were already feeling "very much a part of the school" within less than a week. It was only after analysis of the interview data that a distinction emerged between socialization into the formal structure of the school and the informal social network. Students' reports of feeling comfortable at the school were directed towards such aspects as where their lockers were, who they needed to see when they needed an admit slip, where all their classes were, what teams and clubs they could join, who the principal, vice-principal, and counselors were, what all their teachers were like, and what was going to be expected of them by each. The students indicated that becoming familiar with the physical plant of the school and with the rules was relatively easy to accomplish since the means by which it was done had already been learned at previous schools, that is, those elements do not change dramatically from school to school. When referring to school in general, participants said that students "figure that stuff out fast" and usually within a couple of days.

Integration into the social structure of the student subculture, however, appears to be of a different nature. When asked about any difficulties in becoming a member of the new system, the students repeatedly mentioned meeting people, claiming that "people know people and it doesn't seem like a lot of people want to get to know other people." Transfer students must determine how best to enter an established social structure and find their place in it. When asked about what they missed most about the school they left, the almost universal answer was "friends." The students also claimed that they were having a difficult time "making friends" and feeling a part of the social scene. Thus, it was with respect to the informal social structure of the school that the transfer students felt themselves to be outsiders.

By the end of the first semester, however, the majority of students considered themselves as socialized or more aptly (in their own words) a "part" of the new school and no longer feeling like outsiders. A number of criteria emerged for their feeling of being part of the school, including: having friends, knowing who's who in the social domain of the school, being accepted by others, being with others in the bleachers at the pep rallies, being seen by others as being involved, liking and being proud of the school, feeling that one was contributing to the school, knowing the norms (that is, what was appropriate to wear, say, and do), knowing what teachers were like, and knowing the school and class rules. It seems that to the degree a student met these criteria, she or he was socialized.

Not all students, however, reported success in becoming a part of the school. Of the 15 participants, two dropped out of school, one threatened suicide, and two could not relinquish their emotional attachment to the previous school and wanted very much to return. The variables which these students had in common were less consistent across cases than the variables which seemed to tie together those who succeeded. For the most part, the concerns they articulated centered on not being involved in any school activities and not having any (or few) friends. Because their experiences were unique and they had little in common other than still feeling like outsiders, any generalizations are tentative. Consequently, the report of their experiences is individual and seeks primarily to provide insights into the range of variables which fail to result in successful socialization.

Among those students who were not successful, only one had involvement in any school activity, two acknowledged that there were no others in the school like themselves, and two others had such personal problems that just coping seemed to occupy much of their time. One of the new students was black and reported that "I could only count 11 or so other black kids in the school." He had transferred from a school in which nearly half of the students were black. Another complained at the outset that he was a "waver" in a "rocker" school and anticipated that he would have a hard time adjusting. At the end of the semester he maintained that he still was not a part of the school, hated it, and felt as though the other students hated him. These feelings would seem to be contributing factors to his suicide threat. Both of these students had a problem finding others with whom they could relate socially.

Another student had spent the previous years in and out of orphanages and shelters. She had periodically been in the custody of one parent or another, had been kidnapped by one parent (who later went to jail), and was, at the time the data were collected, living with a mother, brother, and sister whom she had not seen in many years. Being new to the school and

having to adjust to a new family proved to be too taxing and she dropped
out of school. Another student was a returning dropout who stated initially
that her intent was not to become involved in the social scene of the
school, but only to "get her diploma." She considered herself to be different from the other students in that she had been "out on her own" and
had had to take care of herself, something foreign to most of the other
students. She too had dropped out of school by the end of the first term.

Thus, a pivotal variable in the progression from outsider to insider for
these students seemed to involve the number and quality of the friendships the new student was able to form within the first two or three
months after arrival. It is not claimed that this variable is sufficient, but
rather that it is necessary. Figure 6.1 provides a graphic depiction of where
each student could be placed along two axes: (a) degree of socialization
(self report of how "comfortable," "how much I feel at home," how much
I feel "a part," and extent to which I am no longer an "outsider"), and (b)
degree of involvement (reports of actual number of involvements in clubs,
sports, and extracurricular activities).[1]

Figure 6.1 provides a visual representation of an emergent pattern. With
the exception of three of the students, all those who participated in the
study could be placed either in the upper-right quadrant, indicating that
they were both involved and socialized, or in the lower-left quadrant, indicating low involvement and low socialization. None was high in involvement and low in socialization. Three were moderately high to very high
on the socialization scale although not particularly involved in the activities of the school. Of those three, one had become involved with a large
number of other students and had a fairly well developed network of
friends. Consequently, she felt "a part" of the school social scene. Of the
other two, one expressed little desire to become involved in the school
but rather spent most of his time with one friend. In addition, he maintained the attitude that he would be in the same school until he graduated
and so had plenty of time to find his niche. The friend (who was also a new
transfer student but not officially a participant in the study) with whom he
spent most of his time shared this viewpoint. The key to this attitude may
be the notion that they had each other and so did not feel the pressure to
establish a large network of friends or become really "involved." Students
apparently also had different needs in terms of making friends.

Of the group which occupied the low involvement and low socialization
quadrant, one student was anomalous. He was uninvolved and not socialized but was aware of the situation and was striving toward both involve-

---

[1] The two students who dropped out of school during the first term are not placed on the
scatterplot.

ment and socialization. In interviews he expressed concern about how long it was taking to become involved, a situation that had not occurred in previous moves between schools. He was unable to account for it but indicated that he would get involved in clubs if there was someone he knew in them.

One element common to all the students who remained in the study through its completion was an ability to articulate the degree of socialization felt. Each was able to describe how she or he felt. One said "moving here was the best thing that could have happened to me ... the school is great ... I'm really into it!," another "ya, I'm gettin' there.. .just gonna take some more time this time," while still another, "I don't know ... people here don't seem to be willing to accept outsiders ... and I'm still an outsider." Each student seemed to know intuitively where she or he stood on a continuum of outsider to insider.

Question Two: What are the Concerns of Transfer Students as They Socialize into a New High School?

Social/nonacademic and academic concerns. The concerns which students expressed at the beginning of the school year (both on the questionnaires and in the interviews) were primarily social or nonacademic, that is, whether they would be able to make friends, how they would be accepted, if they would adjust, whether people would talk to them, and the pressure that there would be to make friends. The first of these especially was reiterated time and again by the majority of the students. Other concerns expressed were directed at the academic domain. Students worried that they might not get the classes they wanted, that they might not find their classes, and that school would be difficult (e.g., teachers, subject matter).

Additional support for the preeminence of the social/nonacademic category of concern emerged when "Topics of Conversation" were analyzed. Some 60 different topics were identified, of which only 15 directly related to the learning of academic subjects, scheduling, or future academic endeavors (see Table 6.1). For example, talk associated with the academic nature of the school consisted of grades, classes taken, where to go to college, tests taken, subjects taken, answering questions in class, and assignment instructions. Talk associated with the social or nonacademic nature of the school included movies and concerts, homecoming, the prom, social contacts, jokes, helping new students, asking someone out on a date, haunted house, the weather, the federal deficit, sports, having locker "ripped off," concern about others using drugs, and an all-inclusive category they labeled "stuff and school" which was undefined but reported as socially oriented.

Other researchers have made the distinction not only between the social and academic domains, but have further divided the latter into academic procedures and academic performance (Blumenfeld, Hamilton, Bossert, Wessels, & Meece, 1983). In terms of socialization, academic procedures include such activities as finding out how to become a teacher's assistant, learning how to become a "highly distinguished" graduate, determining to whom one must talk to get a class changed, and so on. Academic performance includes learning the subject matter or content of a particular class. For purposes of this chapter, however, academic procedures and performance are combined.

An interesting anomaly that emerged was related to two categories labeled "orienting talk" and "problem-solving talk." On the surface these topics seem to contradict the pervasiveness of the "social talk" in that "orienting talk" and "problem-solving talk" are primarily reported in connection with academic matters. Students mentioned talking to others about how to "do classwork," "become a teacher's aide," "get into driver's education," "get classes changed," "rectify grade mistakes," and "find people and things (like librarians, secretaries, counselors, and such)." With respect to the nonacademic topics, students said they talked about "learning who is who in the school," "determining sports eligibility," and "getting help about the locker being 'ripped off'." It seems as though students were more active in resolving concerns about academic, less personal problems than they were in resolving social concerns which tended to be personal and potentially risky. Admitting ignorance about how to change a class is less personally threatening than admitting a concern about how to make friends.

Social/nonacademic and academic activities. As another indicator of students' primary concern and focus as transfer students, they were asked to identify activities or avenues whereby they could socialize into the new school. From their written and oral responses, it appeared that students viewed school primarily as a social environment. This finding supports Everhart's (1978) hypothesis of the importance of the social dimension. For example, there were twice as many categories subsumed under the heading of Social/Nonacademic (15) than Academic (7) (see Table 6.2). Under the heading of "Organized" activities, the following were reported: Academic—class (with answering questions, and writing papers subsumed); Social/Nonacademic—pep assemblies, school newspaper, band, sports teams, gamer's club, dances, the bonfire at homecoming, prom committee, and homecoming week activities. Under the heading of "Unorganized" activities, the following emerged: Academic—study period, library time, and homework; Social/Nonacademic—lunch, hanging out in the HUB (student union), going to movies, shopping at the mall, hanging out at the Dairy Queen, cruising (in a car), and going over to a friend's house. Regardless of the domain into which it falls, each of the activities reported is an avenue whereby new students can become involved in the new environment, attempt to resolve their concerns, and become socialized to the new school. Not all avenues were identified by all students, rather, Table 6.1 represents a comprehensive list of the avenues reported. Although it is not claimed that these are all the avenues potentially available, it is representative of the ones of which new students are aware.

Question Three: What is the Nature of the Process by Which Transfer Students Socialize into a New High School?

Transfer students reported engaging in a variety of strategies that served to facilitate their socialization into the academic and social domains. As discussed in Chapter Four, the strategies ranged from highly direct to indirect.

Learning the academic domain. Learning the academic domain (that is, school rules and procedures) proved to be easier than learning the social domain. As mentioned, students reported being able to find their way around the school environment within the first week. To account for this, they cited the fact that the school rules were not substantially different from the rules which existed at their previous schools.

Students identified three strategies that helped them ease into the academic domain. First and most direct was asking teachers and counselors about school rules, expectations, and academic requirements. This strategy involved directly approaching a school authority and initiating a question. A second strategy was asking other students in class about academic expectations and specific class assignments. Although it is not generally as face threatening to ask a question of a peer as of an adult, asking a question of a peer who is a stranger still requires some degree of risk. The third and most indirect strategy was that of watching teachers and other students to learn what to do in a particular class. This was a way of determining the more subtle and implicit rules for behavior unique to particular classes. In one class, for example, it was required that students sit quietly and not talk for any reason, while in another there was a great deal of movement permitted and a higher level of noise tolerated. This strategy of observing requires no interaction at all and thus, is indirect.

In addition to learning about the academic domain by engaging in these three strategies, students received information from school authorities. The transfer students indicated that teachers explicitly discussed their class rules and expectations, thus aiding socialization. In addition, students reported receiving a student handbook upon entry into the school. They found the handbook to be helpful in explicating many of the school policies.

Learning the social domain. Gaining information to reduce the uncertainty about the social domain, while reported as being considerably more important than the academic domain, proved also to be far more difficult, complicated, and time consuming for students. As a consequence, the strategies for gaining information were, not surprisingly, more involved and complex. The first order of business for these new students was to identify the different types of people they were seeing on a daily basis. Within the first few weeks, students were able to provide labels for numerous types of people they encountered (e.g., punkers, preps). Students indicated that finding out about informal groups, what was acceptable behavior in the school, what should be worn, and the like, was done by "just watching."

Having identified the informal groups, the next step was to engage in strategies which would bring them in contact with others they had identified as people they would like to know and with whom they would like to become friends. Previous research has established that homophily is a major determinant of friendship formation (Byrne, 1961, 1971; McCroskey, Richmond, & Daly, 1975; Rogers & Shoemaker, 1971). Elliot (1979) defines homophily as "the degree to which pairs of individuals who interact are similar in certain attributes such as beliefs, attitudes, values, education, and social status" (p. 587). Students articulated four strategies they initiated for making friends with others perceived as similar to themselves.

Self-initiated strategies. One strategy was to *join a club or sports activity.* It seemed reasonable to students that by joining a club or participating in a sport they would encounter others with similar interests who would be like them. One student acknowledged that while she had made some friends outside of the swim team, she would have had a much harder time making friends had she not joined the team. Another made the same claim about being involved in the school band. It appeared that having made the friends on the team or in the club reduced the pressure to make other friends, and therefore freed them to look elsewhere at their leisure.

A second strategy articulated by students was to *ask questions of classmates* seated nearby about assignments, the time, and other impersonal topics. While the first of these seems on the surface to be an attempt to clear up an academic matter, it was reported as being both that and a means by which one "broke the ice." After talking about these types of topics for some period of time, the student then began talking to classmates about more personal and social matters. It is at this point that the new student was able to determine if the other(s) was someone she or he wanted to know and have for a friend.

A third strategy was to *listen to the conversation of others and then join in.* This was initially an indirect strategy involving listening to others in order to discover if what was being discussed was something with which the new student was familiar. If so, then she or he engaged in an interactive effort and joined the conversation, thus making herself or himself known to the others as someone with a common interest. One student was somewhat successful with this strategy, but another seemed unable to implement it. He, like the others, would listen to others (because they would not talk to him, he said) and then fill in gaps in their knowledge if the opportunity presented itself. While it was an attempt to become a part of the conversation, he found that the others just thought him "weird" and continued to exclude him or "put him in his place." Not all students were as skilled as others in the ways they engaged in the strategies. It is notable that despite his failure at that strategy, he was consciously aware of it and continued to employ it.

A fourth strategy mentioned by students involved meeting several different people and *acting as a catalyst in the formation of a new group*. One boy reported that some of the members of his new group had known each other previously but did not "hang around" together. Others had not known each other but became a part of the group anyway as a result of knowing one of the members. He saw himself as bringing them together into one group, resulting in all of them "hanging out" together. During one observation at lunch, the school principal commented that this particular group was interesting in that the students were all a little "different" but somehow seem to have found one another. What she meant by "different" was not clear, but it seemed to suggest that they did not fit in like the other "mainstream" students as joiners or outwardly directed. As it turned out, two of the others involved in the study were also part of this group.

What is important to note is that all four of these strategies center on finding others who are similar to oneself. This common theme (seeking homophily) indicates that there is an assumption or belief on the part of the new students that finding others like the self will provide the greatest likelihood of success in making friends.

Other-initiated strategies. In addition to the four self- initiated strategies, the transfer students reported making new friends as a result of the efforts of others. One such strategy involved *an individual friend or a group of friends introducing newcomers* to others whom they knew. One participant reported that she had made many friends this way and that she no longer spent time with the friend who made the initial introductions, indicating she found the new friends more to her liking and so spent more time with them. This was one of the means by which the new student established a network of friends and a group with which she or he could be a part. This same student made it clear that this was just one of the ways she made friends and that she had made other friends on her own. This might indicate a broader repertoire of strategies for finding and making friends.

A second strategy initiated by others involved teachers. Two of the students recounted experiences in which the *teachers in some of their classes had introduced them to the class* as new students. Although this was an embarrassment, they also said that other students then came up to them to talk about where they were from and how they liked the school. In a school the size of this one, it would appear that (and so it was reported) new students arriving at the beginning of the year would not necessarily stand out as being new. Not surprisingly, those who moved from larger schools got the impression that they stood out as new in the smaller school, while those who had transferred from a smaller school felt that they were anonymous and not obviously new.

Those who were not successful with their strategies and did not feel as though they were becoming a part of the school made various attributions for the thwarting of their efforts to "fit in." Those who were not "fitting in" claimed that there were already well established cliques, that the other students were unfriendly, and that a newcomer had little chance of breaking in. This is in marked contrast to those who were successful. The latter indicated that there were no set groups, that everyone was being friendly, and that these were the aspects they liked most about the new school. Two of those who were unsuccessful stated that there was little the school could do to help new students and that they really had to rely on themselves to find their way. They identified their trouble as stemming from not being able to find others like themselves. Those who were successful felt that to some degree they had to make their own way, but seemed much more open about accepting assistance from others. In addition, their strategies turned up sufficient others who were like them and with whom they could spend time in and out of school.

Agents of socialization/information sources. The data were also analyzed to identify the terms students used which refer to the types of people (agents) with whom they interacted and from whom they sought information. Students' use of terms suggests the importance of the peer group. There were far more references made to the different types of "kids" (students) who are encountered at school and fewer references to adults. Of 30 terms students generated that referred to types of people, seven related to adult roles (that is, teacher, principal, counselor, secretary, parents, substitute, coach). The remaining 23 terms referred to various types or categories of adolescents in the school (that is, students, cheerleaders, T.A.s, girlfriends, siblings, punkers, headbangers, preps, freshmen, sophomores, juniors, seniors, college kids, smokers, academic elites, social elites, movers and shakers, outsiders, loners, new kids, snobs, oddballs, nonconformists). In addition, when asked who was most helpful in their becoming a part of the school, the typical response was "definitely the other kids," suggesting that the central focus of the new students' attention was the peer group.

Students did not perceive the adults in the environment as having as vital an impact as peers. Only rarely did they spontaneously mention staff, administrators, or counselors, and then only in the context of problem solving (personal, academic, or scheduling). Teachers were the only adults who were consistently mentioned in the data, and they were discussed almost exclusively in terms of the content they taught or their effectiveness as teachers. The transfer students reported their communication with teachers to be almost entirely devoted to the class content.

Consistent with the perceived importance of peers in the socialization process, the data indicated that students expressed a strong need to gather information about others in order to make friends. Students also reported actively searching for others like themselves. There were several examples.

One student reported that he liked a class because it was all seniors, was A.P. (advanced placement), and the other kids were smart (like him). Along with several others, he stated that "you need a car to get out and meet others" who have cars and can get around. He also indicated that there were places where "anybody who is anybody" goes and one needs to see and be seen there especially with a girl in order to have it be "good for the 'rep' (reputation)." This showed that one was like the other guys with girlfriends. He also claimed that it was important to have a locker in the same area as others of one's class standing. Another student, acknowledging that he was socially backward, still expressed a desire to "know about other people and what they were doing" (he had a need to know about others because he felt it necessary in order to be a part of things). He also said that a commonality of interests was important.

Thus, new students reported a primary reliance on peers as they socialized into the informal school network, and some degree of reliance on peers for socialization into the academic domain. Teachers, counselors, staff, and administrators functioned primarily as agents of academic socialization.

Question Four: What are the Critical Dimensions in the Passage from the Status of Transfer Student to Insider?

There are several important dimensions of the status passage from transfer student to bona fide member of the new high school community. The temporal dimensions of the passage are quite different, for the most part, from those experienced by the students described in Chapters Two through Five. A passage into a new school as a transfer student is an *irregular* occurrence, is *not inevitable*, and is typically *unscheduled*. Many youngsters in American society never have the experience of being a transfer student. For others whose families move frequently, however, being a transfer student may be a regular event.

Unlike routine passages in which students move as a collective (progressing from elementary school to middle school and then on to high school), the move from one high school to another for individual reasons occurs *alone*. Each student must make a place for herself or himself largely unaided by others who are experiencing the same passage. It is interesting to note that although a few of the transfer students were acquainted with one another, they were generally *unaware* that the others were also new to the school and so were unable to be of any assistance. In at least one case, a student knew that his locker partner was a transfer student but thought him too "weird" to try and become a friend. *Communication with others* in the passage did occur on occasion for some of the students, but more because of serendipity than because the transfer students actively sought the company of one another.

All new students were aware of their status as outsiders at the beginning of the school term. For some, the outsider status never changed and they remained beyond the mainstream. For others, the passage to insider came rapidly. In most cases the students were fully cognizant of what was happening to them and could articulate, in some way, how it felt to be at their particular stage of passage: "I don't feel like a stranger any more," "I'm going to be here for three more years so I've got plenty of time for that," or "I'm never gonna be accepted by these people here." For those students who were consciously aware of their status as newcomers, the *signs of the passage* were clear. A lack of familiarity with the new physical environment and not being a part of the informal, social structure of the school were key signs of the status of transfer students. Teachers, administrators, staff, and other students, however, demonstrated few attempts to make the passage a *formal* one.

Passage into the academic and social domains were of different *durations*. In all cases, the passage into the academic domain was relatively short, that is, within the first week or two the new students were settled in as "insiders" in terms of their academic status. The *duration* of their passage into the social domain was more prolonged. As indicated earlier, some students were highly successful at achieving insider status by utilizing a variety of strategies and becoming involved in school activities. Others were unsuccessful and did not achieve insider status during the first term. Such students continually viewed themselves as outsiders and as never having made the passage to insider.

Finally, the status of transfer student was *desirable* for some students and *undesirable* for others. For those who had left an unfavorable school situation, the new status in the new school was an opportunity to begin again. For those who had left a large network of friends in an environment in which they felt secure, the status of transfer student was not a welcome one at all. Several of the students, had they been given a choice, would not have made the move from their previous schools. Regardless of the desirability of the passage, however, the new status was *central* to the identity of these youngsters.

DISCUSSION

For the transfer students described in this chapter, socialization into the social domain of the new school was more difficult to accomplish than socialization into the academic sphere. Being integrated into the social domain and having a friendship network were vital to successful socialization.

School as Primarily Social for Students

The first conclusion that can be drawn from the results relates to earlier research (notably Everhart, 1978) indicating that high school is viewed by teachers, counselors, parents, and administrators as being primarily academic while students view it as primarily social. For the students, the school was the focus of many activities of which learning subject matter was only a small part. Throughout the interviews, students repeatedly made statements such as: "I need to change my classes because all my friends have first lunch," "I like History because I know lots of kids in there," and "I hate Biology 'cause I don't know nobody." They were not heard to comment about the importance or academic value of particular courses. It is not a claim that students do not say these kinds of things, but that the interview responses did not include such academic talk, indicating that it occupied a less prominent position in student concerns. Thus, the socialization process for students was focused more acutely on the social than on the academic sphere.

Since students had already learned at previous schools the ways to make sense of the academic domain, this knowledge seemed to come quite rapidly, usually within the first week or two. The social domain, however, was a different matter. Many of the veteran students in the school already had an established niche while none of the transfer students did. As a consequence, new students engaged in a complicated and time-consuming process of determining where they fit into the existing and ever changing social network, a process which was accomplished over time. The most readily identifiable means by which this was realized was through friendship formation. After analyzing the data to discover the ways in which students seem to get "involved," a process such as the following began to emerge:

Students met other students in class → they became "in school" friends → they discovered activities or clubs which were available → they saw some of the same people in the clubs or at the activities that they had in class → they became "outside school" friends → those friends introduced students to other students → they established a network of friends.

The heavy reliance on the term "friends" in the data led to the conclusion that such peers were integral and necessary to the feeling of "at homeness" which would typify being socialized into the social milieu, that is, relating socially to the others in the culture. Consequently, if the student wanted to have friends, it was necessary to acquire sufficient information about enough other students to provide some basis for selecting friends. The ones chosen were most likely those who were deemed to be similar, as discerned through contact with other students in class, at lunch, at school dances, in clubs, and by watching what others did and where they went or congregated. Communication, both verbal and nonverbal, served as the means by which this was accomplished. Much of what a student needed to know emerged from "just watching what other kids do, how they dress, and what kind of music they listen to." All of these were messages which were inadvertently sent to the newcomers to indicate what was appropriate to become a part of the school culture.

It seemed there was a strong desire to find others like the self and the data indicated that homophily was an important determinant of friendship and affected the friendship-making process. To the degree that students were able to find others like themselves, others who shared their tastes for music, dress, values, and outlook, they began to establish networks of friends and felt "at home" in the new environment.

The findings of the study discussed in this chapter support and complement the results of earlier research. The concept of schools as agents for the transmission of the attitudes and expectations of the greater society (Kimbal, 1974; Parsons, 1959; Spindler, 1955, 1963) is not in any way contradicted. Acknowledging that it is the structure of the school which brings students together in the first place, it appears that those who act as the "agents" may be identified differently from the way they have been previously. If the school is indeed viewed by students as primarily a social institution and a place where they come to see their friends (Everhart, 1978; Kapferer, 1981; Peshkin, 1978; Ritter, 1979), then it could be argued that those friends and peers are the ones who are the most active agents involved in the socialization of students into the social milieu of the world outside the school. This would be a particularly reasonable conclusion given the research of Cohen (1979) and Hollingshead (1949) which examined schools as subcultures in which the grouping of students there reflects the groupings in the larger society.

As a testing ground where students are subjected to pressures which will be experienced later in life (Cusick, 1973; Jackson, 1968), the school described in this chapter reflects those earlier findings but again sheds light on only one aspect of the pressures which students experience. The present results provide a view of a group of students exposed to the difficulties involved in moving from one school to another and encountering an environment about which they have little or no knowledge. What has emerged is that they engage in a variety of direct and indirect strategies designed to cope with their concerns and gain critical information in order to reduce the uncertainty in the new environment. The view of uncertainty reduction is consistent with that formulated by Berger and Calabrese (1975) in which people seek to predict which of the available alternative communicative behaviors others will exhibit, and also determine what was meant by those behaviors once they occurred. In addition, the focus of that sense making has been uncovered as being directed primarily at uncertainty about the social environment. That is not to say that the students did not attend at all to the academic domain of the school, rather, a disproportionate amount of their attention was directed there.

Adult Role in Socialization

A second conclusion was that adults were perceived as being only tangentially related to the core concerns of the transfer students and were viewed as playing minor roles in the socialization process. While students may see it this way, it is more likely that the adults were simply less obviously involved from the students' perspectives. It could be that since they were seen as a part of the stable structure of the school environment, they were "taken-for-granted" and not recognized for the important influence they may have exerted.

Successful Socialization

A final conclusion was that some students socialized successfully into the new school while others did not. The results suggest that there may be some identifiable similarities among those who succeed and those who fail although the data were insufficient to make precise distinctions.

Ide, Haertel, and Walberg (1981) discuss the critical nature of peer influence on a wide range of educational outcomes. The present results were consistent with their view reinforcing the extreme importance placed upon the establishment of friendship networks. Although no tests were administered to the students, it would be reasonable to expect that those who were failing in the social integration process were also not succeeding in the academic domain. Threatening suicide and running away from home would naturally have a profound effect on the academic performance of a student. Conversely, one who has made friends, is involved, comfortable, and content with the new environment is much more likely to have the motivation and social support to succeed academically.

A Concluding Note

Although the fictional Tony did not understand fully what he would be in for as he moved from Jersey City to Rosemont and his new school, he clearly had an understanding of what he would be giving up when he left. Gone would be the familiar; to come would be the unknown. Added to the pain of leaving his friends would be the difficulty of developing new friendships. Like so many others in his situation, he will transfer to a new school and experience a process similar to the one described in this chapter. Although he has had no control over his transfer from one school to another, he certainly will be the most active participant in his socialization experience.

chapter 7
Immigrant Socialization to High School

Co-authored with Kristine L. Fitch

This chapter presents a study of nine immigrant high school students during their first year in American schools. The students are interviewed and observed during their first term in a special bilingual orientation program. Interviews with four of these students continue for the remainder of the first academic year as they leave the bilingual program and move into a regular high school. Although these immigrants have many concerns and needs similar to those of the transfer students, their socialization experience is unique due to language differences and to their being strangers in a new country as well as in a new school.

"Kien? Are you still asleep? Don't you remember that we are supposed to go to school today for the first time?" Kien pulled the pillow over his head. This was the day he had been dreading since their arrival in America two weeks ago. . . .

Kien sighed when he saw the American school. It was huge and surrounded by large grassy fields. . . . A group of boys and girls were drifting toward the big school. Kien looked them over, thinking that they were all bigger than Mai and himself. The Americans looked at the newcomers curiously, and one of them, a boy about Kien's age, smiled and waved. Kien wanted to wave back, but was too nervous. . . .

Steve now led them into the school building to meet Mr. Varney. The principal was a small, plump man who shook Mai's and Kien's hands as he welcomed them. He then spoke with Steve, who looked serious and nodded many times. . . . "Perhaps they are deciding what we must learn here," Mai whispered. Kien nodded glumly. "How are we going to learn anything when we can't understand English?" he wondered. After some time, the principal beckoned to Mai and Kien. He led them down a long corridor flanked on both sides by classrooms. Through windows in the classroom doors, Kien and Mai could see students at their desks. Many were studying, but a few looked to be asleep, others were talking behind their teacher's back, and a few were throwing things at each other. Mai was shocked. . . .

Mr. Varney confused them thoroughly by taking them to many classrooms, introducing them to many teachers. . . . How would they possibly be able to remember all these teachers? Mai looked ready to cry.

But Mr. Varney had understood their confusion. In one of the classrooms they visited, the principal introduced Kien and Mai to two American students called Bob and Alyssa. He explained through gestures that Bob and Alyssa would act as guides around school and help the Vietnamese make friends . . . Thankfully, this was the last stop of their tour around the big school. . . .

Mai shook her head. . . . "School is different here. Everything is different here!" (Wartski, 1980, pp. 24, 27, 28, 30)

Kien and Mai are immigrants to the United States, embarking upon their first day in an American school. The physical surroundings are dramatically different in the new country, but far more dramatic are the differences in the people. As Kien and Mai observed, the people look, sound, and act different from the people "back home." Noticing these differences is usually a reciprocal process in that the immigrant is aware that she or he does not look, sound, or act as the natives do. The ability to accomplish everyday tasks independently is replaced by a dependence on others. Obligations of a daily routine which had been fulfilled almost automatically are suddenly anxiety-producing obstacles. School registration procedures are basic and simple to natives who have experienced the routine. To the immigrant they present a labyrinth of undeciphered terms, framed in unspoken assumptions about schools, students, parents, government regulation, and intergroup relationships. Although there are offers to "answer any questions you may have," just knowing where to begin asking questions is problematic.

Adjustment to American schools is a challenge faced by more than one-and-a-half million immigrants over the last decade. In 1987, there were approximately 139,000 new school-aged immigrants (5 to 19 years old), who were legally entitled to public education (United States Immigration and Naturalization Service, 1988). Since the passage of Title VI of the Civil Rights Act of 1964, the Bilingual Education Act of 1968, and the Bilingual Education Act of 1974, there has been an increased focus on the teaching of immigrants and other non-native English speaking minorities (Teitelbaum & Hiller, 1977). Millions of tax dollars have been spent in implementing bilingual, bicultural, multicultural, and English-as-a-second-language (ESL) programs (Gibson, 1984; Paulston, 1979; Spener, 1988; Trueba, Guthrie, & Hu-Pei Au, 1981; Warren, 1982). Clearly, these immigrant students represent a population of importance in American schools.

The socialization of immigrant students to American schools is similar to the process faced by other students described in this volume in that it involves learning an unfamiliar set of expectations and procedures in order to move from newcomer status to being part of the system. The experience is different and more complex, however, in that learning the system of rules and procedures, as well as mastering the academic content, must be accomplished in a second language (Ziegler, 1980).

Since the competencies required for successful socialization into schools typically reflect white, middle-class interaction patterns (Chattergy, 1983; Hall & Guthrie, 1981), the socialization of immigrants may relate to that experienced by minority groups. American members of ethnic minorities often encounter cultural discontinuities between home and school during socialization that are comparable in magnitude to those faced by immigrants. Ogbu (1982, 1987) speculates, however, that immigrant students actually may encounter fewer difficulties with socialization into American schools than do ethnic minorities because of their more positive evaluation of their own cultural characteristics, and a stronger motivation to learn the new cultural system.

Even if Ogbu's (1982, 1987) speculation is correct, the immigrant student has to overcome the major obstacle of learning a new language before active participation in school is achieved. In studies of learner characteristics which facilitate second language acquisition, it was found that many of these are beyond the control of immigrants. Such aspects as socioeconomic status (Kelly, 1981), occupational level of parents (Connor, 1983), age at the time of immigration (Kim, 1977), and level of education prior to immigration (Paulston, 1979) all correlate with the ease and efficiency of language learning and cannot be altered. Such dimensions as motivation to learn the new language (Gardner & Smythe, 1975) and attitude toward the language (Tucker, 1976) are within control of the immigrants.

School socialization is a different kind of process for immigrants than for Americans in the unique double bind it presents. The mark of having socialized "successfully" into any system is that one "knows the ropes," that is, knows how to perform important tasks effectively. Since the overt task at school is learning, it seems as though being "successfully socialized" into school would consist of academic achievement. Yet Gibson's (1987) study of Punjabi immigrants in an American high school suggests that fitting into the social world of the school was viewed as just as important a marker of success as scholastic performance. The Punjabi students were, in some respects, "better" students than their American classmates, that is, they had a lower absentee rate, took more college preparatory classes, were disciplined less frequently, had a lower dropout rate, and had higher grades.

Nonetheless, American students and teachers viewed the Punjabis as not fully socialized into the school because they dressed differently from the other students, rarely took part in extracurricular activities, and had few American friends. Their parents insisted they maintain Punjabi cultural traditions such as deference to elders, separation of the sexes, and putting schoolwork ahead of housework, jobs, and social activities. School expectations included conforming to the standards of dress of the majority, participating in coeducational activities such as gym class, and volunteering answers in class. Punjabi parents encouraged their children to accommodate to mainstream society sufficiently to compete within it, but not to assimilate to such an extent that they brought shame upon their families. Thus, the Punjabi students faced conflicting demands from home and school.

The Gibson (1987) study focused on students who had been in the United States for several years. They had already learned enough about the American school system to take it for granted, and had found their place (however tenuous) within that system. An empirical description of the process immigrant students undergo to make sense of the new school system can highlight the specific differences they encounter and how communication functions to resolve concern and reduce uncertainty during socialization. In the case of immigrant students, school socialization is a part of acculturation to American society. They face language and cultural differences common to all immigrants. The numbers of immigrant students in American schools provide ample rationale for examination of the socialization process they undergo, that is, such students constitute an increasingly significant population that faces, and presents, special challenges. Beyond that, however, examining American schools, including their definitions of "successful" socialization, from the perspective of a non-native can provide insight into the cultural values embodied in the school system.

PURPOSE OF THE CHAPTER

The purpose of this chapter is to describe the process of becoming part of a school system which is not only unfamiliar as a school, but is also part of a different system of language and culture. The chapter addresses four research questions:

1. What does it mean to be an immigrant high school student?
2. What are the concerns and needs of immigrant students during their first year in American high schools?
3. What is the role of communication in the socialization of immigrant high school students?
4. What are the critical status passage dimensions for new immigrants in American high schools?

METHOD

Research Setting

Participants were 14- to 18-year old immigrant students attending North American high schools for the first time during the 1985–86 school year.[1] The immigrants entered a bilingual education program for a semester, then transferred to "regular" high schools at midyear. This transfer allowed for a comparison of the students' experiences in two different schools within the same system.

These students had their initial contact with American schools through the Center for Bilingual Instruction (CBI), one of several special programs in an urban school district in a large, West coast city. CBI served an overflow function to accomodate new immigrants when programs in the regular high schools were full. Two other alternative high school programs offered by the district, for American students, were housed in the same building with CBI. There were between 190 and 240 students in the program during the time that this study was conducted; the teacher/student ratio was approximately one to 20, compared with one to 30 at the high school level for the district as a whole. The CBI student population was predominantly Asian, with the remainder Hispanic, African, Middle Eastern, and European. They ranged in age from 12 to 21 years, and were designated either as regular bilingual (12 to 18, expected to fulfill requirements and graduate at some point) or overage (18 to 21, not expected to graduate but entitled to bilingual education services). Most teachers were Americans, although one was Chinese and another Vietnamese. Instructional re-

---

[1] As participants, the immigrant students posed some unique difficulties. Their status as minors meant that permission to participate had to be obtained from their parents or guardians. Although the cover term "immigrants" is used to describe these students, both in the school system and in this chapter, their actual status was sometimes that of illegal aliens or exchange students. Therefore, parents were not always available to grant permission, and guardians were understandably cautious about doing so. For the students themselves, the prospect of being observed under circumstances that were already threatening was frequently more than they were willing to commit themselves to voluntarily. Further, the immigrants were enrolled in the bilingual program due to a low level of English fluency. Translators were not a feasible alternative, so students either had to be willing to be interviewed in the basically unfamiliar language of English, or in Spanish, the second language of one of the researchers. Finally, because students transferred to schools throughout the city at midyear, only one group at one school was followed after transfer. Many of these difficulties were compensated for by frequent contact between the researchers and the small group of participants.

sponsibilities were shared by bilingual aides (BAs) and bilingual tutors who represented several of the students' language groups. These individuals were also immigrants, who had been in the United States for several years.

The objectives of CBI were to begin academic instruction, including a heavy emphasis on English as a second language, and to facilitate students' cultural adjustment to the United States and socialization to American schools. Although schooling of the CBI students in their home countries was quite diverse, a few had exposure to education and resources comparable to that of middle-class teenagers in this country. The participants discussed in this chapter were grouped in this category.

At CBI, several nationalities were typically represented in each class. For the most part, there was little contact with American students, as lunch periods were scheduled at different times, and the programs occupied different floors of the building. Efforts were made to encourage contact by planning joint assemblies and by using American students as assistants in CBI classes.

The immigrants' first extended exposure to American students occurred when they transferred to American High School (AHS) at midyear. AHS was a racially mixed urban high school with approximately 1,600 students. Sixty of these were considered immigrants, having arrived in the United States within the last five years.

AHS, which was located near a major university, offered a wide range of vocational and elective coursework in addition to required subjects. The teacher/student ratio was approximately one to 20. Extracurricular activities were also numerous and varied, from music to sports to social events. Seventy percent of its students enter college.

Procedures for Data Collection and Analysis

Data were collected at CBI and AHS through interviews with students and staff and observations in classrooms, the main office, cafeteria, library, and hallways. Data were drawn from 70 hours of observation, 50 at CBI and 20 at AHS. Nine CBI students were observed systematically; two of these were interviewed. Four of the nine students transferred to AHS at midyear, including the two who were interviewed initially. All four of these were observed and interviewed. Nine teachers and staff were interviewed at CBI, eight at AHS. Documents generated by the staff and the school district were made available for examination. These included class handouts, announcements of upcoming events, school newsletters, and general information about school regulations.

Field notes and interviews were transcribed and then coded, in a manner consistent with that described in previous chapters. Procedures of analytic induction were used (Goetz & LeCompte, 1981) and the constant comparison method (Miles & Huberman, 1985).

RESULTS

Question One: What Does it Mean to be an Immigrant High School Student?

Analysis of the data revealed that the identity of immigrant high school students was constructed very differently in CBI and in AHS. In addition, the perspectives of students about what it meant to be an immigrant high school student were distinct from those of the teachers and staff.

CBI

Students' views. To the youngsters at CBI, being an immigrant student had two dimensions of meaning. These included being in a school tailored to them and being valued because they were immigrant students.

To be new and different in a school that is academically, socially, and procedurally tailored to immigrants. The first dimension of the meaning of being an immigrant student related to students' awareness that CBI was organized to accomodate incoming immigrant students. Students' view of this setting was that, although it was new and different from the ones to which they were accustomed, conditions were academically, socially, and procedurally tailored to their needs. In interviews, students mentioned three conditions that facilitated their initial socialization to high school, the presence of which were supported in classroom observations as well: (a) explicit instructions for behavior, (b) abundant academic and social "help," and (c) ready-made friendship groups of same-language (L1) peers.

Explicit instructions for behavior. Although it might seem an easy task to comply with requests of authority figures, it is not so simple in a second language and an unfamiliar culture. The teachers and staff at CBI recognized the danger of such confusion and responded routinely to it by making their expectations for students' behavior extremely detailed. Usually, they were also repeated several times and liberally accompanied with nonverbal illustrators:

> Teacher, to a group of students gathering to have their picture made: I need a line. Students, please make a line here to the side. Make a line here next to me. Once you've finished your picture we'd like you to come out here

(motioned to seats in auditorium) and sit down. Come out here and sit down once you've had your picture taken.

Teachers often made special efforts to speak slowly, especially when BAs were not immediately available to translate. Students reported that it was easy to decipher the "code" of appropriate conduct because instructions were explicit and repeated often.

Freely given academic and social help. Teachers and staff also frequently offered "extra help" to students. This assistance included repetition of instructions, demonstration of desired performance, explanation of translation of unfamiliar words, and permission to receive help from an L1 peer. Such help was often provided even before the student asked (Teacher, giving worksheet to student: "[Name], if you find words here that you don't know, ask me or use your dictionary." School secretary, to new student: "Are you going to need to come on the bus? Go ask Diep, he can explain to you about the bus system in Vietnamese.").

Students commented that one unfamiliar requirement of American classrooms was to speak out as individuals. In their countries, teachers had done most of the talking, and most questions that were asked were responded to as a group or in writing. Teachers at CBI frequently allowed students to "help" each other with oral responses to give the immigrants time to adjust to this new system of communication in the classroom:

Teacher, to student 1:   Would you like to read it, or do you feel shy. Would you like a friend to read it for you?

Student 2:   She think about it.

Teacher: We need someone to read it. Who can read it for us? (A few minutes later)

Teacher, to student 1:   Do you want to read this or would you like to ask your friend to? Come on, you're not shy. OK, the new people can just watch today.

In addition to giving the new student some time to get accustomed to being part of the class before participating, the teacher offered an acceptable account for the student's silence: "shyness," as opposed to implying that the student did not have the ability to read aloud in front of the group.

Ready-made friendship group of L1 peers. It was immediately obvious during observations that students tended to congregate in same-language groups both within the classroom and outside it. During interviews the students commented that having L1 peers was helpful in the sense that it was very easy to make friends in school. In addition to the bond of language, they frequently had experiences in common with L1 peers and shared expectations of friendship behavior. In a world of unfamiliar customs and culture shock, an L1 peer group represented security.

To be valued because of one's unique cultural background and because of one's student status. A second dimension of meaning was to be considered important because of one's unique cultural background and because one was a student. Rather than being expected to reject their home culture or to change their ways in order to fit into the American system, students were reinforced for being able to speak different languages. The students felt that they were seen as valuable resources for Americans, both as educational influences and as important links between their families and American culture.

Unique cultural background. As a group, the immigrants received considerable positive reinforcement for their varied cultural backgrounds. Books were available in the library about several of the most represented countries, and reading materials in the classroom often reflected the experiences of immigrants and refugees. Hallways were decorated with displays of flags, pictures, and artifacts from students' home countries.

One event that reinforced the value of students' cultures was a visit to CBI by 20 American students from a nearby high school. The purpose of the visit was explained to CBI students as a way for the American students to learn about people much different from themselves, "to find out what it is like to speak another language, to find out about other countries and what your experiences have been like coming to this country." Each visitor was paired with a CBI "host" and accompanied that person on her or his daily routines. During the day teachers provided opportunities in class for discussion of differences. American students' comments at the end of the day reflected their impressions of the contact with immigrant students (e.g., "My person told me—she's from Cambodia—she told me she was in this refugee camp for nearly a year, and they escaped on this boat, and then they got here and they've been on Welfare and all—she's really had a tough time, and she's younger than I am!"). Through this experience, the immigrants were reinforced positively for their "differences."

Link between home and American culture. A second way in which the immigrant students felt they were valued was as information links between their families and American culture. It is frequently the case that immigrant children serve such a function in their families' acculturation process, since they may learn English more rapidly and have more contact with the host country natives through schooling than do others in their families. On several occasions, teachers disseminated information to students with the apparent intent of instructing parents about services and resources that might be helpful: how to fill out job applications, where and how to arrange for medical care, how to obtain drivers' licenses, and so on. An instance of this kind of information dissemination came with the first snowfall of the year. It was a day of heavy snow, and many of the immigrants had never seen snow in their home countries. A message was delivered by BAs who came to each classroom and repeated the information in several languages, after which the teacher repeated it once more in English:

> If you get up in the morning and see snow, turn on the radio and listen to what they say. If they say _____ School District is *closed* you don't wanna go stand and wait for the bus for two hours and *freeze*. . . . Sometimes the radio will say, one hour late. You'll hear them read off lots and lots of schools and you listen for _____ School District. If you don't hear anything, that means it's OK, come to school. But be sure to wear *warm* clothes because the bus might take a long time. Snow is fun when you're warm, but not when you're cold.

Teachers' views. From the teachers' perspectives there were two major dimensions of the meaning of immigrant student. These included immigrants as newcomers who warranted special attention and as students who were highly valued.

Immigrant students are newcomers who need and deserve special consideration. Most of the teachers at CBI had taught American students at one time or another, and defined "special consideration" as assistance and information usually perceived as beyond the purview of the school system. One reason, articulated during interviews, that these students needed special consideration was that *they faced unique obstacles to learning.* Beyond the difficulty of being a newcomer in a strange culture and the stress of learning a new language, many students had faced harrowing escapes from war-torn areas, or presently had major responsibilities for care of younger siblings and housework at home. The future of some students was as uncertain as their past. For example, they or their families were illegal aliens or on temporary visas, awaiting decisions on their final immigration status. The parents of some were marginally employed or unemployed. Those with family members still living in their native countries did not know whether those relatives would be allowed to join them in the United States. Teachers expressed their admiration of students who worked diligently at school tasks in spite of traumatic personal circumstances.

Because of the various difficulties the immigrant students faced, the teachers took on responsibilities that extended beyond the school's usual range of duties. One remarked:

> Teachers at this school have to deal with a lot of nonacademic needs. . . . Our students are in the position of dealing with government agencies of many varieties, welfare, clinics, job placement, things like that, and it's up to us to clue them in on all of that on top of the scholastic part of their life.

The head teacher at CBI expressed this idea as a more general philosophy that the school attempted to implement:

> What students need to do well here, more than anything, is total support from the school. We just can't shut our eyes to the conditions in the kids' lives. . . . I think the bilingual program goes way beyond what it was commissioned to do in the way of connecting students to social services and agencies that can help them out. . . . We don't just hand them a list of things they're eligible for—we take them, or we tell them exactly how to get there and who to see and what to say, and we rehearse what they have to know and do to get their needs met.

Another reason for special consideration was the teachers'awareness of the *cultural conflicts between home and school* that students faced. They felt it was the school's responsibility to be flexible in its demands that students adapt to a new way of doing things. One teacher remarked, "I recognize that there's this American way of doing things, and the kids do have to fit into it. But I'm willing to try to mediate between my culture and theirs and try to see that everybody wins." Another teacher talked about times when such situations had been presented to her:

> There are a lot of aspects of their family life that we too often aren't aware of. Like, with the idea of an extended family you have the oldest daughter responsible for all the cooking and taking care of nine adults. . . . I had one student who came to me the day after she was absent once, and said she was sorry she had missed school but her mother was very sick and she had to take her to the clinic. . . . I said to her, "What a good daughter you are to take care of your mother that way". . . . In a case like that we try to make adjustments here, so that the kid has an extra study period to do homework, or some extra help, or something.

Finally, the teachers felt that immigrant students *required constant reassurance in order to participate in class.* The teachers were well aware that the American pattern of individual response to questions was unfamiliar to many cultural groups. Thus, they allowed for more frequent group responses and often allowed students to "help" one another with answers, especially at the start of school. In one class, a teacher urged a Southeast Asian student to come to the front and offer answers aloud, after she had demonstrated that she knew the material well during group responses. The student protested that she was "too shy," while the teacher encouraged her: "Come on, I know you know this!" The student reluctantly came to the front of the room, but asked if she might face the board instead of her classmates while she responded. The teacher agreed and the student showed herself to be competent. Without the teacher's insistence, the student might never have demonstrated the knowledge that she possessed.

Immigrants are highly valued students and resources. Beyond the "special consideration" students required due to their personal circumstances, teachers viewed the immigrants as highly valued students and resources. One important resource function was that of translator for other students. In addition to helping to facilitate communication in a group where language fluency varied widely, students were also eager to assist in any kind of task in the main office, library, or classroom when asked. They seemed pleased to run errands, straighten up books and equipment, or provide assistance to a classmate. One teacher remarked that their willingness to help teachers and each other had left its mark on the school: "Asian and Latin cultures especially tend to put much more emphasis on group harmony, on helping each other out, and we wanted to take that positive part of their culture and extend it into this setting." At the awards ceremony held at the end of the semester, several awards were given for "service to the school" and "teacher's helper," to reinforce those students who had been outstanding in that regard.

In addition to being valued resources, the immigrants were prized students because of their strong motivation to succeed in school. One teacher remarked, "They want to do what's expected of them, even when they're not sure what that is." She mentioned students whose parents had brought them to school the day after they arrived in the United States, and others who had attended despite serious illness—all because of their determination to achieve success in school. This teacher commented: "I left teaching once and said I wouldn't come back until I was with students who wanted to learn. Now that I've found them, I don't plan to leave."

Summary. From the view of both teachers and students, to be an immigrant student at CBI was to be considered a person of special worth, who also had special needs. Teachers and staff saw it as their duty to provide any assistance required to remove the various barriers to instruction in students' lives, and students saw such assistance as readily available to them. This phase of the immigrants' socialization to high school was a relatively smooth, give-and-take process, with the school helping students in their efforts to adapt to the new system. After four-and-a-half months of this entry stage into American schools, the immigrants transferred into a new phase of the process: American High School (AHS).

AHS

Students' views. The immigrants who participated in the second phase of this study were overwhelmed by the complexity of life at AHS during their first few days in the school. They were suddenly isolated from one another in a sea of native speakers, whereas they had been at CBI with some students who spoke their language and all of whom were non-native English speakers.

To be new and different in a school that makes no special allowances for differences. Even after the initial shock abated, the youngsters agreed that to be an immigrant student at AHS meant being new and different in a school that made no special allowances for differences. They felt that teachers and counselors treated them like all other students. Directions were given only once, clarification was not offered unless the students asked for it, and acronyms and specialized jargon were used without explanation. One immigrant student commented that if he were the principal at AHS: "I would tell the teachers to repeat things, to be clear, to be easier. American students sometimes laugh when we don't know a word. If we ask too many questions they think we are stupid."

Immigrant students reported instances when their requests for help were negatively received. One student had done poorly on a physical science test because he did not know the vocabulary. His request to the teacher to define a word was refused: "She told me 'I can't tell you the words or I give you the answers.'"

To make mistakes due to procedural ignorance. The immigrants also said they had made mistakes due to procedural misunderstanding. One student reported finishing a test a few minutes late and being left all alone in the classroom. He placed his test in a work basket and hurried off to his next class. When he got the test back the following day, the grade had been reduced by half. The teacher explained that the test paper was not with the others and, indeed, he had not found it until that day. The teacher thought the student might have taken it home and written all the correct answers. The student said he "didn't think" to argue with the teacher or see a counselor, although he was disturbed about the implication of cheating as well as with his low grade on the test.

To experience frustration due to language. Beyond having procedural difficulties, the immigrant students experienced frustration due to their limited fluency in English. Demonstrating knowledge in fast-paced classroom discussions was challenging even for fluent speakers. Making friends with English speakers was difficult because of immigrant students' fears that they would be laughed at if they made mistakes.

To be ignored and to be invisible. Finally, immigrant students felt that because they were different from the Americans, AHS was not a particularly friendly or welcoming place for them. One student ventured: "Maybe because we came in the middle of the year and the others [students] already had their own friends. They didn't seem too interested in getting to know us." Another said that if he hadn't been so sensitive to being laughed at, he might have made more friends at school. The immigrants felt almost as if they had no status in the school.

Teachers' views. Unlike the teachers at CBI who interacted exclusively with immigrant students, most of the AHS teachers dealt primarily with American students. This colored their views of what it meant to be an immigrant student.

Immigrant students should be treated like American students. Teachers and administrators expressed the view that AHS was a rigorous academic environment in which all students were given the same chance to succeed. The ideology that several of them expressed in interviews was that immigrant students needed to be treated like American students, for the sake of "fairness." The assumption was that "fairness" necessitated treating every student in the same way, and that offering special treatment was not in the best interest of the immigrants.

Specifically, teachers defined "a chance to succeed" as presenting students with opportunities to make decisions and to think and work independently. Several of the observed classes were structured around students' progressing at their own pace. The teacher outlined general expectations for projects and left it up to students to decide the order in which to undertake them. Students who did nothing, or who spent more time visiting with friends than working, suffered by having their grades lowered. Teachers emphasized that assuming individual responsibility for one's actions was the most important value they attempted to convey in the classroom. For that reason, help was given when requested but rarely offered.

Immigrant students are different from American students. Nonetheless, teachers recognized that immigrant students were different from American students in significant ways related to learning. First, they were aware that the immigrants were handicapped by their lack of English fluency, and felt the students might make better grades once their English improved. Second, teachers compared immigrant students favorably to American students: "The bilingual [students] will work themselves to death. They are not heard, there are no complaints," and "But they *try* so hard—they want so much to learn. It's a much more rewarding experience for a teacher."

Teachers perceived that, for the most part, immigrant students were far more involved with schoolwork than in the social life of the school. One teacher commented, "That might make theirs a pretty lonely existence." Several noted that the immigrant students did not get involved in extracurricular activities as often as American students:

> [To be successful at AHS] students need to be involved beyond the classroom: involved in class activities, athletics, the student body, International

Club. There are a number of activities in the school so students can find their niche, be a spectator or participant. [They can] go to the football games even though they don't understand, [so that] they can reach out and make friendships beyond their ethnic group.

Immigrant students receive some special considerations. Despite the ideology that all students should be treated the same, teachers and administrators provided some special considerations. There existed at AHS the grade of "bilingual pass," for immigrant students who worked hard in academic classes but were unable to obtain passing grades. There was an ESL class taken by almost all entering immigrant students to improve their English fluency. There were some part-time "bilingual tutors" (this was their title, although at least one insisted that the students speak English to her at all times "to improve their English") who provided special help to immigrants: assisting with academics, arranging their class schedules, and familiarizing them with school policies. Finally, some classes were offered as "bilingual." Although they were conducted entirely in English, the students were all non-native speakers and the pace was slower than in regular classes.

Obviously, resources were expended on the immigrants' behalf, in compliance with federal guidelines. Additionally, teachers frequently mentioned that a particular student would pass their class regardless of the final average because she or he had "tried hard" to do well. Although the ideology specified "fairness" as treating everyone the same way, there was recognition on the part of the school system that immigrant students needed (and should be provided) some extra assistance in adjusting to school.

Summary. From both teachers' and students' views, conscious efforts were made to treat immigrants like all other students in the school. Teachers considered this necessary in order to be fair to all students, yet at the same time, they tried to give the immigrants some special consideration. The students were aware of the availability of additional assistance (e.g., ESL classes, tutoring), but felt that teachers did not take their limited English into account when evaluating them.

Question Two: What are the Concerns and Needs of Immigrant Students During Their First Year in American High Schools?

CBI

At CBI, two categories of concerns and needs of immigrant students emerged. These clustered around social/cultural and academic/procedural aspects of their lives.

Social/cultural needs and concerns. Students frequently expressed confusion or distress at cultural differences between home and school expectations. Merely being expected to speak up in a classroom full of people was a new and frightening experience for some. Teachers were sympathetic to such difficulties and tried to let them participate in ways in which they were comfortable. Teachers also mentioned that students needed the contrasts between the American system and their home country to be explained in neutral, nonjudgmental, yet specific ways. Two teachers discussed the difficulty of accomplishing this:

> *Teacher 1:* It's hard because you don't want to embarrass [the students] when they come in wearing something strange, and you don't want to seem judgmental but then they could get laughed at on the outside.
>
> *Teacher 2:* What do you do when they come in to class with knee-high hose on and a skirt? You can't exactly say, "that's wrong," because in their country it looks fine. Or try to explain the difference between a party dress and an interview outfit; the idea is you put on something *nice* and they put on their *nicest* clothes.

Emotional support from peers. Teachers verbalized the importance of peer support, especially from L1 peers, for immigrant students to feel comfortable in school. It was apparent from observations that most students felt this concern quite strongly, grouping themselves with L1 peers in class, in the cafeteria, and in hallways. There were some exceptions, for example, an Iranian student who spoke proudly of the Chinese and Korean friends he sat with on the school bus everyday. For the most part, however, the immigrants took comfort in the presence of L1 peers from whom they could request help, share jokes, and generally feel less "out of the ordinary." Those students who had no L1 peers were almost always loners. Sometimes, sharing a first language was an insufficient basis for friendship formation. There were two Ethiopian students (one female, one male) from the same region of the country who spoke the same dialect. Because Ethiopian teenagers are traditionally segregated from the opposite sex, the two seemed unwilling or unable to have more than minimal contact with one another. In their case, the cultural mores of the home country outweighed all else.

Reinforcement for helping abilities. As mentioned previously, teachers felt students needed strong reinforcement of their willingness to help one another and the staff. Attempts to provide that reinforcement had been built into the institution's policies. An administrator remarked that, although helping skills might be considered "prelearning" in some environments, "it's hard to learn anything if you're socially isolated . . . [getting these students to feel comfortable at school] seems like a necessary condition for having positive experiences in that environment." CBI's view was that a constructive way to accomplish the goal of getting students to like school was to incorporate a positive aspect of their home culture, that of helping other people, and then recognize them for doing it well.

Academic/procedural needs and concerns. Teachers perceived a number of academic and procedural concerns of students facing school socialization as a part of the experience of adapting to American culture. Students' perceptions of their concerns and needs were evident largely through observation of their responses to teachers' attempts to meet the needs.

A simplified environment. A need, sometimes academic and sometimes procedural, was that expectations for behavior be explicit. The immigrants seemed fearful of looking ridiculous, hence were reluctant to be first to respond to a novel request or to offer an answer about which they were not entirely sure. Teachers attempted to meet their needs for simplification by delineating details of assignments and procedures carefully, and by assuming that students had little background knowledge.

Individual attention. Teachers and administrators felt that students required a great deal of individual attention appropriate to their varied backgrounds and capabilities. This attention extended from assistance in the classroom to guidance within the school system and to the network of agencies that dealt with refugee issues. Because immigrant students' unstable circumstances outside of school frequently affected their abilities to learn, CBI staff made efforts to be aware of these problems and concerns, and to help resolve them when possible.

Material needs. Circumstances at immigrants' homes included material needs that had to be satisfied before students could learn. Expecting students to come prepared with basic school supplies was often asking too much. At the least, it involved sending a list of unfamiliar items home to a family of limited English speakers who might not even know where to obtain such items. Students who might have arrived in the city only days before beginning school needed information about transportation. Even more basic was the need for appropriate cold-weather clothing. Having lived in tropical climates, most immigrants had little idea of what kinds of clothing were required for cold weather. CBI maintained a "free closet" of winter clothing donated by people in the community. Teachers and staff who noticed students who seemed unprepared for the cold offered them the chance to select warm items.

In sum, the CBI staff's perceptions of immigrant students' needs encompassed everything from explicit instructions for classroom tasks to the most basic human needs for clothing. Although they recognized limits to the school's ability to assist in meeting all of these needs and concerns, they were keenly aware of them and attempted to guide students to people and agencies who could assist them. Observations indicated that teachers were justified in their attention to students' survival needs.

AHS

By the time the immigrant students transferred from CBI into AHS, their initial survival needs had been met. They were able to procure school supplies, to arrange transportation to and from their new school, and to make more inferences from less-explicit instructions regarding assignments. Their English fluency had improved so that communication was less of a struggle. Still, most immigrant students continued to rely heavily on bilingual dictionaries and, when available, translators.

Since there were so few immigrant students at AHS, they felt a more urgent need for English fluency. Teachers were not accustomed to repeating directions, avoiding colloquial usage, and explaining familiar procedures in detail. Teachers would have viewed those as impractical strategies in classes where only one or two students were non-English speakers. Needs and concerns that stemmed from lack of familiarity with the American school system had been resolved through time and exposure at CBI. Their minority status and added emphasis on English fluency, however, exacerbated other social/cultural, academic, and procedural needs they experienced at AHS.

Social/cultural needs and concerns. At AHS, the immigrant students were exposed to a range of behaviors not unlike those witnessed by the fictional Kien and Mai: students complaining about their parents, food fights, open violations of school rules that went unnoticed, casual attitudes toward schoolwork, and open disrespect to authority figures. It is inaccurate to say that the students perceived a need to have this system explained in order to make sense of their place within it. The immigrants looked upon the seeming disorder as if detached from it; they said they tried to be nonjudgmental of this type of American behavior, and were careful not to get involved in obvious violations of the rules.

Their primary concern in such situations was how to "fit in" with the social system well enough to make American friends. The immigrants attributed their difficulties in making friends to a lack of specific strategies for doing so as well as to language limitations. Just as significant is the fact that the immigrants were outsiders in a setting where no one could, or would, make explicit the cultural premises underlying social action.

AHS staff, on the other hand, perceived a need for the immigrant students to get involved in extracurricular activities. Such involvement was viewed as a sign of self-motivation, one of the crucial characteristics of "successful" students as defined by AHS. Somehow, the connection between extracurricular activities, making friends, and success in school was never emphasized to the immigrant students. This may account for the almost total lack of involvement of the immigrants in those activities.

Another social need perceived by AHS staff was that the immigrants gravitate toward academically oriented peer groups, and in this respect the immigrants seemed to succeed. The friends they made were largely other immigrant and bilingual students who were motivated to succeed academically.

Academic needs and concerns. A prominent concern expressed by the immigrant students during interviews was that of making good grades. This was a complex issue for them during their first semester at AHS, in that they had registered for classes later than the students who were already there. Most of their first-choice classes were full, and the immigrants were placed in classes such as typing, business machines, and guitar. Although they expressed some frustration at being closed out of their first-choice subjects such as biology and math, there was some relief that their workload was not too demanding while they got used to the new school.

Partly because of the nonacademic nature of several of their subjects, the immigrants perceived the schoolwork at AHS to be much less demanding than what they had experienced in their countries. In some academic subjects, they actually were ahead of their classmates and were able to do well. In others, the immigrants encountered a great deal of difficulty and were in danger of failing. One student sought help from a bilingual tutor, but found it of limited value in raising her grades in that subject. Another said he had tried asking the teacher for help, but that little was forthcoming. By the end of the year, both students had resigned themselves to low grades in the computer class as an inevitable consequence of their limitations in English.[2]

Procedural needs and concerns. As previously stated, the immigrants often found procedural instructions to be unclear. They hesitated to ask questions for fear of looking silly in front of their classmates. All expressed the concern that Americans might laugh at them for their lack of familiarity with matters that seemed very simple to natives, such as who among their teachers was the "roll teacher," what was the role of a "TA" in instruction, and so on.

To their credit, the teachers seemed aware that immigrant students

---

[2] It must be noted that the four students who participated in the second phase of this study were described as "above average" in academic preparation and ability by their teachers. Although aware that the students experienced difficulty in some subjects, the teachers expressed optimism that they would be successful academically once their English improved.

were sometimes reluctant to show their ignorance in front of classmates. One teacher encouraged a Spanish-speaking immigrant to sit near another student who spoke Spanish and allowed him to ask her questions in class. For the most part, however, the teachers were at a loss as to how to respond to this concern. "Singling out" the students for individual assistance before it was requested was viewed as contrary to encouragement of self-motivation. More concretely, the teachers wanted to avoid embarrassing the immigrants by drawing attention to them. In many cases, the students had no choice but to proceed as best they could on incomplete understanding and contextual cues, and assume that with time and exposure to AHS matters would improve.

Question Three: What is the Role of Communication in the Socialization of Immigrant High School Students?

This question sought to explore several facets of communication as it related to the process of socialization of immigrant students. The functions of communication are examined, including the communication strategies used.

CBI

Communication functions for students. Immigrants engaged in communication that served four functions. These included informative, regulative, innovative, and integrative.

Informative. Students provided help to teachers and their peers by translating, explaining procedures, and demonstrating required performances to their peers. Students reported satisfaction at being able to help one another in this way, and gratitude that such assistance was frequently available to them from L1 peers. With a complex new system of meaning to be learned, sharing information among group members was a valuable communication strategy for doing so.

At the same time, students needed to obtain information. This information seeking often occurred in pairs or groups. For example, two students approached the secretary to find out about the bus, two students jointly formulated questions in class, and three students went to the librarian to ask how to check out a book. Making requests for information into group endeavors seemed to be reassuring to students who were uncertain about how to get needed information. One teacher commented that, having studied a second language herself, she knew that the most intimidating aspect of the process was admitting ignorance to native speakers:

Sometimes it seems like you're asking only the simplest, most obvious questions in the world, that somehow you don't know, and it's easy to feel really dumb. You're not even sure you're asking the questions correctly, and you end up having to be pretty desperate to know something before you're willing to take that kind of chance.

Regulative. Students' early and frequent attempts at communication, beyond seeking and providing assistance, centered around compliance with the stated rules for behavior. They asked teachers for permission to help one another, to share books and materials, and to leave the room on various errands (e.g., asking questions of the BAs, borrowing bilingual dictionaries from students in another class, seeing the school nurse). A teacher remarked that having this degree of flexibility in their behavior was often a new experience for the immigrants who had come from more rigidly controlled systems of education. For those students who had had little or no previous schooling, knowing how to follow classroom procedures was a complicated learning task. One teacher elaborated:

I try to get students real used to these blue slips (indicated pad of excuse slips on her desk). I encourage them to ask me for them, to go to the bathroom or the office or whatever. With a real inexperienced class, even the physiological constraint of only being able to go to the bathroom during class changes takes some getting used to....

Students also reminded each other of the rules and seemed pleased to display their knowledge of them. On one occasion several students were running down a hallway and another student said firmly to them, "No run! WALK!" Another time a teacher started to remind her class that the designated smoking area had been changed:

Teacher: Now instead of room 121, it's outside. Everyone has to go outside to smoke.
Student: No, teacher! Now no smoke!
Teacher: No, I think it's OK to smoke outside, out there in front.
Student: No smoke now anywhere!

Innovative/integrative. A final type of student communication, the performance of novel behaviors that were required in order to become part of the new school system, served both innovative and integrative functions. The immigrants learned several American rituals in their months at CBI (e.g., reciting the Pledge of Allegiance), and participation in them was viewed as a step toward becoming part of the American high school world.

Another new ritual was the celebration of Halloween. Although Halloween may not be celebrated in every high school by students and teachers dressing up in costume, most schools put aside work for a time. The immigrant students were at first astonished at the idea that frivolity would be so rampant in a serious place like school. Several teachers and the principal dressed in costume, and one teacher painted designs on students. Participation in this ritual was a novel kind of holiday experience for students. Perhaps more importantly, they witnessed institutional superiors and subordinates relaxing and laughing together without any subversion of the authority structure.

Immigrant students also engaged in linguistic play in English. In an ESL class, for example, a number of unsolicited verbal "practice runs" were heard as students waited to be called on: "Youuuu speak Englit verry well." (laughter) "Do you speak Englit? Yeah, I speak Englit t'ank you." Much of the lesson was commands: Point to the window, walk around the table, give the green book to her. Then:

Teacher to student:	You be the teacher and tell me what to do.
Student:	Jump to the window. (teacher complied) Jump to the door.
Teacher:	This is too hard! (while complying)
Student:	Jump to the office. (class collapses in giggles)
Teacher:	(smiling) Later I will.

This kind of linguistic play existed as a shared code among teachers and students, and allowed the latter to practice the new language in nonthreatening ways. The immigrants who were part of L1 peer groups faced a double-bind related to language learning. The friends with whom they were most comfortable were the ones with whom they could communicate in their own language, yet speaking their own language slowed the process of learning English. Speaking English to their L1 peers was difficult because "it feels so strange," as one student said, "like you trying to be smarter than them." Speaking English in joking ways, however, provided opportunities to practice the language without alienating themselves from the L1 group. It also offered protection from the fear of making mistakes; if someone laughed at what the speaker said in English, the laughter could be assumed or pretended to pertain to the joking intent, rather than an incorrectly formulated utterance.

Communication functions for teachers. Teachers articulated three assumptions as the basis for their strategies for communicating with students: (a) Much of the information students need to comply with school demands is never written down and must be made explicit orally, for example, information must be repeated more than once. (b) "Help" means watching students carefully and stepping in to provide individual assistance, not merely issuing general directives. Students may be floundering and reluctant, or unable, to seek assistance. (c) Forces outside of school may be hampering students' adjustment. Teachers and staff should make every effort to find out about home life, mental and physical health, and the degree to which students are familiar with American high school ideals and procedures. With that knowledge as background, expectations for students should be geared to them as individuals. Guided by these assumptions, teachers utilized communication to serve four functions.

Informative. Teachers often framed the act of giving information about American high schools in terms of explicit contrasts with the immigrants' home countries. One teacher explained the proper address term for a teacher in this way: "I know in your country you call your teachers 'Teacher' (nods all around.) Here in the U.S. we like our names much better. I would like it if you would call me Ms. _____ ."

Another type of informative communication at CBI had to do with providing "help." As previously described, the preferred mode of giving help was to offer it without requiring a student to ask, to make instructions and explanations as clear as possible, and to repeat everything more than once. A teacher giving the first test of the year to her class, for example, gave the following instructions:

> Please put your books on the floor or under the desk. On the floor, or under your desk. They may go *on* the floor or on the shelf under your desk. You may not have them in front of you. All you need is a pencil. You may put your paper away, I will give you paper. . . .

Another instance of the informative function was that of teachers' requests for help from students and BAs. Teachers utilized students as sources of information about their countries, the customs within school systems, and their languages. Many times, the teachers were simply interested, and had found elicitation of such information to be a good way to get students to talk. Teachers also needed information in order to compare and contrast American schools to the schools students had attended previously. They relied on students to translate and to help one another whenever several students needed attention at one time.

Regulative. Teachers used communication to regulate classroom behavior in two ways. First, they made corrections of several kinds. They corrected students' English output frequently:

> *Student:* Did you was in my country before?
> *Teacher:* What? Did you WALK in my country before?
> *Student:* DID YOU WAS in my country. WAS. (Several repetitions, help from other students trying to clarify sense of the utterance to teacher.)
> *Teacher:* Ohhh. Did you GO to my country before?

Teachers also mandated structure during classroom discussion (e.g., "Hold up your hands, please, if you know the answer. I want one person to answer at a time this time."). Finally, there were times when teachers insisted on use of English. During an ESL class, a teacher was helping a student to construct an oral answer to a question she had asked. When other students began to help him in Arabic, she admonished: "Don't help him unless it's in English."

A second regulative function was sanction of noncompliance with teachers' mandates. Teachers detailed consequences of failure to follow the rules:

> I would like to say "sit down" only once, because we have lots of students. Does everyone understand? If you don't understand I'll move your chair over here so you'll be lonely, no one to talk to. No friends around.

On a broader scale, one of the documents students received on their first day at CBI was a chart that outlined offenses of various severity: smoking in an unauthorized area, unexcused absence, fighting, carrying weapons at school, and so on. There were several disciplinary actions spelled out: detention, grade penalty, note to parents, suspension, expulsion. For each offense, a corresponding sanction was specified.

Innovative. Communication served an innovative function in the socialization of immigrant students to CBI when teachers utilized materials and information from students' experiences as a focus of classroom discussion. A reading comprehension exercise, for example, described the experiences of an immigrant family that had come to the United States. The teacher used the reading to stimulate discussion of the students' own experiences in coming to America. In another class, a teacher showed a film made in Cambodia. Sighs were heard around the room from the Southeast Asian students who recognized landmarks and terrain from their home countries. The film served as a springboard for class discussion, as the students from that region explained the cultural traditions underlying the story.

In interviews, teachers said they made efforts to incorporate materials from students' cultures in order to provide some bridge of familiarity into the process of language learning and socialization. The idea seemed to be that the more students could relate instructional aims to their own recent experiences, the more effective the instruction could be. Teachers were willing to use innovative strategies and seek out materials relevant to students' lives in order to make that connection in the classroom.

Integrative. A final function of communication was to integrate immigrant students into the social network of American high schools. Two aspects of the integrative function were that teachers facilitated positive contact with the American students at CBI and prepared students for the transition to American high schools.

For structural reasons CBI students did not ordinarily have much contact with the American students in the building. Teachers reported, however, attempts to bring the immigrant students into contact with the Americans when the experience would be positive for all involved. For example, several American students volunteered to serve as teacher's assistants for the immigrant program. One teacher said that the assistant in her class had been very helpful in giving individual attention to students who needed it and that the experience seemed favorable for his self-esteem: "You know all the (immigrant) kids just looked at him like he was Superman." There also were attempts to share information about the immigrants' backgrounds with Americans. The visit from the students from another high school, described earlier, was one such effort, and joint assemblies (for immigrants and Americans) was another.

Preparing students for the transition to American high schools was a second integrative function of communication. Teachers led class discussions on strategies for making conversation in English with people they did not know, talked about proper ways of addressing a teacher, and described the procedures that students would encounter when they transferred to their new school. Several of the teachers expressed regret, however, that this particular objective received too little attention in the classroom. They were aware that entry into American schools was a tremendous shock for the immigrant students and wished that they could do more in the way of preparing students for the change.

AHS

Communication functions for students. At AHS, students used communication that served predominantly informative and integrative functions.

Informative. The students' needs for obtaining information greatly increased upon entering AHS. One complained that "teachers say things one time, and if you don't get it, well, that's your problem." Therefore, the major informative function served by communication at AHS was to request help: extra explanation, repetition, or demonstration of the desired performance or procedure. At times they made such requests of the teachers or counselors, but were reluctant to do so too frequently. They more often requested information from other students, especially other immigrants. They may have felt more confident of their question-formulation competence with peers, and/or less concerned that the inquiry itself would be perceived as inappropriate, as sometimes happened with teachers.

A second informative function of communication was the process of learning the school's specialized vocabulary and acronyms. This kind of argot is generally assumed by insiders of a system, in that specialized terms are used in talk without explanation even when newcomers are present. Examples of such argot at AHS were "roll teacher" (the second period teacher who keeps official count of students' absences) and "TA" (an upperclass student who assists a teacher during one class period per day). Some terms, such as "unassigned period," were fairly straightforward in their denotative meaning: a period in which a student has no assigned class. The implications of a period being "unassigned" were not explicated, however, for the immigrant students. Even at the end of the school year, they were uncertain whether they were free to leave campus during an unassigned period or whether they were required to stay on the school grounds.

Knowledge of some aspects of school life that were mysterious to immigrant students was perceived as inaccessible through usual methods of seeking information. They frequently commented, for example, on blatant violations of rules that went without sanction: a student who became angry at a teacher and stalked out of class without asking permission, cigarette smoking in places where it was expressly prohibited, and students wearing shorts to school regardless of the dress code that prohibited them from doing so. Like Kien and Mai in the fictional passage, they were puzzled by students who sat in the back of classrooms doing nothing, or reading paperbacks, without comment from the teacher. All of these examples were aspects of life that were taken-for-granted by the "insiders" of the AHS system, but difficult for newcomers to comprehend or even formulate inquiries. The critical point is that no system of conduct may ever seem entirely intelligible to a nonmember. Contextual cues may eventually reveal the meanings of argot, and trial and error may establish the limits of acceptable variation from behavioral norms. Gathering and transferring information about a complex social system such as a school, however, is never as straightforward as indicated by the admonition to "ask questions about anything you don't understand."

Integrative. Becoming integrated and "feeling like a part of things" at AHS required development of social skills in English. In addition to linguistic fluency, the immigrants felt they needed specific strategies for pursuing nonacademic bonds with Americans. They reported feeling that they lacked those strategies. Although a classroom session observed at CBI involved a discussion of how to make friends with Americans, the immigrants who transferred to AHS felt that their efforts to do so had been largely unsuccessful by the end of their first semester. Their contacts were limited to occasional interactions in the classrooms and in the cafeteria.

A primary strategy for making friends referred to repeatedly by teachers and administrators was participation in extracurricular activities. As mentioned, however, that approach to integration into the school social system seemed not to occur to the immigrant students. Two of the students indicated a desire to participate in sports, but dropped the idea when they were unable to be placed in the necessary physical education class. One student attended the annual International Dinner, but that event drew almost exclusively international students. Teachers and administrators commented that the immigrants' lack of participation in extracurricular activities was the greatest handicap to their being completely socialized into AHS, yet never seemed to encourage them directly to do so. Communication thus served an integrative function in the socialization process of immigrant students into AHS, but from both students' and teachers' perspectives, that function was not fulfilled adequately.

Communication functions for teachers. The teachers engaged in communication primarily to serve informative and regulative functions.

Informative. A pervasive aspect of the informative function was that of detailed oral and written orientation to rules and assignments. Once a rule or assignment had been explained, either orally or in writing, students could then be held accountable for it. A great deal of such orientation took place on the first day of classes, as in the following example:

> *Teacher, talking to class:*   First thing you'll do is buy a disk like this—it has to be activated first, what you've got at THIS point in time is a dead disk. You'll need to have one of these to do your assignments off of. . . . (handed out a typed syllabus; no dates yet, but assignments laid out.). . . . I'll help individuals who are having problems and I'll talk to the class if there's a specific thing everyone has trouble with, but basically you're on your own.

Having outlined the procedures that the class would follow, the teacher's expectation was that all such information was now shared and could be assumed within the group.

Another type of information dissemination was providing extra help to students who requested it. Teachers indicated that they perceived a great deal of extra help was available to any student, including immigrants, who showed herself or himself to be trying hard and who took the initiative to request it. They described themselves as always willing to provide explanation, demonstration of a required performance on a task, or repetition of instructions. They also identified for students other resources that were available: a study skills lab, student assistants for particular classes, tutoring, a career center, and the library. All that was required, they stressed, was individual "motivation" to utilize those resources.

Perhaps because of the belief that help would most appropriately be given to those who actively pursued it, no direct offers of help occurred during classroom observations. The teachers perceived the informative function of communication to be one of informing students of the avenues for extra assistance that were open to them. After that, as one commented, "it's up to them whether they make use of what's available to them."

A final type of informative communication initiated by teachers was that of offering opportunities for students to "participate," that is, to display the individual initiative that was considered so crucial to success. Several teachers made announcements early in the term that the structure of their classes was such that students were expected to make choices about when and how to approach the tasks they were assigned. Making wise choices and taking responsibility for their choices were described by teachers as the most important learning experiences they felt students needed in high school "so they learn to stand on their own two feet."

Regulative. Related to the informative function of communication to provide orientation to assignments were regulative statements of school policies regarding student behavior. Beyond district and schoolwide policies, each teacher had individual standards for grading and discipline that were outlined at the beginning of the semester. These policies were distributed in writing and also elaborated orally, along with consequences for their violation:

> *Teacher to class:*   Absences. When you have 15 absences you're *out.* No questions asked. . . . Tardies. You get three tardies, you go to detention. That's an hour after school. You miss detention, you go to Saturday school.

In addition to the outlining of discipline policies, communication was also used for behavior correction. Such correction was sometimes direct: While students were working on an individual assignment, the noise level of talking and shuffling chairs rose and fell. When it became loud, the teacher said "QUIET!" in a voice that carried through the room, without looking up from his desk. On other occasions, the correction was nonverbal and more subtle. During one classroom observation, a student returned a yearbook to its owner. Looking carefully at the teacher, the student held the book over a table and let it fall with a loud slam. The teacher looked over, made eye contact with the student, and the student picked up the book and handed it gently to its owner. The teacher returned to his previous task without comment, and the student walked quietly back to his desk.

Summary. At CBI, teachers structured the communication environment to accomodate non-native speakers and to reinforce their cultural backgrounds while introducing them to American school procedures. At AHS, in contrast, teachers and administrators communicated their expectations and the opportunities available for students to utilize resources according to their own level of initiative. Socialization was viewed as a process of instilling self-motivation in students, "teaching them to stand on their own two feet," as it was often described.

Question Four: What Are the Critical Status Passage Dimensions for New Immigrants in American High Schools?

The first passage was into CBI, a program specifically for immigrants, where both ESL instruction and liberal use of bilingual aides and materials were part of the curriculum. The second passage was into AHS, a school which included an ESL class and some tutoring assistance for certain language groups, but one that for the most part followed a policy of "mainstreaming" the immigrant students as much and as early as possible. Thus, the temporal dimensions of the passage to the status of student in an American high school followed a definite progression for this group of students. The first semester (September to February) was spent in a context of little contact with American students, while the second semester (February to June) was spent in a school with predominantly American students. Since CBI served an overflow function, passage into it was *not inevitable* and was *irregular* and *unscheduled*. The transfer to AHS, however, was an *inevitable, regular, scheduled* event. Student passage to AHS was not *reversible* in that the district did not permit students, even if unsuccessful in a regular high school, to return to CBI.

The social dimensions of the two passages were distinct. Students entered CBI *alone*. Once there, however, those who had L1 peers began to constitute a collective who sat together at lunch, interacted during free time, and shared concerns. There was an *awareness* of the group and a great deal of *communication* among these youngsters. For those who had no L1 peers or whose only L1 peers were of the opposite sex, however, the passage was experienced as an aggregate. There was an awareness of other newcomers, but little communication because of the language barriers or sex differences.

In contrast, students entered AHS as an *aggregate*. There was an *awareness* that other immigrants had transferred as well, but students were isolated from one another due to differences in grade levels and schedules. Asian students seemed to maintain closer contact with their L1 peers after arrival at AHS than did other language groups. Students who were relatively isolated upon entry into CBI because of a lack of L1 peers continued in this pattern at AHS as well. Thus, some of the immigrants *communicated* with one another at AHS and others did not.

The *clarity of the signs* of the passage to being a student in an American high school was recognized with different degrees of *formality* at CBI and at AHS. CBI marked the entry of new students at the beginning of the school year with an orientation assembly, during which everyone was welcomed and given basic instructions in several languages. As other new students arrived throughout the semester, they were assigned a "buddy" who was responsible for showing them to their classes, explaining the system of bells and lunch shifts, and introducing them to teachers and L1 peers. Teachers routinely took a few minutes to introduce new students to the class:

Teacher, to new student:	How long were you in the camp?
Student:	Ten month.
T:	TEN MONTHS? Wow, that's really a long time. Did you leave by plane or by boat?
S:	Boat.
T:	How long were you on the boat?
S:	One month.
T:	Thirty days, my goodness. Did you have enough food and water?
S:	No. Forty people. My sister die. No food or water. 40 people, 7 die.
T:	I'm sorry to hear that. (Went on to another new student, repeated questions).

As horrifying as this experience was, the teacher drew upon it as a way of acknowledging the student's status as a new immigrant, and thus creating the opportunity for bonds to form with other students.

At AHS, the immigrant students' entry took place after semester break, when a certain amount of change was occurring for all students. They registered for classes, were issued a schedule and a map of the building, and were on their own. Aside from the immigrants themselves and their teachers, this status passage seemed to go unnoticed and virtually without comment. As an immigrant student appeared in a classroom, teachers inspected her or his schedule card to see that the student was in the right place and wrote down her or his name. They frequently added an informal welcome, "Hi, glad to have you. Find a chair somewhere."

Because the researchers had no contact with these students before the school year began, it is difficult to determine whether the first status passage was *desirable* or not. Before the transfer to AHS, however, the students reported eagerness to enter the regular high school. Although somewhat apprehensive that the academic work might be more difficult, the students were excited about the opportunity to meet more Americans and to take a wider variety of subjects.

With respect to the *centrality* of the status passage to the students, it varied according to their acculturation. Socialization into school is but one aspect of the acculturation process to American society. Some students had survived conditions so traumatic (and sometimes were still struggling to survive) that adjustment to school was almost the least of their daily concerns. Other immigrants were absorbed in the task of adapting to the new school, and their primary objective was attempting to do well there.

DISCUSSION

The socialization experience for the immigrant students differed dramatically between the two educational settings. CBI existed as a special program designed to accommodate the unique needs of incoming immigrant students. AHS, in contrast, embodied the general view that immigrant students should be given the same chance to succeed—no less and no more—as any other student in its rigorous, academically-focused environment.

Schools are frequently conceptualized as communities which create and sustain unique patterns of beliefs and thought which influence the behavior of individuals within them. They are therefore often described as constituting "cultures," such that shared meaning exists among students, teachers, and administrators about the central beliefs and values which organize experience in the school. These systems of beliefs and values are in turn described as cultural themes or metaphors that underlie communication within the school.

This characterization seems appropriate for capturing the different experiences the immigrant students in this chapter had during their stay at CBI as contrasted with AHS. Their socialization into "the American high school system" involved learning two highly distinctive cultural systems, in which the functions and nature of communication varied. Even their identity as incoming students was different between the two schools.

Cultural Theme at CBI

A common theme in the socialization process at CBI was "accomodating students' needs." The student body at CBI was perceived as distinctive due to the nature of the "needs," and the system of meaning within the school was largely defined in terms of meeting those needs. Staff members at CBI recognized a potential for students to be caught in cultural conflicts between their home environment and the values of the school. The unfamiliar American system created a need for reassurance and validation of the students' cultures. Instruction was thus adapated to provide that validation.

Communication at CBI clustered around a perception of students' needs that extended beyond instructional content and the school's responsibility to help them to meet those needs. Peer assistance was encouraged and recognition of students' efforts to help each other received a high priority in the reward system of the school. Teachers and aides made active efforts to engage themselves in students' work to provide extra explanation or translation when necessary.

Expectations were made explicit and repeated frequently, down to minute details of school procedure, in an effort to help students to make sense of the unfamiliar system. Violations of procedural rules were usually treated as misunderstanding or forgetfulness, and were corrected rather than punished. Students were assumed to be highly motivated to learn, despite significant barriers to their doing so, such that reassurance and encouragement about their abilities were also high priorities for teachers.

Cultural Theme at AHS

At AHS, by contrast, a theme which was expressed in several forms across different domains of activity was "it's up to you," that is, it is up to the students to determine the quality of their experience in school. A range of choices was made available to students, and the amount they learned was largely dependent on the nature of the choices they made. A cogent statement of this orientation was a sign posted in an office window in the main hallway of the school: "A failure to plan ahead on your part does not necessarily constitute an emergency on my part." This is not to imply that staff members at AHS were uninvolved or unconcerned about the students' circumstances. Teachers were willing to assist any student who asked for guidance, any student, that is, who "chose" to ask for help.

Communication at AHS thus revealed a perception of students as individual choice makers. Teachers laid out assignments; it was up to students to follow directions and complete them. The school district published requirements for graduation; students were responsible for choosing among the classes offered each semester to make sure they had enough credits at the end of four years to meet those requirements.

Perceptions of these themes differed between the staff and the immigrant students in that the staff saw the degree of choice open to students as an opportunity for individual decision making and expression. The students, on the other hand, perceived the emphasis on their own initiative as a lack of interest in their welfare.

Comparison of CBI and AHS

One notable difference between the schools was the conceptualization of students at CBI as newcomers who required instruction about the system as well as academic guidance. The view of students at AHS was of persons who were procedurally knowledgeable, requiring only academic guidance. Socialization to school procedures was thus an explicit agenda at CBI, such that helping students to learn the system was an important theme. At AHS, the implicit socialization agenda was preparation for an adult world where success would be dependent on an ability to make wise choices.

Unsurprisingly, the cultural themes of each school were reflected in the tasks that were accomplished. CBI provided a comfortable, nurturing atmosphere in which incoming immigrant students could learn a great deal about formal schooling and about certain procedural aspects of American public schools. The emphasis on helping and interdependence, however, may not have prepared students adequately for the individualistic orientation of AHS or the more rigorous academic demands. Conversely, AHS provided a more challenging and varied academic program, yet was by some standards unresponsive to the array of needs of immigrant students.

A Concluding Note

The fears and difficulties that faced Kien and Mai in the fictional account, *A Long Way from Home*, were realities for the immigrant students discussed in this chapter. They were newcomers to the country and to the school system. During their first year they had to make sense of two disparate school environments with contrasting philosophies. It was through communication that their socialization occurred.

chapter 8
Conclusion: Communication and Socialization

This final chapter presents a summary and synthesis of the empirical studies described in the previous chapters and discusses how the data fit with the conceptual frameworks explicated in Chapter One. Communication is highlighted as being at the heart of the socialization process.

We were in class when the head master came in, followed by a "new fellow," not wearing the school uniform, and a school servant carrying a large desk. Those who had been asleep woke up, and everyone rose as if just surprised at his work.

The head master made a sign to us to sit down. Then, turning to the class master, he said to him in a low voice:

"Monsieur Roger, here is a pupil whom I recommend to your care; he'll be in the second. If his work and conduct are satisfactory, he will go into one of the upper classes, as becomes his age".....

We began repeating the lesson. He listened with all his ears, as attentive as if at a sermon, not daring even to cross his legs or lean on his elbow; and when at two o'clock the bell rang, the master was obliged to tell him to fall into line with the rest of us. When we came back to work, we were in the habit of throwing our caps on the ground so as to have our hands more free; we used from the door to toss them under the form, so that they hit against the wall and made a lot of dust: it was "the thing."

But, whether he had not noticed the trick, or did not dare to attempt it, the "new fellow" was still holding his cap on his knees even after prayers were over ... "Rise," said the master.

He stood up; his cap fell. The whole class began to laugh. He stooped to pick it up. A neighbour knocked it down again with his elbow; he picked it up once more.

"Get rid of your helmet," said the master, who was a bit of a wag.

There was a burst of laughter from the boys, which so thoroughly put the poor lad out of countenance that he did not know whether to keep his cap in his hand, leave it on the ground, or put it on his head. He sat down again and placed it on his knee.

"Rise," repeated the master, "and tell me your name." The new boy articulated in a stammering voice an unintellible name.

"Again!"

The same sputtering of syllables was heard, drowned by the tittering of the class.

"Louder!" cried the master; "louder!"

The "new fellow" then took a supreme resolution, opened an inordinately large mouth, and shouted at the top of his voice as if calling someone the word, "Charbovari." (Flaubert, 1928, pp. 3–4)

The piteous plight of young Charles Bovary as a "new fellow," although grossly exaggerated by the standards of modern America, is as universal as is the classic *Madame Bovary*. The newcomer phenomenon—entering school for the first time, being a "new kid" in school, being in the lowest grade level in the school, being the "different" student in the school—constitutes an important, often exciting, and sometimes painful, set of experiences for young people throughout the student career.

The chapters in this book describe and analyze the process whereby children become pupils. In contrast with previous research that has emphasized schools as socializing agencies of young people, this volume focuses on how young people, through communication, learn the student role initially and continue to socialize into new and different roles throughout the student career. The book examines six distinct points: (a) kindergarten—entry into the first formal school experience, (b) third grade—entry into a new grade level and a new school, (c) sixth grade—entry into middle school, (d) ninth grade—entry into high school, (e) transfer—entry into high school as a transfer student, and (f) immigration—entry into high school as an immigrant student. The first four points are regular passages in the student career for most Americans, while the points of transfer and immigration constitute "twists and turns" in the career.

As is evident throughout the book, there are differences and similarities in the socialization process of youngsters at various points in the student career. This final chapter provides a summary and synthesis of the student socialization experiences with a focus on: (a) student role variations at each of the particular grade levels and new situations, (b) common threads that exist throughout the student socialization experiences, and (c) the function of communication in the socialization process.

STUDENT ROLE VARIATIONS ACROSS THE CAREER

The descriptions of students at different grade levels and situations indicate that the socialization process varies over the course of the student career. The role of student continually changes as young people confront new school situations. In order to highlight the role variations, a theme is identified that characterizes each particular student role.

Kindergarteners—Students as Novices

To be a kindergartener is to experience the first formal student role. Not only is the school environment a new one, but the role of student itself is new. Kindergarteners are truly novice students in that they have to learn to think, feel, and behave as students for the very first time.

For the children described in Chapter Two and their teachers and parents, becoming a kindergartener was a formal passage to a new status. There were a number of explicit signs and markers, including: going to school only half a day for the first week, lining up in the morning along the fence and being escorted into school, and being the first ones to eat lunch everyday. These unique signs were overt indicators of the novice status of kindergarteners and functioned to mark them as "brand new" students.

Having students learn an appropriate role was an instructional goal in the classroom. Early in the school term, the teacher repeatedly offered definitions of the role (e.g., kindergarteners as children who are special, smart, happy). She also facilitated student learning of the kindergarten role through the use of imperatives, rewards, and negative sanctions.

The school personnel established explicit expectations and procedural routines for the children. There was an overt agenda for orienting the kindergarteners to their classroom and to the culture of the school. There were privileges and restrictions that applied to kindergarteners only (e.g., being able to take an afternoon nap, being permitted to have an afternoon snack, being assigned an eighth-grade buddy for some special occasions, not being able to play on the grassy field at recess with older students). These rules were reflective of the assumption that because kindergarteners were first-time students and the youngest in the school, they needed some special attention and a gradual orientation to "studenting."

Third Graders—Students as Veteran Newcomers

To be a third grader at the school described in Chapter Three is to be a veteran newcomer, that is, one who is experienced in the student role yet new to the particular environment. Although the students were only eight years old, most had attended school for three years prior to beginning the third grade. In various studies of organizational socialization, veteran newcomers refer to those who take on a new role within a familiar organization (Jablin, 1982; Katz, 1980; Staton-Spicer & Spicer, 1987). In the case of the third graders discussed in Chapter Three, however, the students were veterans of the student role and newcomers to an unfamiliar school environment and grade level.

As if in response to the veteran newcomer status, the school administration did not give the new third graders any special consideration. Unlike the passage into kindergarten which was distinguished by explicit markers, the passage into third grade was not characterized by any degree of formality. There were no orientation meetings and the third graders were not set apart from other students in the school either structurally or physically (except for having their own classroom).

The classroom teacher also treated the youngsters in a way that implied her belief that they were not novices, but seasoned students in an unfamiliar setting. She gave little attention to defining the student role per se or instructing the third graders in how to enact the role. She focused instead on bringing the cohort of third graders together as a cohesive group. She assumed that because they were familiar with the student role they already had an understanding of the nature of classroom academic tasks. She emphasized the norms and procedures she wanted operationalized in the classroom and contrasted these with "the way you may have done things in second grade." She wanted them to function as a group more effectively than they had been able to as students in earlier grades. In her classroom talk, the teacher stressed the importance of being responsible, following directions, working independently, and demonstrating a higher level of academic performance. She felt it was reasonable for all students to display these characteristics because they were already familiar with the academic system, that is, veterans of schooling.

Middle Schoolers—Students as Developing Adolescents

To be a middle schooler is to be considered no longer a child in an elementary school, but rather an older, more responsible youngster approaching adolescence. The passage to middle school was a formal one with clear signs. During the spring prior to the opening of school, the youngsters attended an open house at their respective middle school. They reported that their fifth-grade teachers tried to prepare them for middle school. The first week was marked by a formal orientation session for the sixth graders, apprising them of school regulations and procedures. The administrators delineated constrasts between elementary and middle school. Although the orientation of middle schoolers differed from that of kindergarteners, both were formal in nature. The formality served to acknowledge that teachers and administrators viewed these transition points in the student career as major ones.

With entry into middle school came the assumption of greater maturity. Additional responsibilities and privileges accompanied the greater maturity expected of middle school students. They had more freedom and privileges than they had experienced previously (e.g., having a combination lock on one's own locker, selecting one's own coursework, having a variety of selections on the lunch menu).

The school administrators also emphasized greater responsibility by acknowledging that the youngsters were maturing physically. At each of the middle schools where sixth graders were observed, the main speech at the opening orientation assemblies directly addressed the issue of students' "changing bodies." They were cautioned about aspects such as privacy and assured that the administration was there to help them with any problems or violations of the sanctity of their bodies.

Along with the idea of increased maturity and responsibility was an explicit assumption that these youngsters were now capable of committing adult crimes. The opening orientation speeches were peppered with warnings about crimes that must not be committed and consequences for offenders if crimes were committed. The offenses identified were not "childish" ones of chewing gum or wearing inappropriate clothing, but were adult ones such as larceny, assault and battery, and defacement of property. Middle schoolers were considered responsible youngsters, more mature than children, yet still not quite adolescents.

High School Freshmen—Students as Serious Adolescents

To be a high school freshman is to be an adolescent, no longer a child. As the ninth graders described in Chapter Five socialized into high school, teachers and administrators gave them more freedom and autonomy than they had experienced previously in school (e.g., students could leave campus at lunchtime, students could smoke on the school grounds). Teachers focused on academic instruction and did not act as "watchdogs." They expected completion of academic work in a timely fashion and compliance with school rules. At the same time there was not the daily checking on and prodding of students that characterized the lower grade levels.

Although the role of freshman was accompanied by increased academic and procedural freedom, there was an acknowledgment by school personnel that the process of becoming a high school student could be difficult and that students might need assistance and support. Each of the two inner city schools had a required orientation course for freshmen during the first term. The course addressed such topics as developing study habits and using the library, and served as a formal mechanism to facilitate socialization. It should be noted, however, that the administration placed more emphasis on academic issues than on social ones. This is in contrast to socialization into middle school where school personnel at both schools acknowledged that sixth-grade students were entering a new and different system, yet felt that an orientation assembly was a sufficient formal mechanism. The emphasis of the two middle school assemblies was more on social dimensions than on academic ones.

The high school experience was framed as "the real thing." Academics were accorded the highest priority by school personnel and there was explicit comment about grades now counting toward getting into college. This was in contrast to views of elementary and middle school as being mere preparatory academic experiences. Although students and teachers articulated the importance of achieving well in high school in order to ensure future academic opportunities, the emphasis was on high school as important in its own right. Being a freshman was being an authentic, serious student.

Transfers—Students as Social Outsiders

To be a transfer student is to be a social outsider. Despite the isolation of some, the transfer students whose experiences are reported in Chapter Six viewed high school life not as a solitary one, but as eminently social. To be integrated into the high school and to feel a sense of belonging required that one be part of the social scene, that is, to have a network of friends. Making sense of the academic demands, new procedural norms, and the physical environment of the school was a relatively simple, straightforward task for most of the new students. The difficulty was in the social domain.

Transfer students made the passage to the new school alone; they had no cohort or ready-made group of friends. They were social isolates at the point of entry into the new high school. For those who were aware of and able to implement various strategies for making new friends, the socialization process was not too difficult. For those who were reluctant to participate in school activities and who did not seem to make friends easily, the entry process was a trying one. Socialization for the transfer students was a process of becoming social insiders.

In contrast to the socialization experiences of middle schoolers and high school freshmen, there were no formal orientation mechanisms for the transfer students. There was not even an orientation assembly or meeting of all transfer students at the beginning of the school term. There were caring administrators and staff within the school, but the transfer students had to seek support and encouragement for themselves as they enacted their new role.

Immigrants—Students as Strangers

To be an immigrant student is to be a stranger in a new school and in a new country. Although the immigrants described in Chapter Seven had been students in their home countries, they had to learn the role of American high school student. Often that was a disparate role from the one to which they were accustomed. In some instances it required speaking up in class and actively asking questions of the teacher, in contrast to an expectation of student silence in the classrooms of their native countries. The informality in the interaction between teachers and students was another difference that students faced.

During their first academic year as students in America these immigrants were strangers in two schools, the Center for Bilingual Instruction (CBI) and American High School (AHS). Unlike the other students described throughout the book, the immigrants experienced entry socialization twice. They were strangers as they entered both schools, but the experiences were unique (e.g., at CBI there was readily available support and assistance with academic and procedural matters; at AHS there was only minimal special consideration, the assumption being that immigrants should be treated like American students in order for the system to be "fair").

In addition to being newcomers to the school, immigrant students were also strangers to the city, state, and country. They had to make sense not only of the school environment, but also of the larger systems in which the school system was nested. And all of the sense making was undertaken, not in the student's native language, but in a second language. Since the immigrant students were often the most fluent English speakers in their families, they frequently had to take primary responsibility for meeting many of the basic needs of their families. At times, this responsibility detracted from the youngsters' efforts to be students and slowed their transition from stranger to bona fide member of the school.

Summary of Student Role Variations

From the first experiences of kindergarteners as novices to those of high school freshmen as responsible adolescents, the role of student changes, develops, and evolves across the career. Indeed, the requirements for being a "competent" (Mehan, 1980) elementary school student, with an emphasis on compliance with teacher directives, are often in sharp contrast to requirements for being a "competent" high school student (e.g., making sound decisions about what courses to take, managing time in a way that maintains a healthy balance between academics and extracurricular activities). Fortunately, these requirements for the student role are not usually sudden, but are changes that occur gradually throughout the student career.

In the chapters dealing with regular career passages (that is, kindergarten, third grade, sixth grade, ninth grade), there is evidence of a progression from a focus on developing the elementary school students as group members to developing the high school students as individuals. The kindergarteners had minimal freedom and autonomy, in contrast to that of the new middle and high schoolers. Emphasis on responsibility and independence increased with each passage to a higher grade level.

COMMONALITIES OF STUDENT PERSPECTIVES ACROSS THE CAREER

Despite variations in the evolving student role throughout the career, there were also common threads and themes that emerged. All students expressed *uncertainty* about various aspects of the new role and/or school environment and articulated *concern* about the socialization experience. There were also similarities in the dimensions of the *status passage*. This section synthesizes results according to the three conceptual frameworks.

In considering the commonalities, it is important to keep in mind that the experiences occurred during the entry phase. The only data collected during the anticipatory socialization phase were from the kindergarteners who were interviewed three months prior to their entry into school. The only data collected over a duration longer than the first school term were from the immigrant students who were observed and interviewed throughout an entire academic year. Since they entered a different school at the middle of the year, however, it is reasonable to view the immigrants as students who experienced entry socialization twice during an academic year, that is, at CBI and at AHS. Thus, the similarities in the socialization experiences of children and adolescents are contextualized in the entry phase and cannot be generalized to other phases.

Uncertainty During Socialization

Since the entry phase of socialization is a time of uncertainty, students across the span of the elementary-secondary career are in need of role-specific knowledge about a variety of dimensions. As Berger and Luckmann (1966) state:

> Secondary socialization requires the acquisition of role-specific vocabularies, which means, for one thing, the internalization of semantic fields within an institutional area. At the same time "tacit understandings," evaluations and affective colorations of these semantic fields are also acquired. The "subworlds" internalized in secondary socialization are generally partial re-

alities in contrast to the "base-world" acquired in primary socialization. Yet they, too, are more or less cohesive realities, characterized by normative and affective as well as cognitive components. (p. 138)

In their examination of preparing teachers for uncertainty, Floden and Clark (1988) identify two types of uncertainty that are also relevant to student socialization: (a) uncertainty of knowledge, or uncertainty about what is true (related to academics and content), and (b) uncertainty of action, or uncertainty about what to do (related to appropriate behavior). In considering this conceptualization of uncertainty as it relates to Berger and Luckmann's (1966) components of socialization, a three-pronged framework incorporates the types of uncertainty faced by the students described in this volume and the types of information they needed to reduce: (a) knowledge or cognitive uncertainty, (b) behavioral or normative uncertainty, and (c) affective uncertainty.

When students experience *cognitive uncertainty*, they are in need of specific information about academics and the content of instruction. When students experience behavioral or *normative uncertainty*, they need information about the school and its procedures and regulations. When students experience *affective uncertainty*, they require information that will provide emotional support and reassurance. The uncertainty facing the students examined in this volume can be categorized according to the three domains. (See Figure 8.1.)

Cognitive domain. Students across the grade levels expressed uncertainty about the academic dimension of schooling. Kindergarteners and third graders sought information about the classroom learning tasks, that is, what they were supposed to do. The middle schoolers requested specific content information about their homework assignments as well as about their classroom assignments. The high school freshmen and transfer students sought information about the subject matter, the academic program, requirements for graduation, and teacher expectations. The immigrant students also asked content-related questions, first of their same language (L1) peers, then of a teacher or staff member if necessary.

Normative domain. Students at each grade level expressed uncertainty regarding the school norms and procedures. Although teachers and school staff provided a great deal of procedural information, students still engaged in information seeking. They sought general information about the school (e.g., directions for locating specific places in the building, instructions and assistance in opening their lockers), the classroom, and their various teachers. They also requested specific information about what procedures to follow, what routines existed, and what social norms were operating (e.g., rules for classroom interaction, rules for utilization of free time during lunch).

	Cogitive	Normative	Affective
Kinder-garteners	Information about classroom work: -using upper & lower case letters -tracing letters	Information about rules & procedures: -volunteering for class chores -behavior sanctions	-not observed
Third Graders	Information about classroom tasks: -finding the main idea of a story -checking wprk when finished	Information about rules & procedures: -getting out of one's seat -bringing notes from home -getting supplies	-not observed
Sixth Graders	Information about content: -topic for a paper -rounding numbers -spelling particular words	Information about rules & procedures: -how to open locker -how to check out a book -where to sit -how to find classes	Information to reassure that middle school: -will be fun -students will do well -students will get used to it
Ninth Graders	Information about school & subject matter: -academic program -graduation -teacher expectations	Information about rules & procedures: -finding one's way around the school -learning about the school -getting registered	Information: -to reassure -to provide a sense of belonging
Transfers	Information about school & subject matter: -academic expectations -class assignments -academic requirements	Information about norms: -dress code -appropriate place to smoke	Information: -to reassure -to provide a sense of belonging
Immigrants	Information about content: -vocabulary words -assistance with assignments -translation	Information about norms, rules, procedures: -permission to use restroom -checking out a library book -appropriate place to smoke -discipline policy	Information: -about difference between home & American culture as basis for friendship formation -to provide a sense of belonging

Figure 8.1. Types of Uncertainty and Information Needed.

Affective domain. The elementary school children made no overt attempts to seek information to reduce affective uncertainty. The kindergarteners and third graders were not observed engaging in this type of information seeking, nor did they express the need for such information during
interviews. Since the school experience was so new for these young children, one might expect them to seek affective information. What seemed
to be the case, however, was that they focused instead on gathering information about the academic content and about how to follow the school
policies and procedures.

In contrast to the elementary school children, all middle and high
school youngsters expressed uncertainty in the affective domain. The
sixth graders sought information from others assuring them that middle
school would be fun, that they would do well, and that they would adjust
to it. The need to reduce this type of uncertainty did not emerge from
observations of or interviews with kindergarteners or third graders, which
suggests a developmental dimension. The ability to express overtly that
one is uncertain about how well she or he will do in a new environment
requires a certain level of conscious awareness that primary grade children may not possess. This finding also suggests that from students' perspectives, socialization into elementary school is predominantly academic
and procedural, while socialization into middle and high school is largely
affective.

The affective uncertainty experienced by the high school freshmen and
transfer students had to do with their needs for emotional support, for
making friends, and for acquiring a sense of belonging in the new school.
The immigrants also felt uncertainty about a sense of belonging in the
school. To accomplish it was more difficult for them, however, than for
the freshmen or the transfer students. They needed information about the
differences between their home culture and the American culture as a
basis for forming friendships and developing a sense of belonging.

Summary of uncertainty. During the process of socialization, students
faced uncertainty in three domains: cognitive, normative, and affective.
Students across the elementary, middle, and high school levels expressed
cognitive and normative uncertainty. In the affective domain, however,
only the middle and high school youngsters were observed seeking information to reduce uncertainty.

Concern During Socialization

As discussed in Chapter One, the entry phase of socialization can be
viewed as a time when students are likely to have high levels of concern
about *self* (e.g., concern about one's adequacy, about "fitting in" in the

new environment) and about *task* (e.g., concern about how to structure one's time to keep up with homework demands and to participate in sports). Although a concern may be related to an uncertainty, the two are distinct. An uncertainty is a lack of information about a particular domain or issue; a concern is a personal frustration or a problem situation that one seeks to resolve. Information serves the function of reducing an uncertainty. Information does not necessarily function to resolve a concern; reassurance and support may also be required. Students at all grade levels observed, and in all situations described throughout the book, had concerns about their socialization experience that could be categorized as self or task. (See Figure 8.2.)

Self concern. Self concerns were evident for all of the students except for third graders. These concerns were identified or inferred from observations, interviews, and questionnaires. Kindergarteners and immigrants had similar self concerns about *social* aspects. Middle schoolers, freshmen, transfers, and immigrant students expressed similar self concerns about *social* aspects. Finally, middle schoolers and freshmen had similar *status* concerns about self.

Certain types of self concern are similar conceptually to uncertainty expressed in the affective domain. Concern about fitting into a new school situation may manifest itself in feelings of uncertainty which may result in the student seeking information to reduce the uncertainty. A reduction in uncertainty may then function to resolve the concern.

A type of self concern that was shared by kindergarteners and immigrant students was *social* concern about public embarrassment and face saving. There were a number of public embarrassment concerns for the kindergarteners that resulted in crying: wetting pants, being reprimanded in class, being unable to answer a teacher's question, and spilling milk in the lunchroom. Additional support is given to the idea of public embarrassment being a concern in that the children would not admit to having cried, even when they knew the researcher had witnessed it. For the immigrants, there was a concern that they not appear foolish in the presence of classmates. They were reluctant to speak out, to ask questions, and to respond to questions about which they were uncertain, for fear of being wrong and subject to ridicule. Although this concern may differ from the kindergarteners' on a surface level, the essence of the concern is the same.

The *social* concern articulated by middle schoolers, freshmen, transfers, and immigrants related to feelings of being alone in the new school, needing to meet people and make friends, being anxious about fitting in and being accepted by others, and feeling insecure about the many new dimensions of school life. Although there were a variety of concerns expressed, the core concern for these secondary school students was the same.

	Self Concerns	Task Concerns

Kinder-
garteners
	Social—separation anxiety
	   being around older & larger students
	   public embarrassment
		Academics—doing harder work

Third Graders	—not expressed	Academics—doing harder work

Sixth
Graders
	Social—fitting in
	   meeting people
	Status—being picked on & pushed around
		Academics—doing more difficult work
		   doing homework
		   turning in assignments on time
		Environment—how to get around in the new school

Ninth
Graders
	Social—fitting in
	   meeting people
	Status—being put down
		Academics—doing more difficult work
		   doing more homework
		   getting good grades
		Environment—how to get around in the new school

Transfers	Social—fitting in
	   meeting people
		Academics—doing more difficult work
		   doing more homework
		   getting good grades

Immigrants	Social—fitting in
	   meeting people
	   public embarrassment
	   (not appearing foolish)
		Academics—explicit expectations
		   getting good grades
		Environment—how to get around in the new school

Figure 8.2. Concerns.

Related to the *social* concern of the adolescents were two types of self concern expressed by the kindergarteners. One expressed repeatedly by two of the kindergarteners was that of separation anxiety (from parents and home). This concern was manifested by the children crying and clinging to the parent each day when they came to school. Another type of self concern related to anxiety about being in a new and unfamiliar setting where older students were present. Again, there were instances of crying when a child got lost in the building or had a problem with older students on the playground. These are related to the concerns about insecurity expressed by the adolescents.

The *status* concern expressed by sixth and ninth graders related specifically to their respective roles as youngest in the school. The sixth graders expressed concern about the older students and the threat of being "picked on" and "pushed around." The ninth graders were concerned about being "put down" by older students (verbally) and about physical harm.

Task concern. There were two types of task concern common to children and adolescents. Students at all grade levels expressed task concern about *academics*. In addition, the middle schoolers, freshmen, and immigrants articulated task concern about the *environment*.

Both the kindergarteners and the third graders expressed concern about doing the academic work. The concern surfaced during interviews with the youngsters, not as anxiety about their ability to perform more difficult work, but as a business-like task concern about how to do "harder work." Similarly, the middle schoolers expressed task concern about the difficulty of the academic work, the increased responsibility of doing homework, and turning in assignments on time. Again, this type of concern did not center on the self (e.g., my own adequacy and ability), but on the actual task (e.g., how does one accomplish difficult assignments and always remember to get them in on time without reminders from the teacher?). The task concern of the freshmen and transfer students centered around doing more homework, doing more difficult work, making good grades, and being assigned the desired classes. The immigrants expressed academic concern about how to get explicit expectations from teachers and how to make good grades.

There was also task concern expressed by the middle schoolers, freshmen, and immigrant students that related to the new *environment*. One aspect of concern for sixth and ninth graders was that of being in a much larger physical facility and the idea of simply "getting around." Interestingly, this concern was noticeably absent among the transfer students. Perhaps because all had been in a high school setting previously, they knew how to approach the task of finding their way around. (Or perhaps because they were older, these students would not admit to having such a relatively simple concern.) A different type of environmental task concern of the immigrants related to how to find their way around the city as well as the school. Such dimensions as using the city bus system and knowing where to go for school supplies are examples.

Summary of concern. Students expressed a variety of self and task concerns about their socialization experiences. With the exception of the third graders, students across grade levels and school situations expressed *self* concern related either to their *status* in the new role or their *social* situation in the new school. For the third graders, it cannot be said that they did not have any such concerns, merely that none was expressed or observed. All of the students expressed *task* concern related either to *academics* or to learning the new *environment.*

Status Passage Dimensions

Throughout the book the characteristics of the passage to a new student status have been examined. As presented in Chapter One, 18 properties of status passage served as the framework to guide the analysis. To facilitate a comparison of these properties across grade levels and situations, it is helpful to cluster them into categories: *temporal dimensions:* whether (a) inevitable, (b) regular, (c) scheduled, (d) prescribed, (e) reversible, (f) repeatable, and (g) the length of time or duration in the passage; *social dimensions:* (h) whether alone, in a collective, or an aggregate, (i) awareness of the collective, and (j) communication with others in the passage; *procedural dimensions:* (k) degree of choice, (l) degree of control, (m) legitimation required, (n) clarity of signs, (o) whether signs are disguised, and (p) degree of formality; and *value dimensions:* (q) desirability, and (r) centrality.

For the routine status passages that are experienced by almost all American youngsters (that is, kindergarten, third grade, sixth grade, ninth grade), there are commonalities across the four categories of dimensions. The two passages that constitute unusual points in the student career (that is, transfer, immigrant) are similar generally to one another, but different from the more routine passages. (See Figure 8.3.)

Temporal dimensions. For kindergarteners, sixth graders, ninth graders, and immigrants entering AHS, the passage was considered inevitable and was viewed as a regular, scheduled event that was a "taken-for-granted." Kindergarten was accepted as the first step in the student career and there was no classroom talk, either overt or implied, about any likelihood of the children not progressing. Similarly, the passages to middle and high school were planned events, assumed, and there was no evidence of talk about the passage being reversed or repeated. For the immigrants, passage from

	Kinder-gardeners	Third Graders	Sixth Graders	Ninth Graders	Transfers	Immigrants CBI	AHS
Temporal 1. Inevitable	Yes	Yes	Yes	Yes	No	No	Yes
2. Regular	Yes	Yes	Yes	Yes	No	No	Yes
3. Scheduled	Yes	Yes	Yes	Yes	No	No	Yes
Social 4. Alone, Aggregate, Collective	Collective	Collective	Collective	Collective	Alone	Alone	Aggregate
5. Awareness	Yes	Yes	Yes	Yes	No	Some	Some
6. Communication	Yes	Yes	Yes	Yes	No	Some	Some
Procedural 7. Clarity of Signs	Yes	Some	Yes	Yes	Student perceived-yes By school-no	Yes	No
8. Formality	Yes	No	Yes	Yes	No	Yes	No
Value 9. Desirability	Yes	Yes	Generally	Generally	Mixed	No data	Yes
10. Centrality	Yes	Yes	Yes	Yes	Yes	To some degree	To some degree

Figure 8.3. Salient Status Passage Dimensions.

the bilingual center to a regular high school was an established part of the school system routine about which there was no question.

In contrast, teacher talk in the third-grade classroom often focused on the issue of what had to happen and what students must accomplish in order to progress to fourth grade. Although the passage into third grade was assumed, the teacher frequently articulated that passage to the next status was not inevitable, and that third grade could be repeated if students did not work at the appropriate level.

The temporal dimensions of the passage for transfer students and immigrants entering CBI were largely different from the dimensions for all of the other students. Entry into a new school as a transfer student is usually an irregular occurrence that is unscheduled and not inevitable. Because this type of passage often occurs as a result of parental job transfer or divorce, it is typically unpredictable and occurs without much forewarning. Similarly, entry into the bilingual program at CBI was unscheduled and not inevitable. Since CBI accomodated students when other programs were full, entry into it was not inevitable.

Social dimensions. All groups of students experienced their respective passage as a collective except for the transfer students and the immigrants. Kindergarteners, third graders, middle schoolers, and freshmen began the school year as a cohort; all were newcomers together to the new environment. (The social dimensions are discussed in more depth in a later section of this chapter.)

Procedural dimensions. The two procedural dimensions most salient for the elementary, middle, and high school youngsters were the degree of formality and the clarity of the signs of the passage. For the most part, the signs of the passages were clear and marked with a degree of formality.

As discussed, passage into kindergarten was formal, with a number of overt signs. Additionally, the teacher made direct references to "kindergarteners" and talked about what kindergarteners do and how they act. The passage into third grade was not so formal; the third graders were not singled out by procedural markers as were the kindergarteners. The passages to middle and high school were considered formal and accompanied by distinct signs (e.g., the orientation assemblies).

School personnel did not attempt to formalize the transfer student passage or make available clear signs. Perhaps because students embarked on this type of passage alone, it was not considered as formal as those passages in which a large number of students are involved. For the students themselves, however, the signs of their status as outsiders were explicit: a lack of familiarity with the new physical setting and a lack of integration into the social network of the school.

For the immigrant students, entry into CBI was a formal event replete with various signs of the passage (e.g., an orientation assembly and assignment of a "buddy") and somewhat like that experienced by the middle schoolers and new freshmen. The passage to AHS, however, was similar to that experienced by the transfer students in that it was unheralded by school personnel and was not accompanied by any formal markers.

Value dimensions. The passage into the new status seemed to be highly desirable for the elementary school children, and generally desirable for the middle schoolers and freshmen. For the transfer and immigrant students, however, the desirability was mixed.

Prior to the opening of school all kindergarteners expressed a desire to attend. Once school began, the talk centered around kindergarteners being distinct and being special in the school. Thus, the passage was seen as desirable and central to the children. Being a third grader did not have quite the same distinctiveness that being a kindergartener did, yet it was clearly a desirable passage and central to them. Students articulated various new privileges they possessed as third graders, and generally expressed positive feelings about being a "big kid."

The passages to middle and high school were considered generally desirable and central to the students, thus constituting positive value dimensions. The sixth graders felt older, more grown up, and glad to be out of elementary school. In their view a higher status was accorded them as middle school students. Similarly, the status of high school freshman was a central one that the new ninth graders internalized very quickly. To be a high school freshman was more than an external label, and seemed actually a part of the self-concept for many of the students. For both the sixth graders and the ninth graders, their respective passages were welcome, but they expressed some misgiving about being once again the youngest students in the school.

The passage to transfer student cannot be clearly designated as either desirable or undesirable, because the desirability varied with individual student motivations. Some of the students were glad to have left the former school and embraced the move to a new one; others sorely missed friends from the previous school and were not newcomers by choice. So too, the passage to immigrant student at CBI was desirable for some and undesirable for others. The transfer from the bilingual center and into the regular high school, however, was desired and eagerly anticipated.

Summary of status passage. Ten of the 18 properties which initially guided the description of the status passages across grade levels and school situations emerged as most helpful in comparing the various passages. These included: (a) whether inevitable, (b) whether regular, (c) whether scheduled, (d) whether the person goes through alone, as an aggregate, or as a collective, (e) awareness of others in the passage, (f) communication with others in the passage, (g) clarity of signs, (h) degree of formality, (i) desirability, and (j) centrality.

COMMUNICATION DURING SOCIALIZATION

Communication was defined in Chapter One as the process by which people attempt to create and negotiate shared meanings and understandings with others in society. The children and adolescents described in this volume interacted with a variety of others (e.g., teachers, administrators, peers, family members) to create and negotiate appropriate student roles and to make sense of the new school environments. As demonstrated throughout each chapter, communication is integral to the socialization process.

In this section, communication is discussed as it relates to the reducing of uncertainty and the resolving of concern, the status passage dimensions, and the functions it serves. Communication is the means by which students seek (and teachers and others provide) information and reassurance to reduce uncertainty and resolve concern about the new student role and school situation. Communication is also a critical aspect of several of the most salient status passage dimensions. Finally, it serves important informative, regulative, and integrative functions during socialization.

Communication to Reduce Uncertainty and Resolve Concern

It is through communication that students gain the needed information and reassurance to reduce uncertainty and resolve concern as they socialize into new student roles and school environments. Students engage in communication strategies to seek information and reassurance. Similarly, teachers utilize communication to provide information and reassurance to students. As students reduce uncertainty and resolve concern, they progress toward becoming socialized students.

Communication strategies of students for seeking information and reassurance. Students used a range of information seeking strategies for reducing uncertainty in the cognitive, normative, and affective domains, and for resolving self and task concerns. The ways in which the elementary school children sought information in the normative and cognitive domains were similar. Both the kindergarten and third-grade children listened to their teachers as they explained subject matter and work assignments, and outlined policies and procedures. They complied with teacher directives and engaged in occasional reprimands of others, that is, peer discipline. Some kindergarteners also engaged in acts of noncompliance with teacher directives and of imitating other students. Through these strategies youngsters learned and negotiated what it meant to be an "acceptable" student in the classroom.

Although listening to teacher directives and complying with them can be considered indirect, the strategies of peer discipline and noncompliance require initiative and risk. A student would seem to possess self-confidence in order to reprimand others for deviating from class rules. Similarly, noncompliance, or testing the limits of the rules, is an assertive behavior. A child who does not comply with teacher directives is deviating from the student role prescribed by the teacher and is active in constructing and negotiating her or his own role.

With respect to all three types of uncertainty, the middle schoolers engaged in communication strategies that ranged from highly direct to indirect. These included: overt means, being interpersonal, asking indirect and rhetorical questions, testing limits, observing behavior, getting around in the school on one's own, and "hanging loose."

The high school freshmen identified communication strategies for information seeking only in the affective domain. They reported several strategies: participating in school activities, being interpersonal, being introduced by a common friend, being themselves, and impression management. They did not mention any particular strategies for acquiring information about academics or about school regulations.

The transfer and immigrant students gained information about the academic content (cognitive domain) and the school rules (normative domain) by asking direct questions and by watching others. In the affective domain, the transfer students engaged in strategies of participating in clubs and sports, asking questions of classmates, joining in conversations, and meeting others through common friends, teachers, or parents. The immigrant students asked questions of peers, teachers, aides, and other school staff. At AHS, the need for obtaining information was greater than at CBI, but there were fewer instances of the immigrant students asking direct questions of teachers. At AHS, the strategy of asking questions of peers was most frequent.

Teacher-initiated communication to provide information and re-assurance. As evidenced throughout the book, most students sought information and reassurance as needed. What also emerged from the observational data, however, was that teachers often provided information and reassurance before students expressed such need. Thus, teacher-initiated communication to reduce uncertainty and resolve concern is another important aspect.

At the elementary school level, there was a great deal of teacher talk that functioned to provide information about the student role. The kindergarten teacher, for example, made explicit comments defining what it meant to be a kindergartener. She also used verbal imperatives, rewards, and negative sanctions as ways of gaining student compliance with desired behavior. Similarly, the third-grade teacher offered comments characterizing "what third graders do." She used verbal communication strategies of giving explicit directions, reprimanding violations, asking questions, praising, and repeating rules in order to clarify the desired student behavior. She also engaged in nonverbal strategies such as finger snapping, disapproving facial expressions, use of a particular tone of voice, and hand and arm gestures.

At the middle school level, teachers provided information and attempted to influence student role learning through explicit classroom talk about their expectations for student behavior. Teachers communicated their expectations proactively by stating rules, and reactively by issuing verbal reprimands for violations of their expectations. The middle school teachers also provided general information to students about school activities and offered frequent encouragement and praise without solicitation from students.

At the high school level, teachers also gave information and reassurance. The freshmen reported that teachers were an important source of information about what the school had to offer, how the school worked, and directions. The transfer students did not mention the same degree of teacher-initiated communication as did the freshmen, although they indicated that teachers provided information about academic content and introduced them to their classmates. Teachers of the immigrants at CBI engaged constantly in providing and repeating unsolicited information about academic content, school and classroom procedures. They also offered continual affective support and reassurance. Unsolicited information giving at AHS was not as prominent, although most of the teachers initiated oral explication of rules, procedures, and class assignments at the beginning of the term.

Communication During Status Passage

Communication is an important aspect of several of the critical status passage dimensions examined in the empirical studies. Three of Glaser and Strauss' (1971) status passage dimensions are centered in communication: (a) whether the newcomers experience the passage as a collective, an aggregate, or alone, (b) whether the newcomers are aware of the collective or aggregate, and (c) whether the newcomers communicate with one another. As Glaser and Strauss describe, the "simplest visualization of how important those conditions can be is to imagine the differences ... of whether someone goes through passage in concert with others rather than as a solo passage" (p. 116). Taken in conjunction, these three dimensions constitute a *social* cluster in which communication is central.

Kindergarteners, third graders, sixth graders, and ninth graders all experienced the passage to a new status as a collective. Because each group constituted a cohort in the respective new school, each had a ready-made set of peers with similar problems, needs, and concerns. The passage was formal with clear signs, although less so for the third graders than the others. School personnel made explicit the signs of the passage (e.g., the sixth grade orientation assemblies warned students about the consequences of committing crimes).

The elementary school children who experienced the passage as a collective were generally aware of the group and communicated freely with one another. Their teachers often referred to the five-year olds as "kindergarteners" and gave them a considerable degree of freedom to talk with one another, during class, recess, and lunch. As discussed in Chapter Two, the regular teacher used a family metaphor to develop a sense of unity: "We are like brothers and sisters. We are together every day. We see each other every day." In the third-grade class there were fewer references to the group as a whole, although the teacher talked about looking out for one another (e.g., asking the children to account for those who were absent) and being "good neighbors." She also make frequent use of the term "we" in response to an individual act (e.g., "I know we're tired. We need to yawn more quietly.").

The sixth and ninth graders were also fully aware of the cohort and there was a great deal of explicit communication among the youngsters and on the part of the school personnel about the collective. Students were recognized as being newcomers who needed information about the new role and the new school environment. In one of the middle schools, for example, most classes for sixth graders were located on one hallway of the same floor, with the lockers located outside of the classrooms. This physical proximity served to promote interaction among the sixth graders and fostered their communication about the new experience.

Consistent with the middle school students, freshmen at all four of the high schools experienced the passage as a collective, with full awareness of the collective, and many opportunities to communicate with one another about it. The social dimensions of the status passage were important in that the schools made conscious efforts to bring the students together as a group. School personnel referred to them, not as high school students, but as "freshmen." Distinctions were made often between freshmen and the upperclassmen, ensuring that everyone was aware of the students as a cohort. The ninth graders attended classes primarily in the company of one another and had numerous forums for communication. The "orientation course" was one particular place in which talk among the students about the freshman experience was encouraged.

Unlike the students who experienced the regular passages as a collective, the transfer and immigrant students made their passage either alone or as an aggregate. Overall, the socialization experience for these youngsters was more difficult (and was accomplished less easily) than for the other groups of students. The transfer students and the immigrants who entered the bilingual program began school as isolates and had no immediate peer group with whom they could share concerns, exchange information, and interact. Nor did the four immigrant students who transferred from CBI to AHS constitute a cohort. Because they knew one another at CBI, there was an awareness of an aggregate of immigrant students, but no real sense of a community of newcomers. Unlike the elementary and middle school students who were in the same classes, the transfer students enrolled in different courses. The immigrants were placed in classes at AHS as individuals, not on the basis of their status as immigrants. The one exception to this was the bilingual class. Because of the stigma attached to it (that is, bilingual classes were considered remedial and served students only until they were ready for regular classes), it did not function to bring the youngsters together in a meaningful way. Thus, the lack of communication among the transfers and immigrants seemed to have been a factor in the difficulty of their socialization.

Functions of Communication

Across Chapters Two through Seven, communication has emerged as the means by which students seek (and teachers and others provide) information and reassurance to reduce uncertainty and resolve concern about the new student role and school environment. It is also an important aspect of the passage to a new student status. As a way of synthesizing this view of communication, Greenbaum's (1974) functional framework is useful. Three of the categories of his four-function model are most applicable in delineating the functions of communication in the process of student socialization: (a) informative—communication related to the giving and seeking of information about cognitive and task dimensions, (b) regulative—communication related to the giving and seeking of information about normative and task dimensions, and (c) integrative—communication related to the giving and seeking of information and reassurance about social or affective dimensions. (See Figure 8.4.)

Informative. For all students in new situations described throughout the book, communication was the means by which they sought and acquired cognitive and task information and reassurance. They utilized a variety of communication strategies to reduce uncertainty and resolve concern about academic matters (e.g., subject matter content, academic program, classroom and homework assignments, teacher expectations, grades). Similarly, it was through communication that teachers provided academic information and support to students. Finally, for the older stu-

	Informative	Regulative	Integrative
Kinder-garteners	Cognitive uncertainty - content Task concern - academics	Normative uncertainty - procedures	Self concern - social
Third Graders	Cognitive uncertainty - content Task concern - academics	Normative uncertainty - procedures	-not observed
Sixth Graders	Cognitive uncertainty - content Task concern - academics	Normative uncertainty - procedures Task concern - environment	Affective uncertainty - reassurance Self concern - social & status
Ninth Graders	Cognitive uncertainty - content Normative uncertainty - procedures Task concern - academics environment	Normative uncertainty - procedures	Affective uncertainty - reassurance Self concern - social & status
Transfers	Cognitive uncertainty - content Normative uncertainty - procedures Task concern - academics	Normative uncertainty - procedures	Affective uncertainty - reassurance Self concern - social
Immigrants	Cognitive uncertainty - content Normative uncertainty - procedures Task concern - academics	Normative uncertainty - procedures Task concern - environment	Affective uncertainty - belonging Self concern - social

Figure 8.4. Functions of Communication.

201

dents, there was a continual exchange of normative information about school procedures (e.g., freshmen, transfers, immigrants) and the physical environment (e.g., freshmen, transfers).

Regulative. Communication was the means by which students sought and acquired normative and task information. Students used a number of information seeking strategies to learn about school policies and procedures to which they were expected to conform. Through communication, teachers and administrators conveyed expectations to students about their definition of an appropriate student role. Communication was also the mechanism by which the new middle schoolers and immigrants learned their way around the new school environment (e.g., by following directions provided by or solicited from teachers, peers, administrators).

Integrative. Communication was the means by which students sought and gained affective and self-related information to resolve their concerns. Students needed and received reassurance and emotional support about their new role and status through communication with a variety of others. Teachers and parents conveyed to youngsters that the new student role would be fun, that they would do well, and that they would "fit in." Through interacting with peers, students learned how others in the school viewed their status. And finally, through communication, students made friends and developed a sense of belonging.

CONCLUSION

In Chapter One socialization was broadly defined as a dialectical process in which individuals enter new sectors of society and learn new roles. In Chapters Two through Seven the three conceptual frameworks of uncertainty reduction, concern, and status passage were used to illuminate student perspectives and to describe the socialization experiences. Socialization can be viewed as a communication process of acquiring information and gaining reassurance to reduce uncertainty and to resolve self and task concern during the passage to a new student status. Synthesis of the research presented throughout the book supports this conceptualization. To socialize successfully into a new student role in a new school environment requires cognitive, normative, and affective knowledge. According to Mehan (1980), in order for students to socialize into the classroom community, they must learn the rules of the community, interpret the context, and integrate the interactional form and academic content. As this occurs, young people move toward becoming competent students. The students described throughout this book continually sought information and expressed concern about academic, normative, and affective dimensions of their new student roles and their new school environments.

Although all students needed knowledge and reassurance in the three domains, being a competent student was not equivalent at the different career points. This was due to variations in the student role across the career. Indeed, the socialization process for elementary students (kindergarteners, third graders) focused primarily on academic and procedural issues and concerns, while the process for secondary students (middle schoolers, freshmen, transfers, immigrants) centered in the affective domain. As indicated by the description of students' concerns and information seeking, the elementary students expressed a greater need for academic and procedural information than for affective information or reassurance. For the secondary students, however, the reverse was the case. The information they sought and the concerns they articulated were directed more toward affective dimensions.

Kindergarteners, as novice students, had to learn the student role for the first time. Accordingly, they sought a great deal of cognitive and normative information. Although some self concerns were manifested (e.g., separation anxiety, public embarrassment), these were not predominant and were resolved early in the school term. For the third graders who were veteran students, there were no self concerns expressed, but a focus instead on gaining information about classroom work, rules, and procedures. These youngsters, to become competent, needed cognitive and normative information about the new role and environment.

For the new middle schoolers and freshmen, the emphases were on greater responsibility and greater autonomy, respectively. Although both of these groups of students still needed content and procedural information, the affective domain emerged as most important to them. Students needed reassurance and a sense of belonging. Unlike the elementary school children, they expressed social concerns about fitting in and meeting people, and status concerns about being picked on, pushed around, and put down. For these young people to feel comfortable in the student role required a strong sense of self as secure in the social environment, in addition to knowledge of academics and procedures.

Finally, although the transfer and immigrant students also needed content and procedural information, socialization for them was tied integrally to the affective domain. These students entered the unfamiliar role and school as outsiders and strangers to the system. Because of prior schooling, they had some knowledge of academic content and school rules. In order to function effectively in their new student roles, they had to carve a niche in the social structure and become bona fide members of the system.

Regardless of the distinctions in the student role, it was through communication that young people developed the role and strove to socialize successfully. As discussed in Chapter One, a dialogic view of communication is one in which the focus is on the person "in relation" to others. This book has presented empirical data of classroom communication occurring between students and teachers, and between students and students. In addition, from interviews with students and from their written comments, reports have been provided of the important people with whom they interact and the information and reassurance they seek to reduce uncertainty and resolve concern. Finally, the functions of communication in the socialization process have been discussed. From the empirical data presented, it is evident that young people learn and construct the role of student as they communicate with others. Indeed, the role of student exists only *"in relation"* to others.

When students socialize successfully into a new status, there is communication that serves informative, regulative, and integrative functions. The communication interactions have been reported to be or observed to be essential in providing them with needed cognitive, normative, or affective information. And it is through communication that students resolve their self and task concerns.

Similarly, when difficulties occur during socialization, students and teachers alike attribute them largely to communication problems, (e.g., absence of a collective with whom to communicate, restricted communication among those in the cohort, limited repertoire of communication strategies for making friends, lack of fluency in the language of the school, limited understanding of the school rules and procedures, lack of knowledge about appropriate role expectations). Thus, communication is the key to understanding socialization.

A FINAL NOTE

The socialization experiences examined in this book have marked similarities with those presented in the various fictional passages. Just as Christopher Robin feared that he would be unable to do "Nothing" anymore, and Ramona Quimby had "quivery feelings" about starting the third grade, and Kien was facing the dreaded first day of school, the actual students discussed in these pages expressed concern and misgiving about taking on a new student role and entering a new school environment. Similar to Judy Blume's Tony, the transfer students described in Chapter Six entered an unfamiliar system alone, as social isolates without a cohort of other newcomers. And like the fictional girl with the middle school blues, the sixth graders discussed in Chapter Four also expressed feelings about being lost in the new and larger school. So too, as ninth grade Elsie was concerned about her image—not looking like a freshman or "sweating her new sweater," the students described in Chapter Five felt the importance

of fitting in and not looking "like a nerd." Finally, although not accompanied by the public humiliation felt by Charles Bovary on his first day in a
new school, most of the students had the experience of being unfamiliar
with the procedures, routines, and habits that were a part of the new
school environment.

The concern and uncertainty expressed about the new student role and
school environment are part of a universal phenomenon of student socialization. And it is through communication that they are resolved and the
socialization process occurs.

References

Alexander, W.M., & George, P.S. (1981). *The exemplary middle school.* New York: Holt, Rinehart & Winston.

Anderson, B.D., Haller, E.J., & Smorodin, T. (1976). The effects of changing social contexts: A study of students who transferred between high schools. *Urban Education, 10,* 333–355.

Anyon, J. (1980). Social class and the hidden curriculum of work. *Journal of Education, 163,* 67–92.

Apple, M.W. (1980). The other side of the hidden curriculum: Correspondence of theories and the labor process. *Interchange, 11,* 5–22.

Balaban, N. (1985). *Starting school: From separation to independence.* New York: Teachers College Press, Columbia University.

Ball, S.J. (1980). Initial encounters in the classroom and the process of establishment. In P. Woods (Ed.), *Pupil strategies: The sociology of the school* (pp. 143–161). London: Croom Helm.

Barrett, C.L., & Noble, H. (1973). Mothers' anxieties versus the effects of long distance move on children. *Journal of Marriage and the Family, 35,* 181–188.

Bate, B. (1988). *Communication and the sexes.* New York: Harper & Row.

Bennett, W.J. (1986). *First lessons: A report on elementary education in America.* Washington, DC: U.S. Dept. of Education.

Berger, C.R. (1979). Beyond initial interaction: Uncertainty, understanding, and the development of interpersonal relationships. In H. Giles & R.N. St. Clair (Eds.), *Language and social psychology* (pp. 122–144). Oxford: Basil Blackwell.

Berger, C.R. (1986). Communicating under uncertainty. In M.E. Roloff & G.R. Miller (Eds.), *Further explorations in interpersonal communication.* Beverly Hills, CA: Sage.

Berger, C.R., & Calabrese, R.J. (1975). Some explorations in initial interaction and beyond: Toward a developmental theory of interpersonal communication. *Human Communication Research, 1,* 99–112.

Berger, P.L., & Luckmann, T. (1966). *The social construction of reality.* New York: Anchor Books.

Bernstein, B. (1972). A sociolinguistic approach to socialization; with some reference to educability. In J.J. Gumperz & D. Hymes (Eds.), *Directions in sociolinguistics* (pp. 465–497). New York: Holt, Rinehart & Winston.

Bloome, D. (1985). The individual, the collective, and classroom education. *Review of Education, 11,* 123–126.

Blume, J. (1971). *Then again, maybe I won't.* Scarsdale, NY: Bradbury Press.

Blumenfeld, P.C., Hamilton, V.L., Bossert, S., Wessels, K., & Meece, J. (1983). Teacher talk and student thought: Socialization into the student role. In J.M. Levine & M.C. Wang (Eds.), *Teacher and student perceptions: Implications for learning* (pp. 143–192). Hillsdale, NJ: Lawrence Erlbaum.

Blumenfeld, P.C., Hamilton, V.L., Wessels, K., & Falkner, D. (1979). Teaching responsibility to first graders. *Theory into Practice, 18,* 174–180.

Blumenfeld, P.C., & Meece, J.L. (1985). Life in classrooms revisited. *Theory into Practice, 24,* 50–56.

Blumer, H. (1969). *Symbolic interactionism: Perspective and method.* Englewood Cliffs, NJ: Prentice-Hall.

Bollenbacher, J. (1963). A study of the effect of mobility on reading achievement. *Reading Teacher, 15,* 356–365.

Borman, K. (1978). Social control and schooling: Power and process in two kindergarten settings. *Anthropology and Education Quarterly, 9,* 38–51.

Bossert, S.T. (1979). *Tasks and social relationships in classrooms.* Cambridge: Cambridge University Press.

Brophy, J. (1985). Interactions of male and female students with male and female teachers. In L.C. Wilkinson & C.B. Marrett (Eds.), *Gender influences in classroom interaction* (pp. 114–142). Orlando, FL: Academic Press.

Brophy, J.E., & Good, T.L. (1974). *Teacher-student relationships: Causes and consequences.* New York: Holt, Rinehart & Winston, Inc.

Brown, B.A. (1988). The vital agenda for research on extracurricular influences: A reply to Holland and Andre. *Review of Educational Research, 58,* 107–111.

Bryan, K.A. (1980). Pupil perceptions of transfer between middle and high schools. In A. Hargreaves & L. Tickle (Eds.), *Middle schools: Origins, ideology, and practice* (pp. 228–246). London: Harper & Row.

Buber, M. (1965). *Between man and man.* New York: Macmillan.

Byrne, D.E. (1961). Interpersonal attraction and attitude similarity. *Journal of Abnormal and Social Psychology, 62,* 713–715.

Byrne, D.E. (1971). *The attraction paradigm.* New York: Academic Press.

Calvert, B. (1975). *The role of the pupil.* London: Routledge & Kegan Paul.

Canaan, J. (1987). A comparative analysis of American suburban middle class, middle school, and high school teenage cliques. In G. Spindler & L. Spindler (Eds.), *Interpretive ethnography of education* (pp. 385–406). Hillsdale, NJ: Lawrence Erlbaum.

Carroll, T.G. (1981). Learning to work: Adaptive communication of the organizing principles of work in a suburban elementary school. In R.T. Sieber & A.J. Gordon (Eds.), *Children and their organizations: Investigations in American culture* (pp. 44–57). Boston: G.K. Hall & Co.

Cazden, C.B. (1986). Classroom discourse. In M.C. Wittrock (Ed.), *Handbook of research on teaching* (3rd ed., pp. 432–463). New York: Macmillan.

Cazden, C.B. (1988). *Classroom discourse: The language of teaching and learning.* Portsmouth, NH: Heinemann.

Chapple, E.D., & Coon, C.S. (1942). *Principles of anthropology.* New York: Henry Holt and Co.

Chattergy, V. (1983). Beyond the needs of children from minority cultures. *Educational Perspectives, 22,* 26–28.

Cleary, B. (1981). *Ramona Quimby, age 8.* New York: Dell Publishing Co., Inc.

Cohen, J. (1979). High school subcultures and the adult world. *Adolescence, 14,* 491–502.

Coleman, J.S. (1961). *The adolescent society: The social life of the teenager and its impact on education.* New York: The Free Press.

Coleman, J.S. (1979). Current views of the adolescent process. In J.S. Coleman (Ed.), *The school years: Current issues in the socialization of young people* (pp. 1–23). Cambridge: University Press.

Connor, U. (1983). Predictors of second language reading performance. *Journal of Multilingual and Multicultural Development, 4,* 271–288.

Cornille, T.A., Bayer, A.E., & Smith, C.K. (1983). Schools and newcomers: A national survey of innovative programs. *The Personnel and Guidance Journal, 62,* 229–236.

Cramer, W., & Dorsey S. (1979). Are movers losers? *Elementary School Journal, 70,* 887–890.

Cronkhite, G. (1986). On the focus, scope, and coherence of the study of human symbolic activity. *The Quarterly Journal of Speech, 72,* 231–246.

Cusick, P.A. (1973). *Inside high school: The student's world.* New York: Holt, Rinehart & Winston.

Cusick, P.A. (1983). *The egalitarian ideal and the American high school: Studies of three schools.* New York: Longman.

Cusick, P.A., Martin, W., & Palonsky, S. (1976). Organizational structure and student behavior in secondary school. *Journal of Curriculum Studies, 8,* 3–14.

Darling, A.L., & Staton, A.Q. (in press). Socialization of graduate teaching assistants: A case study in an American university. *International Journal of Qualitative Studies in Education.*

DeClements, B. (1983). *How do you lose those ninth grade blues?* New York: Scholastic Inc.

Denzin, N.K. (1977). *Childhood socialization.* San Francisco: Jossey Bass.

Dewey, J. (1964). *John Dewey on education—Selected readings.* (R. Archambault, Ed.), New York: Random House.

Durkheim, E. (1956). *Education and sociology.* (Trans. by S.D. Fox). New York: Free Press.

Eccles, J.S., & Blumenfeld, P. (1985). Classroom experiences and student gender: Are there differences and do they matter? In L.C. Wilkinson & C.B. Marrett (Eds.), *Gender influences in classroom interaction* (pp. 79–114). Orlando, FL: Academic Press.

Egan, K. (1983). Educating and socializing: A proper distinction? *Teachers College Record, 85,* 27–42.

Eggert, L.E. (1984). Psychosocial development in adolescence. In L.K. Mahan & J.M. Rees (Eds.), *Nutrition in adolescence* (pp. 21–39). St. Louis: Times Mirror/Mosby College Publishing.

Eichhorn, D.H. (1966). *The middle school.* New York: The Center for Applied Research in Education.

Elliot, S. (1979). Perceived homophily as a predictor of classroom learning. In D. Nimmo (Ed.), *Communication Yearbook 3.* New Brunswick, NJ: Transaction Books.

Erickson, F. (1982). Classroom discourse as improvisation: Relationships between academic task structure and social participation structure in lessons. In L.C. Wilkinson (Ed.), *Communicating in the classroom* (pp. 153–181). New York: Academic Press.

Erickson, F. (1984). School literacy, reasoning, and civility: An anthropologist's perspective. *Review of Educational Research, 54,* 525–546.

Erickson, F. (1986). Qualitative methods in research on teaching. In M.C. Wittrock (Ed.), *Handbook of research on teaching* (3rd ed., pp. 119–161). New York: Macmillan.

Erickson, F., Boersema, D.B., Pelissier, C., & Lazarus, B.B. (1985). *Toward a theory of student status as socially constructed* (Occasional Paper No. 88). East Lansing, MI: The Institute for Research on Teaching.

Everhart, R.B. (1978). The fabric of meaning in a junior high school. *Theory into Practice, 18,* 152–157.

Falik, L.H. (1969). *The effect of high geographic mobility on the academic and social adjustment of children to their school environment. Dissertation Abstracts, 30,* 1015A.

Fasick, F.A. (1984). Parents, peers, youth culture and autonomy in adolescence. *Adolescence, 19,* 143–157.

Federbush, M. (1974). The sex problems of school math books. In J. Stacey, S. Bereaud, & J. Daniels (Eds.), *And Jill came tumbling after: Sexism in American education* (pp. 178–184). New York: Dell Publishing Co.

Feinberg, W., & Soltis, J.F. (1985). *School and society.* New York: Teachers College Press, Columbia University.

Fenstermacher, G.D. (1986). Philosophy of research on teaching: Three aspects. In M.C. Wittrock (Ed.), *Handbook of research on teaching* (3rd ed., pp. 37–49). New York: Macmillan.

Fernie, D.E. (1988). Becoming a student: Messages from first settings. *Theory into Practice, 27,* 3–10.

Fine, G.A. (1981). Friends, impression management, and preadolescent behavior. In S.A. Asher & J. M. Gottman (Eds.), *The development of children's friendships* (pp. 29–52). Cambridge: Cambridge University Press.

Flaubert, G. (1928). *Madame Bovary.* (Trans. by E. Marx- Aveling). New York: E.P. Dutton & Co., Inc. (London: J.M. Dent & Sons LTD).

Floden, R.E., & Clark, C.M. (1988). Preparing teachers for uncertainty. *Teachers College Record, 89,* 505–524.

Florio, S., & Shultz, J. (1979). Social competence at home and at school. *Theory into Practice, 18,* 234–243.

Frazier, I.J.B. (1970). *Relationships of local pupil mobility to reading achievement and intelligence test results of educationally disadvantaged children. Dissertation Abstracts, 31,* 1508–1509.

French, J., & Raven, B. (1959). The bases of social power. In D. Cartwright (Ed.), *Studies in social power* (pp. 150–167). Ann Arbor, MI: Institute for Social Research.

Fromberg, D.P. (1989). Kindergarten: Current circumstances affecting curriculum. *Teachers College Record, 90,* 392–403.

Fuller, F.F. (1969). Concerns of teachers: A developmental conceptualization. *American Educational Research Journal, 2,* 207–226.

Fuller, F.F., & Bown, O.H. (1975). Becoming a teacher. In The National Society for the Study of Education (Ed.), *Seventy-fourth yearbook of the National Society for the Study of Education* (pp. 25–52). Chicago: The National Society for the Study of Education.

Fuller, F.F., Watkins, J.E., & Parsons, J.S. (1973). *Concerns of teachers: Research and reconceptualization.* Austin, TX: University of Texas Research and Development Center for Teacher Education.

Galton, M., & Delamont, S. (1980). The first weeks of middle school. In A. Hargreaves & L. Tickle (Eds.), *Middle schools: Origins, ideology, and practice* (pp. 207–227). London: Harper and Row.

Gamoran, A., & Berends, M. (1987). The effects of stratification in secondary schools: Synthesis of survey and ethnographic research. *Review of Educational Research, 57*, 415–435.

Gardner, R., & Smythe, P.C. (1975). Motivation and second language acquisition. *Canadian Modern Language Journal, 31*, 218–230.

Garfinkel, H. (1967). *Studies in ethnomethodology.* Englewood Cliffs, NJ: Prentice-Hall.

Gibson, M.A. (1984). Approaches to multicultural education in the United States: Some concepts and assumptions. *Anthropology and Education Quarterly, 15*, 94–119.

Gibson, M.A. (1987). Punjabi immigrants in an American high school. In G. & L. Spindler (Eds.), *Interpretive ethnography of education* (pp. 281–310). Hillsdale, NJ: Lawrence Erlbaum.

Glaser, B.G., & Strauss, A.L. (1971). *Status passage.* Chicago: Aldine Atherton, Inc.

Goetz, J.P. (1981). Sex-role systems in Rose Elementary School: Change and tradition in the rural-transitional south. In R.T. Sieber & A.J. Gordon (Eds.), *Children and their organizations: Investigations in American culture* (pp. 58–73). Boston: G.K. Hall & Co.

Goetz, J.P., & LeCompte, M.D. (1981). Ethnographic research and the problem of data reduction. *Anthropology and Education Quarterly, 12*, 51–70.

Goffman, E. (1967). *Interaction ritual: Essays on face-to-face behavior.* Chicago: Aldine.

Gordon, D. (1983). Rules and the effectiveness of the hidden curriculum. *Journal of Philosophy of Education, 17*, 207–218.

Gordon, R.M. (1984). Freedom of expression and values inculcation in the public school curriculum. *Journal of Law and Education, 13*, 523–579.

Goslin, D.A. (1969). *Handbook of socialization theory and research.* Chicago: Rand McNally.

Grant, C.A. (1979). Classroom socialization: The other side of a two-way street. *Educational Leadership*, pp. 470–473.

Green, J.L. (1983). Research on teaching as a linguistic process: A state of the art. In E.W. Gordon (Ed.), *Review of research in education 10* (pp. 151–252). Washington, DC: American Educational Research Association.

Green, J.L., & Harker, J.O. (1982). Gaining access to learning: Conversational, social, and cognitive demands of group participation. In L.C. Wilkinson (Ed.), *Communication in the classroom* (pp. 183–221). New York: Academic Press.

Greenbaum, H.H. (1974). The audit of organizational communication. *Academy of Management Journal, 17,* 739–754.

Hall, W.S., & Guthrie, L. (1981). Cultural and situational variation in language function and use: Method and procedures for research. In J. Green & C. Wallat (Eds.), *Ethnography and language in educational settings* (pp. 209–228). Norwood, NJ: Ablex.

Hamilton, S.F. (1983). The social side of schooling: Ecological studies of classrooms and schools. *The Elementary School Journal, 83,* 313–334.

Hamilton, S.F. (1984). The secondary school in the ecology of adolescent development. In E.W. Gordon (Ed.), *Review of research in education 11* (pp. 227–258). Washington, DC: American Educational Research Association.

Hampel, R.L. (1986). *The last little citadel: American high schools since 1940.* Boston: Houghton Mifflin Co.

Hatch, J.A. (1987). Impression management in kindergarten classrooms: An analysis of children's face-work in peer interactions. *Anthropology and Education Quarterly, 18,* 100–115.

Holland, A., & Andre, T. (1987). Participation in extra-curricular activities in secondary school: What is known, what needs to be known? *Review of Educational Research, 57,* 437–466.

Hollingshead, A.B. (1949). *Elmstown's youth: The impact of social classes on adolescents.* New York: John Wiley and Sons.

Hollingshead, A.B. (1975). *Elmstown's youth and Elmstown revisited.* New York: John Wiley and Sons.

Hymes, D.H. (1972). Models of the interaction of language and social life. In J.J. Gumperz & D. H. Hymes (Eds.), *Directions in sociolinguistics: The ethnography of communication* (pp. 35–71). New York: Holt, Rinehart, and Winston.

Ide, J.K., Haertel, G.D., & Walberg, H.J. (1981). Peer group influence on educational outcomes: A qualitative synthesis. *Journal of Educational Psychology, 73,* 472–484.

Jablin, F.M. (1982). Organizational communication: An assimilation approach. In M.E. Roloff & C.R. Berger (Eds.), *Social cognition and communication* (pp. 255–286). Newbury Park, CA: Sage.

Jackson, P. (1968). *Life in classrooms.* New York: Holt, Rinehart, and Winston.

Kantor, M.B. (1965). Some consequences of residential and social mobility for the adjustment of children. In M.B. Kantor (Ed.), *Mobility and mental health.* Springfield, IL: Charles C. Thomas.

Kapferer. J.L. (1981). Socialization and the symbolic order of the school. *Anthropology and Education Quarterly, 12,* 258–274.

Kassem, L. (1986). *Middle school blues.* New York: Avon Books.

Katz, R.L. (1980). Time and work: Toward an integrative perspective. *Research in Organizational Behavior, 2,* 81–127.

Kelly, A. (1988). Gender differences in teacher-pupil interactions: A meta-analytic review. *Research in Education, 39,* 1–23.

Kelly, G.P. (1981). Contemporary American policies and practices in the education of immigrant children. In J.K. Bhatnagar (Ed.), *Educating immigrants.* London: Croom Helm.

Kim, Y.Y. (1977). Communication patterns of foreign immigrants in the process of acculturation. *Human Communication Research*, *4*, 66–77.

Kimbal, S.T. (1974). *Culture and the educative process.* New York: Teachers College Press, Columbia University.

Kroger, J.E. (1980). Residential mobility and self-concept in adolescence. *Adolescence*, *15*, 967–977.

Lacey, C. (1970). *Hightown grammar: The school as a social system.* Manchester: Manchester University Press.

Lacey, C. (1977). *The socialization of teachers.* London: Metheun & Co.

Larkin, R.W. (1979). *Suburban youth in cultural crisis.* New York: Oxford University Press.

LeCompte, M. (1978). Learning to work: The hidden curriculum of the classroom. *Anthropology and Education Quarterly*, *9*, 22–37.

LeCompte, M.D., & Goetz, J.P. (1982). Problems of reliability and validity in ethnographic research. *Review of Educational Research*, *52*, 31–60.

Lee, P.C., & Gropper, N.B. (1974). Sex-role culture and educational practice. *Harvard Educational Review*, *44*, 369–410.

Leemon, T.A. (1972). *The rites of passage in a student culture.* New York: Teachers College Press, Columbia University.

Lightfoot, S.L. (1978). *Worlds apart: Relationships between families and schools.* New York: Basic Books, Inc.

Lightfoot, S.L. (1983). *The good high school: Portraits of character and culture.* New York: Basic Books, Inc.

Lofland, J. (1971). *Analyzing social settings: A guide to qualitative observation and analysis.* Belmont, CA: Wadsworth.

Lofland, J., & Lofland, L.H. (1984). *Analyzing social settings.* Belmont, CA: Wadsworth Inc.

Louis, M.R. (1980). Surprise and sense-making: What newcomers experience in entering unfamiliar organizational settings. *Administrative Science Quarterly*, *25*, 226–251.

Lubeck, S. (1985). *Sandbox society: Early education in black and white America.* London: The Falmer Press.

Mackay, R.W. (1974). Concepts of children and models of socialization. In R. Turner (Ed.), *Ethnomethodology* (pp. 180–193). Middlesex, England: Penguin Books.

MacLeod, J.S., & Silverman, S.T. (1973). *You won't do: What textbooks on U.S. government teach high school girls.* Pittsburgh, PA: Know.

Magoon, J.A. (1977). Constructivist approaches in educational research. *Review of Educational Research*, *47*, 651–693.

Mankowitz, M.F. (1970). *Mobility and its relationship to the achievement and personal problems of seventh-grade pupils. Dissertation Abstracts*, *30*, 3648A.

Martin, A. (1985). Back to kindergarten basics. *Harvard Educational Review*, *55*, 318–320.

McCroskey, J.C., Richmond, V.P., & Daly, J.A. (1975). The development of perceived homophily in interpersonal communication. *Human Communication Research*, *1*, 321–332.

Mead, G.H. (1934). *Mind, self and society.* Chicago: University of Chicago Press.

Mead, G.H. (1938). *The philosophy of the act.* Chicago: University of Chicago Press.

Mehan, H. (1980). The competent student. *Anthropology and Education Quarterly, 11,* 131–152.

Mehan, H. (1982). The structure of classroom events and their consequenses for student performance. In P. Gilmore & A.A. Glatthorn (Eds.), *Children in and out of school: Ethnography and education* (pp. 59–87). Washington, DC: Center for Applied Linguistics.

Merton, R., Reader, G., & Kendall, P. (1957). *The student physician.* Cambridge: Harvard University Press.

Miles, M.B., & Huberman, A.M. (1985). *Qualitative data analysis: A sourcebook of new methods.* Beverly Hills, CA.: Sage.

Miller, V.D., & Jablin, F.M. (1987). *Newcomers' information seeking behaviors during organizational encounter: A typology and model of the process.* Paper presented at the annual meeting of the Speech Communication Association, Boston, MA.

Milne, A.A. (1928). *The house at Pooh Corner.* New York: E.P. Dutton.

Moore, S.G. (1986). Socialization in the kindergarten classroom. In B. Spodek (Ed.), *Today's kindergarten: Exploring the knowledge base, expanding the curriculum* (pp. 110–136). New York: Teachers College Press, Columbia University.

National Education Association. (1977). *Sex role stereotyping in the schools* (Revised ed.). Washington, DC: National Education Association.

Noblit, G.W. (1987). Ideological purity and variety in effective middle schools. In G.W. Noblit & W.T. Pink (Eds.), *Schooling in social context: Qualitative studies* (pp. 203–217). Norwood, NJ: Ablex.

Ogbu, J.U. (1982). Cultural discontinuities and schooling. *Anthropology and Education Quarterly, 13,* 290–307.

Ogbu, J.U. (1987). Variability in minority responses to schooling: Nonimmigrants vs. immigrants. In G. & L. Spindler (Eds.), *Interpretive ethnography of education* (pp. 255–278). Hillsdale, NJ: Lawrence Erlbaum.

Page, R. (1987). Lower-track classes at a college-preparatory high school: A caricature of educational encounters. In G. & L. Spindler (Eds.), *Interpretive ethnography of education* (pp. 447–472). Hillsdale, NJ: Lawrence Erlbaum.

Parsons, T. (1951). *The social system.* London: Routledge & Kegan Paul.

Parsons, T. (1959). The school class as a social system: Some of its functions in American society. *Harvard Educational Review, 29,* 297–318.

Paulston, C.B. (1979). Bilingual/bicultural education. In L.S. Shulman (Ed.), *Review of research in education 6* (pp. 186–228). Itasca, IL: F.E. Peacock Pub., Inc.

Perrone, V., & Associates. (1985). *Portraits of high schools: A supplement to High School: A report on secondary education in America.* Princeton, NJ: The Carnegie Foundation for the Advancement of Teaching.

Peshkin, A. (1978). *Growing up American: Schooling and the survival of community.* Chicago: University of Chicago Press.

Peshkin, A. (1986). *God's choice: The total world of a fundamentalist Christian school.* Chicago: University of Chicago Press.

Peters, J.F. (1985). Adolescents as socialization agents to parents. *Adolescence, 20,* 921–933.

Pollard, A. (1985). *The social world of the primary school.* London: Holt, Rinehart & Winston.

Powell, A.G., Farrar, E., & Cohen, D.K. (1985). *The shopping mall high school: Winners and losers in the educational marketplace.* Boston: Houghton Mifflin Co.

Puleo, V.T. (1988). A review and critique of research on full-day kindergarten. *The Elementary School Journal, 88,* 427–439.

Riseborough, G.F. (1985). Pupils, teachers' careers and schooling: An empirical study. In S.J. Ball & I.F. Goodson (Eds.), *Teachers' lives and careers* (pp. 202–265). London: The Falmer Press.

Ritter, E.M. (1979). Social perspective-taking ability, cognitive complexity and listener-adapted communication in early and late adolescence. *Communication Monographs, 46,* 40–51.

Robinson, S.L. (1987). Kindergarten in America: Five major trends. *Phi Delta Kappan, 68,* 529–530.

Rogers, E.M., & Shoemaker, F.F. (1971). *Communication of innovation.* New York: The Free Press.

Rohrkemper, M.M. (1984). The influence of teacher socialization style on students' social cognition and reported interpersonal classroom behavior. *The Elementary School Journal, 85,* 245–275.

Rothstein, S.W. (1979). Orientations: First impressions in an urban junior high school. *Urban Education, 14,* 91–116.

Saario, T.N., Jacklin, C.N., & Tittle, C.K. (1973). Sex role stereotyping in the public schools. *Harvard Educational Review, 43,* 386–415.

Salmon, P. (1979). The role of the peer group. In J.C. Coleman (Ed.), *The school years: Current issues in the socialization of young people* (pp. 95–121). Cambridge: University Press.

Samson, G.J. (1966). *A study of the relationship of mobility to achievement, study methods, and attitudes of tenth grade students in the Chicopee, Massachusetts, school system. Dissertation Abstracts, 20,* 242–246.

Savin-Williams, R.C. (1980). Social interactions of adolescent females in natural groups. In H.C. Foot, A.J. Chapman, & J.R. Smith (Eds.), *Friendship and social relations of children* (pp. 343–364). New York: John Wiley & Sons Ltd.

Schwartz, A.J. (1975). *The schools and socialization.* New York: Harper & Row.

Schwartz, F. (1981). Supporting or subverting learning: Peer group patterns in four tracked schools. *Anthropology and Education Quarterly, 12,* 99–121.

Shimahara, N.K. (1983). Polarized socialization in an urban high school. *Anthropology and Education Quarterly, 14,* 109–130.

Shulman, L.S. (1986). Paradigms and research programs in the study of teaching. In M.C. Wittrock (Ed.), *Handbook of research on teaching* (3rd ed., pp. 3–36). New York: Macmillan.

Shultz, J.J., Florio, S., & Erickson, F. (1982). Where's the floor: Aspects of the cultural organization of social relationships in communication at home and in school. In P. Gilmore & A.A. Glatthorn (Eds.), *Children in and out of school: Ethnography and education* (pp. 88–123). Washington, DC: Center for Applied Linguistics.

Sieber, R.T. (1978). Schooling, socialization, and group boundaries: A study of informal social relations in the public domain. *Urban Anthropology, 7,* 67–98.

Sieber, R.T. (1979). Schoolrooms, pupils, and rules: The role of informality in bureaucratic socialization. *Human Organization, 38,* 273–282.

Sieber, R.T. (1981). Socialization implications of school discipline, or how first-graders are taught to "listen." In R.T. Sieber & A.J. Gordon (Eds.), *Children and their organizations: Investigations into American culture* (pp. 18–43). Boston: G.K. Hall & Co.

Sizer, T.R. (1984). *Horace's compromose: The dilemma of the American high school.* Boston: Houghton Mifflin Co.

Skarpness, L.R., & Carson, D.K. (1987). Correlates of kindergarten adjustment: Temperament and communicative competence. *Early Childhood Research Quarterly, 2,* 367–376.

Smith, L.M., & Geoffrey, W. (1968). *The complexities of an urban classroom.* New York: Holt, Rinehart & Winston.

Snipes, W.T. (1970). *The effect of moving on reading achievement, grade 11, Anderson City schools, Anderson, Indiana, 1968–1969. Dissertation Abstracts, 30,* 2780A.

Spencer-Hall, D.A. (1981). Looking behind the teacher's back. *The Elementary School Journal, 81,* 281–289.

Spener, D. (1988). Transitional bilingual education and the socialization of immigrants. *Harvard Educational Review, 58,* 133–153.

Spicer, C.H., & Staton-Spicer, A.Q. (1983). *Communication strategies of newcomers to groups.* Paper presented at the annual meeting of the Speech Communication Association, Washington, DC.

Spindler, G.D. (Ed.). (1955). *Anthropology and education.* Stanford: Stanford University Press.

Spindler, G.D. (1963). The transmission of American culture. In G.D. Spindler (Ed.), *Education and culture: Anthropoplogical approaches.* New York: Holt, Rinehart and Winston.

Spodek, B. (Ed.). (1986). *Today's kindergarten: Exploring the knowledge base, expanding the curriculum.* New York: Teachers College Press, Columbia University.

Spradley, J.P. (1979). *The ethnographic interview.* New York: Holt, Rinehart & Winston.

Staton, A.Q., & Darling, A.L. (1989). Socialization of teaching assistants. In J.D. Nyquist, R.D. Abbott, & D.H. Wulff (Eds.), *The training of teaching assistants* (pp. 15–22). San Francisco: Jossey- Bass.

Staton-Spicer, A.Q. (1982). Qualitative inquiry in instructional communication: Applications and directions. *The Communicator, 12,* 35–46.

Staton-Spicer, A.Q. (1983). The measurement and further conceptualization of teacher communication concern. *Human Communication Research, 9,* 158–168.

Staton-Spicer, A.Q., & Bassett, R.E. (1979). Communication concerns of preservice and inservice elementary school teachers. *Human Communication Research, 5,* 138–146.

Staton-Spicer, A.Q., & Darling, A.L. (1986). Communication in the socialization of preservice teachers. *Communication Education, 35,* 215–230.

Staton-Spicer, A.Q., & Darling, A.L. (1987). A communication perspective on teacher socialization. *Journal of Thought, 22,* 12–19.

Staton-Spicer, A.Q., & Spicer, C.H. (1987). Socialization of the academic chairperson: A typology of communication dimensions. *Educational Administration Quarterly, 23,* 41–64.

Stewart, J. (1978). Foundations of dialogic communication. *The Quarterly Journal of Speech, 64,* 183–201.

Stubblefield, R.L. (1955). Children's emotional problems aggravated by family moves. *American Journal of Orthopsychiatry, 25,* 120–126.

Sullivan, H.S. (1953). *The interpersonal theory of psychiatry.* New York: Norton.

Teitelbaum, H., & Hiller, R.J. (1977). Bilingual education: The legal mandate. *Harvard Educational Review, 47,* 138–170.

Thornberg, H.D. (1980). Early adolescents: Their developmental characteristics. *The High School Journal, 63,* 215–221.

Tooley, K. (1970). The role of geographic mobility in some adjustment problem children and families. *Journal of the American Academy of Child Psychiatry, 9,* 366–378.

Trecker, J. (1974). Women in U.S. history high school textbooks. In J. Stacey, S. Bereaud, & J. Daniels (Eds.), *And Jill came tumbling after: Sexism in American education* (pp. 249–268). New York: Dell Publishing Co.

Trueba, H.T., Guthrie, G.P., & Hu-Pei Au, K. (1981). *Culture and the bilingual classroom: Studies in classroom ethnography.* Rowley, MA: Newbury House.

Tucker, G.R. (1976). Affective, cognitive and social factors in second language acquisition. *Canadian Modern Language Review, 32,* 214–226.

United States Immigration and Naturalization Service. (1988). *Statistical yearbook of the Immigration and Naturalization Service, 1987.* Washington, DC: U.S. Government Printing Office.

Vangelisti, A.L. (1988). Adolescent socialization into the workplace: A synthesis and critique of current literature. *Youth and Society, 19,* 460–484.

van Gennep, A. (1960). *The rites of passage.* (Trans. by M.B. Vizedom & G.L. Caffe). Chicago: University of Chicago Press.

Van Maanen, J. (1976). Breaking in: Socialization to work. In R. Dubin (Ed.), *Handbook of work, organization, and society* (pp. 67–130). Chicago: Rand McNally.

Van Maanen, J., & Schein, E.H. (1979). Toward a theory of organizational socialization. *Research on Organizational Behavior, 1,* 209–264.

Varenne, H. (1982). Jocks and freaks: The symbolic structure of the expression of social interaction among American senior high school students. In G. Spindler (Ed.), *Doing the ethnography of schooling* (pp. 210–235). New York: Holt, Rinehart & Winston.

Wallat, C., & Green, J. (1979). Social rules and communicative contexts in kindergarten. *Theory into Practice, 18,* 275–284.

Wallat, C., & Green, J. (1982). Construction of social norms by teacher and children: The first year of school. In K.M. Borman (Ed.), *The social life of children in a changing society* (pp. 97–121). Hillsdale, NJ: Lawrence Erlbaum.

Warren, R.L. (1982). Schooling, biculturalism, and ethnic identity: A case study. In G. Spindler (Ed.), *Doing the ethnography of schooling: Educational anthropology in action* (pp. 382–409). New York: Holt, Rinehart & Winston.

Wartski, M.C. (1980). *A long way from home.* Philadelphia, PA: The Westminster Press.

Weinstein, R.S. (1983). Student perceptions of schooling. *The Elementary School Journal, 83,* 287–312.

Whalen, T.E., & Fried, M.A. (1973). Geographic mobility and its effect on student achievement. *The Journal of Educational Research, 67,* 163–165.

Wheeler, S. (1966). The structure of formally organized socialization settings. In O.G. Brim, Jr. & S. Wheeler (Eds.), *Socialization after childhood: Two essays* (pp. 51–116). New York: John Wiley & Sons, Inc.

Wilcox, K. (1982). Differential socialization in the classroom: Implications for equal opportunity. In G. Spindler (Ed.), *Doing the ethnography of schooling* (pp. 268–309). New York: Holt, Rinehart & Winston.

Wilkinson, L.C. (Ed.). (1982). *Communicating in the classroom.* New York: Academic Press.

Willes, M.J. (1983). *Children into pupils: A study of language in early schooling.* London: Routledge & Kegan Paul.

Wilson, C.E. (1986). *Organizational socialization, uncertainty reduction and communication networks.* Paper presented at the annual meeting of the Speech Communication Association, Chicago, IL.

Wise, S.R. (1971). *A study in the three Alabama counties to determine the relationship between migrant and nonmobile rural disadvantaged students in selected curriculum area as measured by a standardized testing instrument. Dissertation Abstracts, 31,* 5106A.

Women on Words and Images. (1972). *Dick and Jane as victims: Sex stereotyping in children's readers.* Princeton, NJ: Women on Words and Images.

Woods, P. (1980). The development of pupil strategies. In P. Woods (Ed.), *Pupil strategies: The sociology of the school* (pp. 11–28). London: Croom Helm.

Woods, P. (1983). *Sociology and the school: An interactionist viewpoint.* London: Routledge & Kegan Paul.

Zeichner, K.M. (1980). *Key processes in the socialization of student teachers: Limitations and consequences of oversocialized conceptions of teacher socialization.* Paper presented at the annual meeting of the American Educational Research Association, Boston, MA.

Ziegler, S. (1980). School for life: The experience of Italian immigrants in Canadian schools. *Human Organization, 39,* 263–267.

Ziller, R.C., & Behringer, R.D. (1961). A longitudinal study of the assimilation of the new child in the group. *Human Relations, 14,* 121–133.

Author Index

Subject Index

222